THE CIRCLE
OF MOUNTAINS

A Basque
Shepherding Community

Moving a flock to its mountain pasturage in May

THE CIRCLE
OF MOUNTAINS,

A Basque
Shepherding Community

SANDRA OTT

CLARENDON PRESS · OXFORD
1981

Oxford University Press, Walton Street, Oxford OX2 6DP
Oxford London Glasgow
New York Toronto Melbourne Wellington
Kuala Lumpur Singapore Jakarta Hong Kong Tokyo
Delhi Bombay Calcutta Madras Karachi
Nairobi Dar Es Salaam Cape Town

Published in the United States
by Oxford University Press, New York

British Library Cataloguing in Publication Data
Ott, Sandra
The circle of mountains.
1. Sainte-Engrâce, France – Social life and customs
2. Basques – Social life and customs
301.29'44'79   DC801.S17| 80-40976
ISBN 0-19-823199-7

Printed in Great Britain
by Butler & Tanner Ltd
Frome and London

For Fee and Pidge

PREFACE

I

THE commune of Sainte-Engrâce extends along a mountain valley in the south-eastern corner of Soule, one of the three Basque provinces in France. The people of Sainte-Engrâce insist, however, that they live not in a valley but in 'the circle of mountains' (*bortüko üngürü*). They visualize their community as a circle; but this is not the only reason why the title of this book is appropriate. The same word which the people use to describe the 'circle' of mountains in which they live is applied by them to a diverse range of phenomena which they conceive as 'making a rotation' (*üngür bat egiten*); for *üngürü* also means rotation, in the sense of 'the action of moving round a centre or of turning round on an axis' (*OED*). The notion of rotation, in English, as a regular and recurring succession of persons or objects is conveyed by another Basque word—*aldikatzia*, which denotes what I shall call 'serial replacement', as well as 'alternation', in its strictest sense. In Sainte-Engrâce, I found that *üngürü*, in the sense of rotation, and *aldikatzia* are the two fundamental principles which order—in particular but among other things —two systems of asymmetric exchange and a range of other institutionalized forms of co-operation.

Üngürü and *aldikatzia* have a general importance as organizing notions in Sainte-Engrâce society—a fact which, I was pleased to discover, many of the people themselves recognize. When I returned to the commune during the summer of 1979 and showed the people the doctoral thesis upon which this book is based, I was asked continually to summarize in Basque the main theme of my 'book'. On one occasion, when I told a couple that my book was about *üngürü* and *aldikatzia*, the husband looked at me approvingly and exclaimed, 'Well, in that case you've got it all! If you've understood *üngürü* and *aldikatzia*, then you understand Sainte-Engrâce!'

It was, of course, gratifying to have an informant confirm my own views about the importance of these two notions; but I have by no means written a complete ethnographic study of Sainte-Engrâce, nor was it my intention to do so. I chose instead to make a selective analysis of certain formally interesting features of the society and thus have focused primarily upon a few main topics that are interrelated. This approach has certain defects. For example, topics such as kinship are touched upon only briefly and raise many questions that I could not answer fully in this book without digressing from my main themes. It is hoped, however, that my approach will be justified by the interest of the institutions that I do explore fully and by the strength of my analyses of them.

Much of this book is concerned, in one way or another, with the concepts of *üngürü* and *aldikatzia* and with three main institutions in Sainte-Engrâce society: the household, 'first neighbours', and the pastoral institution of the *olha*. My aims are to show that the same fundamental ideals of co-operation and reciprocity are the essential basis of these three institutions; to describe and to analyse the systems (such as those constituted by the asymmetric exchange of certain ritual goods and services) and the relationships within systems that are ordered by the principles of *üngürü* and *aldikatzia*; and, finally, to show how the male domain of the mountain herding hut is sociologically, ideologically, and symbolically a re-creation of the female domain of the house in the valley.

The book is divided into six parts. Part One deals with historical, environmental, and socio-economic considerations, and is intended to provide a background for the parts which follow. Part Two is concerned with three institutions in the valley: the household, 'first neighbours', and the Church. The facts presented in the chapter dealing with 'first neighbours' and an appreciation of the logic underlying this institution are necessary to an understanding of Part Three of this book, which is largely concerned with Sainte-Engrâce systems of asymmetric exchange.

Part Four represents a shift from institutions in the valley to that of the *olha* in the mountains. A general description of this shepherding institution is followed by a detailed analysis of transformations that have taken place within it. The third chapter in this part provides facts about the process of cheese-making that are crucial to an understanding of the notion of human conception held by the Sainte-Engrâce people and described in Part Five. A summary of recurring themes and patterns contained in this book is given in Part Six. One theme is singled out as having a formal importance not only in Sainte-Engrâce, but also in certain rural European societies outside the Basque country.

II

My interest in the Basques was initially guided by three factors: first, the Basques are often regarded as 'the mystery people' of Europe; the literature about them is extensive and covers a period of several hundred years; yet surprisingly the Basques have not received the attention they deserve from social anthropologists.

My literary research about the Basques was begun in February 1976. In the spring of that year I discussed my interests in the French Basques with Julian Pitt-Rivers, who kindly suggested several villages in which I might work. During that period I also began my study of the Basque language. On the advice of Julian Pitt-Rivers, I approached William Douglass, Co-ordinator of the Basque Studies Program at the University of Nevada (Reno). Through him I contacted Eugène Goyheneche, a Basque scholar whom I met when I first went to the Basque country in July 1976.

My first month in the Basque country was spent travelling from village to village and talking to priests. During that month I visited Sainte-Engrâce on three separate occasions. On my third visit I met Dominique Peillen, a Basque scholar and teacher who spends holidays in the commune. With his assistance I found a family with whom I lived for most of my stay in Sainte-Engrâce.

In preparation for my field-work, I enrolled in a Basque language school in August 1976, and received tutorials in the Souletine dialect. Although these were held in Uhart-Mixe, I lived with a Basque family in the nearby village of Pagolle.

In September of 1976 I spent two and a half weeks in Saint Michel, a small village three kilometres south of St-Jean-Pied-de-Port. I lived with a Basque-speaking family who provided me with many valuable insights into the way of life in a lowland French Basque community.

I chose to work in Sainte-Engrâce for the following reasons. The commune is relatively isolated, both socially and geographically, in its mountain cul-de-sac; the people speak Souletine Basque as their first and daily language; and I had heard that the pastoral institution of the *olha*, which is unique to Soule, remained intact in Sainte-Engrâce. In the lowlands I heard, too, that the Sainte-Engrâce people were 'different' from all other Souletine Basques and in some ways 'peculiar'—a judgement which merely served to enhance my curiosity.

The majority of the field-work upon which this book is based was conducted in Sainte-Engrâce over a period of twelve months in 1976/7 and 1979. In 1976/7 I lived in the upper half of the commune with a widow, her son, and his wife, who bore their first child in 1977.

In 1979 I arranged to stay in the lower half of the commune for two months. I rented a flat in a house which belongs to the mayor and lies next to his own. Although I spent most of my time with the people in their houses and fields, I found out what I have always suspected—namely, that there are many things about a people that one is unlikely to learn unless one lives with a local family. During this period my husband and three step-children spent a fortnight with me and the Sainte-Engrâce people, who gave my family an enthusiastic welcome, as well as vast quantities of food and drink. Although they were extremely appreciative when my family greeted and thanked them in Basque, they were distressed not to be able to converse with my family in Basque and thereby 'to get to know them'.

The conditions in which my field-work was conducted were favourable in every respect. I am very fond of the people and enjoyed virtually every moment of my stay with them. From the start and with few exceptions, the people were friendly, hospitable, and helpful. They took a keen interest in me and in my work and were proud of the fact that I had chosen to study them. The extent of their cultural pride and of their trust in me is perhaps best illustrated by the fact that they asked me not to change the name of their community or to conceal its location in this book.

When I first arrived in the community, I asked the people to speak to me only in Basque, though I could compose and understand only the most simple sentences at the time. They took my request seriously and respected my decision and determination to conduct all my work in their native language. Many of them were demanding, uncompromisingly strict teachers; but they were also patient and careful to correct my many mistakes. The linguistic instruction and encouragement that I received from them enabled me to begin my work in earnest by the end of my first month in the commune. Although we never spoke French to one another, I asked them occasionally to provide French glosses.

Although my best informants rightly advise me that I do not yet speak 'pure Basque', I found in 1979 that my speaking-knowledge of their language enabled me to gain immediate access to households, inside and outside Sainte-Engrâce, where I was not personally known.

I was not excluded from any social, ritual, or economic activity in which the people themselves participated. I was invited to attend baptismal and wedding feasts and to participate in mortuary rituals. I harvested hay, maize, and fern with the people, herded sheep and cattle, helped them clean their barns and feed their livestock, raked and spread manure on the winter pastures, and assisted twelve households with their pig-killing. During the period of summer transhumance, I was never excluded from the otherwise exclusively male domain of the mountain herding huts. In fact, I was encouraged by both sexes to stay in the huts with the shepherds whenever and as often as I liked. So far as I know, my sleeping in the same bed as the shepherds (for there is only one large bed in every hut) never gave rise to any scandal in the valley. From the point of view of the women, my staying in the huts was a necessary part of my research. The women reasoned that if I were to write about the male world of the hut I should see for myself what life is like in the mountains, though they themselves have not.

III

During the course of my research I was helped in various ways by many people inside and outside the Basque country. I am grateful to Eugène Goyheneche of Ustaritz for his assistance during my first month in the Basque country and for having recommended Sainte-Engrâce to me. The late Fr. Officialdeguy of Lantabat, Fr. Marcel Etchandy of the Abbaye du Belloc, Fr. Jean Casenave of Saint Palais and Saint-Engrâce, Fr. Joseph Arhex of Sainte-Engrâce, and Jean Etchegoren, former archpriest of Mauléon provided many useful insights into traditional ritual practices in Soule and Basse-Navarre.

My thanks are due to Francesca Zawadzki, formerly of Wolfson College, Oxford, and Joseph Etchebarne of Camou-Cihigue for having given me tutorials in the Basque language. I am also grateful to Dominique Peillen and Fr. Jean Casenave for having corrected the spelling of several Souletine words which were rendered phonetically in the first draft of this book. They also advised me to employ *tx* rather than *tch* in words such as *etxekandere*, as the former is now regarded as more acceptable by Basque scholars. Opinions about the correct orthography of Souletine Basque are, however, regularly revised.

Much of my literary research was conducted in the library of the Basque Studies Program at the University of Nevada, Reno. William Douglass, Jon Bilbao, and Virginia Chan all helped to make my stay in Reno profitable.

I appreciate the financial assistance provided by Wolfson College and by the Philip Bagby Trust (Oxford), who gave me two generous grants in 1976 and 1977, and the technical assistance of Peter Narracott (Pitt Rivers Museum, Oxford), who made the prints for the plates in this book.

Much of the material contained in Chapter XII appears in an

article, 'Aristotle Among the Basques: The "Cheese Analogy" of Conception', which was published in *Man* (December 1979). Another article, 'Blessed Bread, "First Neighbours" and Asymmetric Exchange in the Basque Country', which was published in the *Archives Européennes de Sociologie* (vol. xxi, 1980), contains material included in Chapters V, VII, and VIII of this book. I am grateful to the editors of these two journals for having permitted me to reprint this material.

The doctoral thesis on which this book is based was submitted at Oxford in 1978. Many of the revisions and additions that have been made are the result of queries and comments made by my examiners, John Campbell and Julian Pitt-Rivers, and by William Douglass. Rodney Needham supervised my doctoral thesis. The instruction, support, and encouragement that these individuals have given me are deeply appreciated. If there are points in this book which they queried and I have not answered satisfactorily, the fault is mine, not theirs.

My greatest debt of thanks is owing to Peter Rivière, who has been a patient assistant, critic and friend, and to the people of Sainte-Engrâce. Since I cannot thank the latter individually, I shall single out the following people to represent them: Anna and Mathieu Arospide; Anna and Borthol Carricart; Kattlin Curutchague; Elizabeth, Madeleine, and Alexis Etchebarne; Maddy and Felix Goillart; the late Grabile Harriguileheguy; Ambrosi Junet and his family; Jeanetta and Borthol Larbonne; Louisa and Joseph Lascoumes; Marienna, Pethi, and Dominique Salaber. Special thanks are also due to the shepherds of Ligoleta. *Eskerrik hanitx eta izan untsa.*

St. Antony's College, Oxford
January 1980

CONTENTS

LIST OF ILLUSTRATIONS

MAPS

TABLES

PART ONE

I. THE BACKGROUND

SAINTE-ENGRÂCE is a Basque mountain community located in the province of Soule on the south-eastern edge of the Pyrénées-Atlantiques. Soule (Xiberoa, or Zuberoa) is one of seven Basque provinces in Üskal-Herria, 'the Basque Country'.[1] The three northern provinces of Labourd, Basse-Navarre, and Soule are in France; the four southern Basque provinces of Navarra, Alava, Vizcaya, and Guipúzcoa lie in Spain.

Although there were well over 1,000 people in Sainte-Engrâce during the latter half of the nineteenth century, the resident population is now only 376 (see Appendix).[2] The majority of the people, like their forefathers, are pastoralists who cultivate small farms scattered along the valley. Approximately 66 per cent of the adult male population are shepherds, whose daily lives are largely devoted to caring for their 4,000 sheep.[3] Although most of the people are now bilingual in Basque and French, Basque is still their first and daily language. They speak the Souletine dialect, *Xiberotarra*, the grammar and vocabulary of which differ considerably from those of the other seven major Basque dialects.[4] When spoken the Souletine dialect also has a melodic quality which the other dialects lack; and of all the Souletine Basques, the Sainte-Engrâce people have the most musical accent.

I

Although the literature about the Basques is extensive, it contains few references to Sainte-Engrâce; and these are primarily concerned with the history and architecture of its eleventh-century church. The series of articles by Foix (1921, 1922, 1923, 1924) is an exception,

---

[1] Outside Soule, the following variations are employed: Eskal-Herria, Eskual-Herria, Euskal-Herria. [2] This figure is my own.

[3] This figure was given to me by the priest who, as town hall secretary, tries to keep an up-to-date account of the number of sheep in the commune.

[4] According to the linguistic atlas of Prince Louis-Lucien Bonaparte (1883), these are: Vizcayan, Guipúzcoan, Upper Navarrese (northern), Upper Navarrese (southern), Labourdin, Lower Navarrese (western), and Lower Navarrese (eastern). Although the number of Basque dialects is a subject of some dispute, Bonaparte's atlas is generally accepted by Basque scholars as the most authoritative source.

1

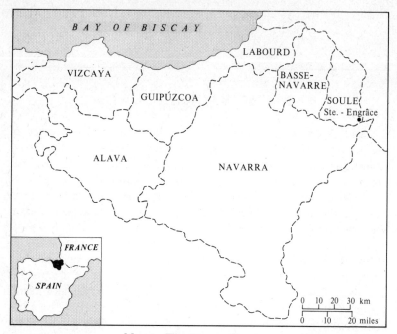

Map 1. The Basque Country

in as much as it provides us with some information about both the ecclesiastical and the social history of the commune.

The recorded history of Sainte-Engrâce covers a period of nearly 1,400 years, and begins with the defeat of the Franks in the seventh century. Under the leadership of Arimbert, the Frankish army invaded the Vascons of *Subola* (Soule) in 635. The ambush and subsequent defeat of Arimbert took place in Ehüjarre, a deep and narrow gorge which lies within the present boundaries of Sainte-Engrâce.

By the tenth century Catholicism had already been established in the community, which was known then as Urdax (or Urdaix).[5] The ancient church of Sainte Madeleine, which stood on the south-eastern edge of the commune, is thought to have been built in that century. Although no visible traces of the church remain, the remnants of the Cross of Sainte Madeleine still stand on the site.

In the eleventh century the community of Urdax was renamed Sainte-Engrâce du Port, in honour of the Portuguese virgin and martyr. Variations of the name appear in the literature: Sancta

[5] Colas (1923: 66) refers to the community as Urdax se Sumopuerto, or Urdax du sommet du port.

Gracia in the twelfth century, Sancta Engracia in the thirteenth century, and Senta Grace Deus Ports in the fifteenth century (Cuzacq 1972: 2).

At the time of her martyrdom, Sainte Engrâce was travelling to Saragossa with eighteen of her relatives, who were also Christians. According to the legend, her breasts, liver, and heart were torn from her body; those who accompanied her were decapitated. Soon after the conversion of Constantine the Great, the city of Saragossa built a shrine in her honour.

A band of thieves pilfered the shrine in the eleventh century. In order to obtain the jewels with which the hands of the saint were laden, the thieves reportedly cut off her arm and fled to the mountains of Soule. The version of the legend commonly accepted in Sainte-Engrâce claims that the thieves hid the arm in the hollow of an oak tree beside the Fountain of the Virgin Mother at the south-eastern end of the commune. The waters of that fountain are still thought to have curative powers.

The miraculous discovery of the relic is attributed to a bull, whose horns blazed 'like two candles on the altar' as it knelt in front of the oak (Cuzacq 1972: 3). The relic was placed in the sacristy of the church of Sainte Madeleine, but returned time and again to the oak in which it had been discovered. This second miracle was interpreted as a sign that the saint wished for a church in her honour on that site. The new church was built in the late eleventh century or early twelfth century; and it is perhaps the finest example of roman architecture in the Basque country today.

In approximately the middle of the eleventh century, an Augustinian collegiate was founded in the community. The monastery probably served as a refuge and hostel for pilgrims travelling from Soule to Navarra. The earliest extant reference to the collegiate appears in a Charter of 1085, in which Sanche I, King of Navarra and Aragon, placed it under the suzerainty of Leyre in Navarra. Leyre was one of the most celebrated and wealthy abbeys in the Middle Ages. Although the monks of Leyre were Benedictine, the canons of Sainte-Engrâce remained Augustinian and refused to recognize the royal decree of annexation. An agreement between the two rival abbeys was reached in 1125, by which the collegiate was obliged to give Leyre two salmon once every year and two cows on Ascension and St John the Baptist.

Conflict between the abbeys resumed in the fourteenth and fifteenth centuries. The Sainte-Engrâce canons objected to the taxes imposed upon them by Leyre; and in 1491, they were threatened with excommunication. In the fifteenth century the canons were involved in a dispute concerning pasturage rights and four *cayolars* of which Leyre claimed ownership (Foix 1922: 504). So far as I know, the account of this dispute is the earliest extant reference to the Souletine *cayolar* (*olha* in Basque), the pastoral institution with which a substantial part of this book will be concerned.

Following the usurpation of Haute-Navarre by Ferdinand the Catholic in 1512, relations between Leyre and the collegiate were probably severed. The collegiate was temporarily disbanded at the end of the sixteenth century, when its canonates were allocated to priests in other parts of Soule.

At the beginning of the sixteenth century, Sainte-Engrâce was one of six royal boroughs. One of the most important documents in the history of the commune was drawn up in that century—namely, the *Coutume de Soule*. During the reign of François I and under the direction of the jurist Jean Dibarrola, a general assembly of Souletine nobles and clergy was convened in 1520. The purpose of the assembly was to codify the customary laws and privileges of the province. Sainte-Engrâce was represented by one of its canons (Nussy Saint-Saëns 1955: 35). The *Coutume* covered several different aspects of Souletine law; but a substantial portion of it was devoted to 'the right of the *cayolar*'.

The *Coutume* was first written in Gascon, the official administrative language of the period. For this reason, the Gascon term *cayolar*—rather than its Basque equivalent *olha*—is employed in the text. Etymologically *cayolar* is derived from another Gascon word, *couye*, meaning 'ewe' (Lefebvre 1933: 192). As defined by the *Coutume*, the *cayolar* is a pastoral syndicate which consists of a group of shepherds, their communal herding hut, corral, and the mountain pastures on which their flocks graze during the months of summer transhumance.

The 'law of the *cayolar*' decreed that the members of each pastoral group should live 'socialement' in the hut, and that their primary duties were to tend their communal flocks and to make cheese from the milk of the ewes (Lefebvre 1933: 192). The emphasis placed upon the cohabitation of the shepherds 'socialement' is especially interesting, because it continues to receive expression in the present *olha* groups of Sainte-Engrâce. (See Chapter IX.)

The 'right of the *cayolar*' defined in the *Coutume* provides my account of the modern *olha* with an historical depth of more than 400 years. The 'right' was threefold: the right of pasturage on a specified tract of mountain land was reserved exclusively for the members of the pastoral group; the *cayolar* was granted ownership rights to the hut, the corral, and the land on which these stood; and thirdly, the members of the *cayolar* received the right to use timber from the nearby forests for firewood and for the construction and repairs of the hut and corral (Nussy Saint-Saëns 1955: 89). These rights are still accorded to the Sainte-Engrâce shepherds by the commune.

Shortly after the *Coutume de Soule* was written, the Protestant forces of Jeanne d'Albret invaded Catholic Soule. In 1570 the Sainte-Engrâce church was burned by the Huguenot army of Montgomery. Although the archives, interior, and ornaments of the church were destroyed, the walls remained intact. The relic of the saint is said to have been surrendered to the enemy by one of the local priests (Foix 1923: 80).

In order to punish the Sainte-Engrâce people for having refused to embrace Protestantism, Jeanne D'Albret gave a large tract of their communal forest and pasturage to the neighbouring Béarnais communes of Lannes, Aramits, and Arette. Nearly 300 years later, in 1866, the Sainte-Engrâce people contested the legitimacy of her action in the Court of Appeal at Pau and demanded that the land should be returned to them. The court rejected their claims; and some of the people are still obliged to pay the Béarnais communes for the use of those pastures.

When Arnaud II de Maytie became Bishop of Oloron in 1622, the collegiate of Sainte-Engrâce was re-established; and two of its priests were sent to Saragossa to obtain a new relic of the saint. This relic, the third finger of her right hand, is now kept in the sacristy of the church.

In the eighteenth century local attempts to preserve the autonomy and independence of the collegiate suffered further defeat. In the first quarter of that century the Bishop of Oloron received royal authorization to annex the collegiate, and thereby to increase the revenue for his newly founded seminary (Foix 1923: 83). The bishop promised that two places in the seminary would be reserved each year for Souletine students; and that special preference would be given to candidates from Sainte-Engrâce. The three priests and the priest-sacristan of the commune opposed the annexation; and the case was taken to the Council of State. In 1725 Louis XV supported the Bishop of Oloron, and the decree of union was re-confirmed (Foix 1923: 85).

During the Reign of Terror, many of the Souletine clergy escaped to Spain; but the priest and vicar of Sainte-Engrâce steadfastly remained in their mountain cul-de-sac. The Sacraments were administered covertly in the grange of the former presbytery (Cuzacq 1972: 11). In order to conceal his true profession, the vicar is reported to have enlisted himself as a mule-driver in a military caravan. His expertise in deceiving the authorities was further demonstrated when customs officers were sent to the commune. According to local tradition, Haritchabalet played a vital role in the flourishing contraband trade by staging mock funeral processions. The coffin was filled with smuggled goods; and while the officers knelt to express their respect, the coffin was transported safely past them.

During the career of Haritchabalet, the customs officers received their board and lodging in local houses. In 1840 his successor convinced the municipal council that the officers should be provided with their own station—ostensibly to control the contraband trade more effectively. But his primary objective was to check the reported promiscuous behaviour of the young officers.

In 1838 the Syndicate of Soule was established by royal decree with a view to regulating the exploitation of natural resources in the province, and to promote the growth of the Souletine economy. In keeping with its previous attempts to remain independent, Sainte-Engrâce was one of only two communes which refused to join. By doing so the community retained possession of its forests, mountain pasturage, and common lands, which otherwise would have become the communal property of the Syndicate.

In 1841 the church was classified as an historical monument; and under the direction of Etchecopar, one of the few priests whom Sainte-Engrâce has produced, the church was completely renovated between 1850 and 1864.

With the exceptions of Haristoy (1893) and Foix (1921, 1922, 1923, 1924) the late nineteenth- and early twentieth-century references to Sainte-Engrâce contain little material of sociological interest. Haristoy gives us a fairly detailed account of the procession to the Three Crosses at Lechartzu, a col located on the north-western edge of the commune, on Corpus Christi; and he makes the interesting observation that the processional cross was carried *à tour de rôle* by the men whose lands were traversed by the pilgrims.[6] People who participated in the procession before the Second World War confirmed his report in 1976/7.

---

[6] The notion of *à tour de rôle* is expressed in Basque as *aldizka*, derived from the same root as *aldikatü* meaning to alternate, to take turns, to replace serially.

II

It is outside the specific aims of this book to explore fully the recent history of Sainte-Engrâce, which, in the French Basque country, is widely regarded as the most geographically and socially isolated community in the region; but it is important to the achievement of certain aims to examine selectively events which have brought the Sainte-Engrâce people into contact with the outside world during the latter part of the nineteenth century and until 1979. In this way it will be possible to appreciate the extent to which the people have been exposed to outside influences and yet have retained many aspects of traditional Basque culture which have been lost or are becoming obsolete in other parts of the Basque country.

During the nineteenth century and until the 1920s the period of summer transhumance brought the Sainte-Engrâce men into close contact with three groups of outsiders: the shepherds from lowland Souletine villages whose households owned shares in herding huts located on the mountain pastures of Sainte-Engrâce and who spent the milking and cheese-making season in these huts; Spanish Basque shepherds from Isaba, the village in north-eastern Navarra that is closest to Sainte-Engrâce; and shepherds from southern Navarra who travelled with their flocks to the mountain pastures bordering the southern edge of Sainte-Engrâce.

Formerly, the Isaba and southern Navarrese shepherds regularly hired Sainte-Engrâce men to milk their ewes and to make cheese for them in June and July. According to the Sainte-Engrâce men, they and their forefathers were hired to perform these tasks because they were widely acclaimed to be the most skilful shepherds and cheese-makers in the region. During the two-month period the Sainte-Engrâce men lived in huts owned by Isaba shepherds and which lay between five and fifteen kilometres south of the commune. Those who were hired were generally young, unmarried men whose fathers and/or brothers remained in Sainte-Engrâce to act as shepherds for their own households. The Sainte-Engrâce men continued to work for Isaba shepherds until about 1927, by which time few of the large Isaba flocks remained intact and, according to the Sainte-Engrâce men, when 'the Isaba shepherds lost interest in the arts of cheese-making and shepherding'.

During the months of summer transhumance, the Isaba and lowland Souletine shepherds occasionally came down from the mountains to drink in Sainte-Engrâce cafés; and some were regular visitors in local households. I am told that conversations between the Isaba shepherds and the people were generally conducted in Basque, though the two groups had difficulty in understanding their respective dialects.

In the nineteenth century and until 1913, the Sainte-Engrâce people were also well known among the merchants and traders of Isaba, which was formerly regarded as 'the first neighbour village' (*herri-aizoa*) of Sainte-Engrâce. In this part of the Basque country, a community has only one 'first neighbour village', with which a trading relationship is established. Some of the elderly people vividly recalled having made the thirty-five-kilometre journey to Isaba on foot or on mule when they had livestock, cheese, and woollen cloth to sell or to trade in return for goods such as salt, sugar, cotton cloth, and metal tools.

When the paved road from lowland Soule to the north-western end of the commune was completed in 1913, Tardets became the 'first neighbour village' of Sainte-Engrâce. As a result, commercial ties between Sainte-Engrâce households and traders from Isaba and other nearby Navarrese villages were weakened; but they were by no means severed, for the Sainte-Engrâce shepherds continued to rely upon certain traders to supply them with contraband goods such as wine and spirits. A fairly large-scale contraband trade flourished in the area until the Second World War.

Before the completion of the road, Sainte-Engrâce was accessible to lowland Soule only by means of narrow, rough trails. The few French Basques who were not shepherds and who travelled to Sainte-Engrâce regularly were mostly priests and bishops. Published accounts of their experiences are largely devoted to descriptions of the inclement weather, the treacherous terrain, and the arduous journey by mule. One elderly bishop, who travelled to the community for its annual confirmation ceremony, is reputed to have uttered the following equivocal words:

> Sainte-Engrâce, Sainte-Engrâce,
> Jamais plus tu ne verras ma face!

According to my eldest informants, the majority of the Sainte-Engrâce people rarely travelled to lowland Soule before 1913. Severe winter weather sometimes forced the shepherds to move their flocks to lowland pastures, which they rented near Tardets; but the shepherds rarely stayed there for more than a few weeks. Contact with other Souletine Basques was not, however, confined to the periods of summer and winter transhumance; for, during the nineteenth century and until the 1940s, Sainte-Engrâce households regularly sent their young, unmarried members to work as servants in lowland Souletine villages. This and other forms of temporary migration by unmarried members of a household are part of a long-standing tradition in rural Basque society (cf. Douglass 1975: 120–3). Before the First World War, some young people worked as *domestiques* in Béarnais households in the valley of Baretous; and a few of them learned to speak the *patois* of their employers, though they rarely mastered French. The duration of their employment in a Souletine or Béarnais household ranged from one to as many as seven years. In the majority of cases, a *domestique* from Sainte-Engrâce began his or her career shortly after having taken First Communion at the age of twelve and worked as a servant until the age of eighteen or nineteen.

During the period 1900–17, several groups of outsiders, most of whom were French, travelled to the commune; but their presence seems to have been largely ignored by the people. As early as 1903 a party of tourists attempted to penetrate the gorge of Khakueta, which is roughly three and a half kilometres in length and separates the upper and lower halves of the commune on the western side of the valley. An increasing number of tourists came to the gorge after 1906, when a series of foot-bridges was built along the bottom of Khakueta.

In 1907/8 a speleologist was commissioned by the French government to study the numerous caves, chasms, and caverns in the region of Sainte-Engrâce and Pierre-St-Martin. As a result of this research, the government built a dam in the lower half of the commune between 1914 and 1917, and a hydro-electric plant in the neighbouring community of Licq. The dam and plant were intended to provide power for electric traction railway lines in the western Pyrénées; they now provide power for domestic and commercial use in the Pyrénées-Atlantiques and in the western half of Béarn.

Government officials also came to the commune when a tramway linking Sainte-Engrâce and the Tardets sawmill was constructed in 1910. So far as I know, the tramway was used only to transport lumber and forestry officials. Foix (1921: 710) reports that the small locomotive travelled from Tardets to the commune twice daily and that the journey took an hour and a half. The tramway was abandoned in 1914.

In 1932 the paved road linking Tardets and the Caserne of Sainte-Engrâce was extended to the south-eastern end of the commune. Although the extension of the road made Sainte-Engrâce and lowland Soule more easily accessible to each other, travel within the community remained difficult; for the majority of the houses could be reached from the road only by means of the old trails. In the lower half of the commune, these trails were not replaced by more direct and paved roads until the 1960s and 1970s. The first motor cars in the commune, introduced between 1932 and 1935, were owned by three local people: the proprietor of the only hotel in Sainte-Engrâce, the postmistress, and a man who ran one of the cafés, as well as a taxi service. In the late 1930s, the parish priest also bought a motor car. Although these vehicles were occasionally used to transport people and livestock to the Tardets market, the majority of the people travelled to and from the market on foot or on mule until the late 1940s.

The Second World War is remembered as a 'black period' by the Sainte-Engrâce people. Many of those who served in the French army were captured by the Germans and spent several years in prisoner of war camps; and in 1942/3, the commune was occupied by the German army. The people were rarely permitted to travel to the lowlands and were required, under penalty of death, to be inside their houses by eight o'clock every evening. German sentries were stationed in many of the Sainte-Engrâce herding huts along the frontier; and two of the eight men who died in the war were executed by the Germans for having taken refugees across the frontier into Spain. Houses were searched regularly; and every household in the commune was required to provide the German officers with one kilo of meat once a month. If a household was unable to meet its monthly quota, its members sought the assistance of a 'first neighbour'. Meat provided by a 'first neighbour' was classified as *dohañik*, or free, though it was collectively understood that any gift of meat would be 'paid for' in kind if the 'first neighbour' were unable to meet its own quota later on.

III

At the time of my research in 1976/7, Sainte-Engrâce was still a small, face-to-face society that remained relatively isolated, both socially and geographically, from the outside world. Although a few of the elderly women travel to Paris or Bordeaux to spend a few weeks with their children and grandchildren once every year, the majority of the adult population rarely go further than Mauléon, the capital of Soule, or the nearby Béarnais town of Oloron.

With the exception of a school bus, which operates between Sainte-Engrâce and Tardets, there is no public means of transport linking the community with lowland Soule. In 1976/7 roughly one-third of the households in the commune had motor cars. By 1979 more than half of the households either owned motor cars or had access to vehicles recently purchased by young people who work in the lowlands during the week and return to their natal households at week-ends.

At the time of my research, seventeen young men between the ages of nineteen and twenty-eight were employed by the electricity board to repair cables in Soule and in Béarn. The men are required to travel extensively and are well paid by regional standards. During the week, they take their meals and sleep in a hotel in Pau. All of them return to Sainte-Engrâce every week-end.

From the point of view of many young, unmarried people, the motor car is not only an essential acquisition if one wishes to work in the lowlands and to return regularly to one's natal community; it is also an essential feature of their social lives both inside and outside Sainte-Engrâce. During the summer and on major holidays, large groups of young people between the ages of sixteen and twenty-five regularly attend dances and festivals in other Souletine villages and in some nearby Béarnais villages. At other times of the year many of them travel to the lowlands at least once every week-end to drink in cafés, to hear Basque bands and singing groups, and to socialize with young people from other Souletine villages.

Unlike these young people, the majority of adult men and women neither have the desire nor feel that they have the time to go to the lowlands unless the journey is absolutely necessary for economic, medical, or certain social reasons such as the death of a close relative in another community.

Unless they have lambs to sell at the livestock markets in winter and spring, the men rarely go to Tardets more than once a month. If they attend the market they often gather in a Tardets café that is owned by a Sainte-Engrâce man before returning to the commune.

The frequency with which the Sainte-Engrâce women go to Tardets varies considerably. Most of the elderly women rarely or never make the journey, though there are a few who enjoy attending the market occasionally to exchange news with other Sainte-Engrâce people. The younger female heads of household generally attend the market once a month to purchase supplies for the household. The Tardets market is held in the plaza once every fortnight, but only a few young women go to every market. These women, all of whom drive motor cars, are often asked to buy goods for neighbours and close relatives who do not wish to make the journey themselves.

People also travel to Tardets to collect pensions, to go to the local bank, and to receive medical treatment from one of the two doctors, one of whom speaks Basque and has served the Sainte-Engrâce people for forty years. A few people occasionally go to the only dentist in the town. In preparation for certain special occasions, such as a wedding, some of the women now go to one of the local hairdressers to have their hair cut and styled. The journey to Tardets is also made when an individual or household group wishes to make a marriage or property contract and requires the assistance of the notary.

With the exception of those who are young and unmarried, few of the Sainte-Engrâce people regularly travel in the French Basque country further than Tardets. Some of the men attend the livestock market in Mauléon when they have lambs to sell in the spring. A few household groups who own motor cars occasionally spend a Sunday with a close relative who has married and settled in Oloron, Saint Palais, or in a village in the neighbouring Basque province of Basse-Navarre; but most people prefer to have their kin and affines come to Sainte-Engrâce.

During the period of summer transhumance, the shepherds make regular trips to a hostel in Navarra which is only a few hours' walk from their herding huts and where they buy spirits and wine.

Within the commune itself, the only outsiders with whom the people have any regular contact are the Basque baker from Sauguis who travels to the commune three times a week and upon whom the people rely for their bread; a Basque grocer from Tardets who travels from *quartier* to *quartier* twice weekly to sell tinned and some fresh food; and two livestock dealers to whom the people sell their calves, cows, and mares. Only one of these men speaks Basque. In late winter and spring, a French-speaking employee of a Béarnais *fromagerie* visits the commune once every two days to collect ewes' milk. Three other outsiders come to Sainte-Engrâce when asked to do so: the two doctors from Tardets and the veterinarian from Mauléon.

The two French schoolmasters who live in the commune are not well known and are rarely seen by the majority of the local people, though one of them has lived in Sainte-Engrâce with his wife and children for ten years. They have a flat in the school that is attended by children from the lower half of the commune until the age of twelve. The other schoolmaster lives alone in a flat above the school in the upper community. Neither schoolmaster speaks Basque, though the local children told me that the schoolmaster in the lower community can understand some of their conversations in the language.

There are two other households in the commune whose members are French and who are not well known by the vast majority of the local people. In 1974 a couple and their three children came to Sainte-Engrâce from the French Alps and bought the house of an elderly bachelor who moved into the geriatric ward of the Tardets hospital. The family do not speak Basque. The man worked in the low-lands but is now rumoured to have gone to Africa. His wife opened a curio shop near the entrance to Khakueta during the tourist season in 1979. Only one of her neighbours has made an attempt to know and to help her look after her farm and livestock; but her two large, ferocious dogs do not encourage neighbours to approach the house.

In 1979 another French couple bought an old house in the same *quartier*. They are reportedly friends of the first couple. The husband works in the shoe factory in Licq, and his wife has a job in a chocolate factory in Oloron; but they apparently intend to buy sheep and 'to learn how to live like Sainte-Engrâce people'. They have been be-friended by the same household whose members often assist the owner of the curio shop with her livestock.

During the past five years, an increasing number of French people have expressed an interest in buying barns and derelict houses in Sainte-Engrâce for conversion into holiday homes. At the time of my research, three derelict barns and three houses had been renovated or partially restored for use during the summer. With two exceptions, the owners of these properties are not known and are rarely seen by the local people.

In 1976/7 the Sainte-Engrâce people rarely conversed with the tourists, hikers, and speleologists who passed through their com-munity during the summer. The owners of two of the five cafés did not seem anxious to attract a large tourist clientele and often sent prospective customers to one of the other cafés when they and their families wanted to spend the day haymaking.

Every summer several thousand tourists pay 5 francs per person to see the gorge of Khakueta, which is widely renowned for its beauty. The woman who collects admission fees also runs a café on the ground floor of her house, which is located near the entrance to the gorge. Proceeds from the sale of tickets generally total 40,000 francs per annum and, together with proceeds from the sale of timber taken from the commune's forests, contribute greatly to the monetary wealth of Sainte-Engrâce, which is widely regarded as the wealthiest commune in Soule.

The eleventh-century church at the south-eastern end of the commune also attracts tourists in summer.

In 1976/7 tourist accommodation was available in the hotel, which has six rooms to let; in the town hall, which has several small flats; in a house owned and renovated by the mayor; and in a house owned by a Sainte-Engrâce widow living in Saint Palais. During this period, however, only a small proportion of the tourists who came to the commune spent the night there.

When I returned to the commune in 1979 I found that local attitudes towards tourists had changed considerably and rapidly. Many of those who had formerly opposed any plans which aimed to promote tourism in Sainte-Engrâce observed gloomily that their own society is doomed to extinction, since 'none of the young people want to be farmers and shepherds any more or to have lots of babies', and reasoned that it would be better to have tourists as neighbours than to have no neighbours at all. Some people have also come to regard tourists as a seasonally reliable source of cash. The café owners who used to turn away customers in order to go haymaking have converted their cattle and sheep barns into a tourist hostel. Another café owner, who does not keep livestock, now uses the field beside the café as a camping site for hikers.

One other step was taken in 1979 which will encourage the growth of the tourist industry in Sainte-Engrâce. For several years the local people have opposed government plans to build a road from the south-eastern end of the commune to the Spanish frontier near Pierre-St-Martin. In 1979 the majority of the people decided to support the plan, not, they claim, because they want more tourists to pass through their community. The road would come within a kilometre of many of their herding huts and would enable the shepherds to travel to and from their mountain pastures by motor car. As one shepherd observed, 'with the road I could go up to the mountains to see my sheep and cattle as often as I liked in summer, and I'd have more time to spend helping my household with the hay'. In 1979 the municipal council received permission from the people to proceed with plans to widen the road, which is now no more than a rough track. The road is expected to be completed as far as the frontier by 1982.

July and August not only bring tourists to the commune. Although many of the people who left Sainte-Engrâce in this century have never returned, a large proportion of those who have emigrated since the 1940s return to their natal community every summer. The majority of emigrants have settled in Paris and Bordeaux and have

French spouses. During the summer nearly every household in the commune is visited by at least one group of close relatives from these cities. In cases where there are several siblings who wish to bring their spouses and children to their natal household, these siblings and their families are expected to take turns, of roughly equal duration, staying in the house; but when the holidays of emigrant siblings and/or offspring coincide, a household group may have as many as fourteen close relatives staying with them for a fortnight or more.

The members of most households look forward to, and greatly enjoy, having their emigrant kin with them for a few weeks every year. During their stay, relatives are generally expected to assist the household with the routine chores, as well as with the hay harvests. Affines who are neither natives of Sainte-Engrâce nor Basque are rarely excused from haymaking, though they are generally unfit and unaccustomed to the work which is expected of them.

Nearly all of the emigrants whom I met in Sainte-Engrâce speak Basque fluently and clearly enjoy having an opportunity to use their first language; but in the presence of one's own or someone else's French affines, French is often spoken as a matter of courtesy.

Emigrants who return to the commune regularly have contributed greatly to the people's knowledge of urban French society and of a way of life which differs radically from their own; and, as is the case elsewhere in the Basque country (cf. Douglass 1975: 125), the close ties which exist between emigrants and their natal households provide a channel for further migration to the cities. From at least as early as the 1860s, Sainte-Engrâce emigrants living in Paris, Bordeaux, and Bayonne have been an invaluable source of assistance to relatives seeking temporary or permanent employment in these urban centres.

Many of the young people who are now between the ages of seventeen and thirty have visited close relatives in Paris or Bordeaux at least once; and several worked for their emigrant relatives before returning to Sainte-Engrâce to settle. Those who did return admit that they were impressed with the material advantages that an urban way of life can bring. But they were anxious to return to their natal community and to the way of life which they know best, to which they feel best suited, and of which they are extremely proud.

II. THE SETTING AND THE PEOPLE

SOULE is the smallest of the seven Basque provinces; it extends approximately sixty kilometres from north to south and roughly thirty kilometres from east to west. The province has a total land area of 785 square kilometres (Goyheneche 1961: 21). The total land area of the seven provinces is more than 20,000 square kilometres, but only one-seventh of that total lies in France (Douglass and Bilbao 1975: 14).

I

Soule is divided into four regions: Basse-Soule, Grande Arbaille, Petit Arbaille, and Haute-Soule. The latter region is further divided into the Val Dextre and the Val Senestre. Sainte-Engrâce lies in the Val Senestre of Haute-Soule, the most mountainous part of the French Basque country.

With 589 hectares Sainte-Engrâce has the largest land area of the seventeen communities in Haute-Soule. The mountain pastures and forests of the commune extend as far as Béarn in the east, Spanish Basque Navarra in the south, and the Souletine commune of Larrau in the west. The pastures and forests east and south-east of Sainte-Engrâce belong to the Béarnais communities of Lannes, Arette, and Aramits.

From north-west to south-east the commune has a length of eleven kilometres and averages six kilometres in width. The mountain valley, along which the Sainte-Engrâce houses are scattered, has been formed by the often treacherous waters of the Gave de Sainte-Engrâce. At the northern end of the commune, the river joins the Gave de Larrau to form the Saison, the beginning of which lies roughly five kilometres north of the dam and reservoir. The waterfall created by the dam plunges several hundred feet into a narrow, steep-walled gorge.

The Gave de Sainte-Engrâce, which the people refer to simply as Uhaitza, 'the River', flows through the centre of the commune, though it is said to have little *indarra*, or force, until it joins the main tributary from Khakueta and flows north into the Saison. My

16

inquiries about the spatial orientation of the river revealed, however, that few people know terms for the cardinal points, to which virtually no importance is attached in Sainte-Engrâce ideology. With some prompting, people identified north and south as *ipharra* and *hegoa* respectively but tended to associate these terms with the north and south winds, rather than with the cardinal points. After considerable debate among themselves, they gave two words for west: *ekhisargia*, literally 'the entering sun', and *ekhi-itzalgia*, 'the setting sun'. No one could think of a word for east.

Although I was unable to elicit any information about the river within the context of traditional cosmological views, I found that the river did feature prominently in a particular ritual that was performed until recently (see Chapter VII), though no informant had any clear understanding of the river's symbolic importance in that ritual.

By motor car there is only one means of access to Sainte-Engrâce. A narrow, winding road follows the Saison from Tardets to Licq-Athérey and forks at the mouth of the Sainte-Engrâce and Larrau rivers. The road branching off to the south-west leads to Larrau; the road running south and south-east leads to Sainte-Engrâce. The only direct routes to the commune from Spain are sheep trails.

The Souletine community closest to Sainte-Engrâce is Licq-Athérey, the communal pastures and forests of which border the commune on its northern side. The two small, spatially separate villages of Licq and Athérey lie between six and seven kilometres north of the Sainte-Engrâce/Licq-Athérey border. Tardets lies eighteen kilometres north of this border; and from the lower, northern half of Sainte-Engrâce, it can be reached by motor car in about twenty-five minutes. Mauléon, the capital of the province, lies roughly twenty-nine kilometres north-west of Sainte-Engrâce.

The paved road, which links the commune and lowland Soule, extends from the extreme northern end of Sainte-Engrâce to the head of the valley in the south-east. The road winds along the eastern side of the valley and follows the course of the river for several kilometres. In 1976/7 the road led to the church in Senta, a settlement in the upper half of the commune, where it joined a dirt track along which several households are located. This track was paved during 1978/9 and ends abruptly at the head of the valley.

The people themselves do not, however, classify the valley which runs through the centre of their community as a valley (*ibarr*). In their opinion, the valley is too high and too narrow to qualify as an *ibarr*; it is, for them, the lowest part of the circle of mountains (*bortüko üngürü*) in which they live, yet high enough to be classified under the general heading of *bortiak*, or mountains. The valley is often referred to as an *üngürünea*, which conveys the notion of a circular region. The middle part of the circle of mountains consists of *mendiak*, steep hills which rise from the valley floor; whereas the third and highest part of the circle consists of *bortiak*, or mountains. I shall return to the notion of the commune as a circle in later chapters.

From the point of view of its inhabitants, Sainte-Engrâce is bounded on all sides by mountains, each one of which has a name. According to several experienced shepherds, the entire circle of mountains was formerly referred to by one name, Ünhürüz, the meaning of which is no longer known. Ünhürüz is also the name of a particular mountain near the south-western rim of Khakueta; but it does not seem to have any special significance for the people.

Although the men and some women claim to know the names of all the mountains in the circle, they were unable to tell me exactly how many mountains Sainte-Engrâce has; nor did they see any point in counting them. (According to my own calculations, there are more than ninety named mountains in the commune.) For the people, the number is unimportant; the essential fact is that the mountains form an *üngürü* or circle around Sainte-Engrâce.

The mountains within the commune range in elevation from 850 to 1,800 metres. Along the boundary between Béarn and Navarra and within five to ten kilometres of Sainte-Engrâce, the Pic d'Arlas, Pic d'Anie, and the Table of the Three Kings reach elevations of 2,044 to 2,504 metres. To the south and south-west the commune is flanked by the highest of the western Pyrénées. In the neighbouring commune of Larrau, the Pic d'Orhy has an altitude of 2,021 metres. The Pic Lakhoura (1,877 m) marks the southern boundary of Sainte-Engrâce and the political boundary between France and Spain. In the west the Sainte-Engrâce/Larrau boundary lies on a chain of mountains which range in elevation from 1,069 to 1,885 metres.

II

On the northern slope of the western Pyrénées the climate is temperate, maritime, and is characterized by a relatively low annual range of temperatures; but in the mountains of Haute-Soule the maritime climate is modified by elevation, aspect, and winds (Gómez-Ibáñez 1975: 12). Rainfall is abundant on the northern slope. The lowlands receive at least 1,000 mm annually; but mountain communities such as Sainte-Engrâce may receive from 1,500 to 1,800 mm per year.

Temperatures in December, January, and February generally range from −2 to 10°C; but when the dry, warm south wind from Spain sweeps across the mountains, temperatures may reach as high as 17 °C. The people welcome the warm, clear weather brought by the south wind in autumn and spring; but a south wind in December, when the sausages and hams are hung to dry, is greatly feared. The wind brings flies and consequently maggots that can quickly spoil the newly salted meat.

In Sainte-Engrâce the first frost may occur as early as the beginning of November. Frost and a light snowfall are not uncommon as late as April. In the mountains and on the ridges above 1,200 metres the first snow generally falls in early November and remains until April. In the valley, which ranges in elevation from 600 to 800 metres, the depth of the snow now rarely exceeds a few centimetres; but the people recall winters when their community was snow-bound for several weeks at a time.

In March the temperature ranges from about 3 to 14 °C. The low, pot-bellied stoves, which have replaced the open hearths in most houses, are not put into storage until April. Mild weather can generally be expected in April and May, when some of the heaviest rainfalls occur. In April the forests are still barren and black against the snow-capped peaks and bright green pastures in the valley; but by the middle of May the forests of beech and oak form a thick, green canopy above the gorges, ravines, and pastures that slope toward the valley bottom.

In late spring and in summer the expanse of green meadows, forests, and mountain pastures is a truly impressive sight. July and August are usually the hottest months with temperatures ranging from 18 to 24 °C. The two summers that I spent in Sainte-Engrâce taught me something about the extremes to which this mountain climate is subject. The summer of 1976 was hot; the skies were clear nearly every day, and there was just enough rainfall to bring an abundant harvest. In 1977 it rained almost continually from April until early September. A sharp frost in June ruined most of the potato crop. The heavy summer rains either washed away or flooded the fields. By the end of August the maize was only a few centimetres high.

Autumn weather in Sainte-Engrâce is less changeable. The days are generally crisp and clear; but when the south wind rattles the shutters the days become warm and hazy. In late October the fern becomes a burnished copper on the hillsides, and the leaves turn yellow and gold. With the exception of early frosts, the first signs of

winter—snow on the peaks and the mournful cry of migratory cranes
flying high above the valley—do not appear until late November.

III

From the base of the valley to the top of the mountains there are
four distinct zones of vegetation: meadow, heath, forest, and alpine
meadow. Most of the valley meadowlands and arable fields range
from 600 to 800 metres in elevation. The meadow grasses provide
winter fodder for the livestock; and in midsummer they provide
three harvests of hay. In the lower, northern end of the commune,
the winter pastures and fields form a broad, undulating plain on the
north-facing slope; but on the south-facing slope and in the upper
half of the commune, most pastures are on steep inclines.

Heaths are interspersed between the meadowlands and patches
of forest. Bracken, furze, gorse, and heather thrive on the ridges of
the south-facing slope. Immediately above the heath are short
grasslands, used for grazing cattle in the spring and autumn.

The forests are predominantly on the western, south-western, and
southern sides of the valley at altitudes ranging from 600 to 1,000
metres. The eastern side of the valley has only small patches of
forest. Pedunculate oak and chestnut are scattered along the bottom
of the valley. The forests from 800 to 1,000 metres are largely beech;
but in some places there are large tracts of fir as well. Between 1,100
and 1,300 metres the beech and fir forests gradually give way to the
broad expanse of alpine meadow on the mountain-tops.

Alpine vegetation in the western Pyrénées consists of various
grasses, sedges, and legumes. As soon as the snow melts in late
spring, the shepherds burn large sections of alpine meadow. They
claim that burning the 'old grass' induces the birth of new and richer
grass, on which their flocks graze in summer.

IV

Sainte-Engrâce is divided into two geographically and socially
separate communities: the lower community, which extends
approximately seven kilometres from the north-western end of the
commune to the gorge of Khakueta; and the upper community,
which runs from Khakueta to the head of the valley in the south-east.
The upper community has a length of roughly four kilometres.

The lower community consists of six rural *quartiers* in which
there are sixty-seven permanently inhabited houses: Caserne,

Ekhi-Begia, and Altsaso lie on the eastern side of the valley; Ükhü-mürrütia, Dolainty-Ükhümürrütia, and Athoro lie on the western side. Roughly two-thirds of the population live in this half of the commune.

As one approaches the commune from the neighbouring community of Licq-Athérey, the first houses are obscured from view by a steep embankment on the eastern side of the road. As the road winds along the rim of the valley gorge houses scattered across the eastern and western escarpments become visible. Patches of beech and rolling pastures are interspersed among the two-storey grey and white fieldstone houses, the architecture of which is similar to that of farmhouses in Béarn.

Souletine houses have neither the long, sloping red tile roofs nor the façades ribbed with wooden beams which are so characteristic of houses in Labourd and Basse-Navarre. In Sainte-Engrâce, as in other Souletine communities, the dull slate roofs of the houses are steep and pointed; the façades of some houses are whitewashed but they are never decorated.

In the lower *quartiers* of Sainte-Engrâce, large rectangular barns are often attached directly to the houses. Cultivated fields and fenced pastures are clustered around each dwelling, so that a complex of sheds, barn, and house forms a nucleus in the centre of each farm. The average size of a lower farm—including winter pasturage, arable land, heath, and forest—is roughly fifteen hectares.

Farms in the west-facing *quartiers* are generally recognized as having a more favourable spatial orientation than those in east-facing *quartiers*, since the former receive sunlight later in the day. This factor is particularly important during the hay harvests, when people in west-facing *quartiers* are able to dry and to gather their crops long after the other side of the valley has been cast into shadow and haymaking there has ceased for the day.

The lower, west-facing *quartier* of Ekhi-Begia (literally 'the eye of the sun', figuratively 'a very sunny place') receives the warmest and latest sun; and some households there have an additional advantage in being within an hour's walk from their herding huts and mountain pasturage. Ekhi-Begia is, however, widely thought to have one major disadvantage; it is the steepest *quartier* in Sainte-Engrâce. Fields and winter pastures there often have a vertical incline of 45 to 60 degrees, which prohibits the use of tractors and most other types of modern farm machinery.

In the lower half of the commune Caserne is the only *quartier* that has any nucleus whatever. The town hall, a school, and two houses

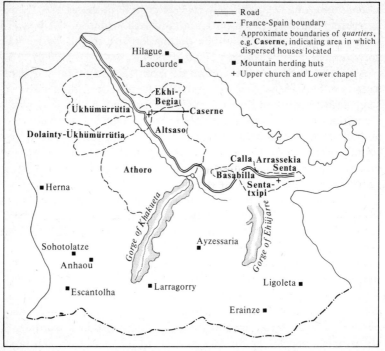

Map 2. The commune of Sainte-Engrâce

border a paved plaza, on which a fronton court stands. One of the houses contains a café and the only shop in the entire community. The other five houses in Caserne are scattered along the main road and the ridge above the town hall. The chapel, which was constructed in 1952, lies on the southern edge of Caserne. The ruins of the former chapel lie on a hillock overlooking Caserne in the *quartier* of Dolainty-Ükhümürrütia.

The number of houses in the other lower *quartiers* ranges from ten to twenty-two. The houses are fairly evenly dispersed along both sides of the valley, though the majority of houses are located on the east-facing slope in the *quartiers* of Athoro and Dolainty-Ükhümürrütia. The distance between lower households ranges from one-half to one and a half kilometres. Until 1976 most houses were accessible to one another and to the main road only by narrow, rocky footpaths. Mules and horses were used to transport all agricultural and domestic supplies to the houses from Caserne. At the time of my research, the commune completed a series of serpentine paved roads leading from the main road to nearly every lower house.

Roughly one kilometre of forest, heath, and pasturage separates the upper and lower communities. The total land area of the upper community is approximately half that of the lower community. The valley narrows as it winds south and eastward from Caserne. The amount of arable land is further decreased by the encroaching beech forests, the lack of sunshine on the east-facing slope, and the precipitous fields. The average land area of an upper farm is only about nine hectares.

There are thirty-two permanently inhabited houses in the upper community and these are divided among five named settlements: Basabilla, Calla, Sentatxipi, Arrassekia, and Senta. The distance from Basabilla, the northernmost upper *quartier*, to Senta at the head of the valley is only two kilometres.

Basabilla consists of five houses and a small hotel, which attracts tourists in summer but stands virtually empty in winter. The hotel is owned by an elderly Sainte-Engrâce couple. In 1976 the business was leased by a local man and his Basse-Navarrese wife. The young man left the community about ten years ago and served as an apprentice chef in several Béarnais and Basque hotels before returning to his native commune.

Dances are held in the hotel on most major holidays; and these are attended by the young people of Sainte-Engrâce and other Souletine communities. In 1977 five households held their First Communion feasts in the hotel; but the two wedding feasts in the same year were held in the lowlands, ostensibly because the local hotel cannot accommodate a wedding party of one hundred people.

On a hillock above the hotel and Basabilla, Calla is the largest nucleated settlement in the commune. Ten houses and several barns are clustered around a small, paved plaza. Two of the ten houses face the main road rather than the plaza, across which people, livestock, and the one Calla tractor frequently pass. One of these houses presents a striking contrast to the other dwellings: it has a gleaming white façade, a double garage, paved drive, manicured gardens, and a wrought iron gate. 'S.V.P.' (s'il vous plaît) is printed neatly beneath the doorbell. The house belongs to a wealthy, retired French industrialist and his Sainte-Engrâce wife, whom he met in Paris. The couple use the house occasionally at week-ends and during the holidays. The husband, now in his seventies, rarely ventures out of their house except to visit the natal household of his wife and that of her brother-in-law. The only other household with which he and his wife have established fairly close and friendly ties is one of their 'first neighbours'. Their relationship with that household will be discussed in Chapter V.

The other Calla houses, like those elsewhere in the commune, are three-storeyed dwellings with gray or white fieldstone walls, slate roofs, and bright green or red shutters. During the first two months of my stay in 1976/7, I lived in the vacant house of the Saint-Palais widow; but I worked and ate with her sister and sister's son, whose house is also in Calla and with whom I had hoped to stay from the start. The 'woman of the house' (*etxekandere*) explained that she wanted me to sleep in the vacant house because her twenty-five-year-old son was still unmarried. He had a local *emaztegeia*, a 'potential wife', and his mother feared that my sleeping in the same house would inspire gossip. I moved into their house on the day after her son was married and remained there for the duration of my research in 1976/7. In 1979, I lived in a lower house owned by the mayor of Sainte-Engrâce.

From Calla the paved road winds around the upper schoolhouse toward the three houses of Sentatxipi. The four houses of Arrassekia border a footpath which links Calla and Sentatxipi. On the southern side of the road the land is divided into small, enclosed pastures and fields of maize. A low, steep hillock occupies the centre of the valley basin. Behind the one house perched on the brow of the hillock the magnificent gorge of Ehüjarre cuts sharply into the mountains on the frontier.

The valley of Sainte-Engrâce ends abruptly in Senta, roughly eight kilometres from Caserne. Four Senta houses flank the paved road near the eleventh-century church: the priest's house, the holiday house of a Frenchman and his Sainte-Engrâce wife, and two houses with kitchens which serve as cafés. The other seven Senta houses are dispersed along the ridges and paved road which ends at the head of the valley.

V

In order to differentiate themselves from all other Souletine Basques (Xiberotarrak), the people of the upper and lower communities are collectively known, and know themselves as Santaztarrak, 'Sainte-Engrâce people'. Like the people of most other Souletine communities, they also have a nickname: Xahakotarrak, 'the goatskin flask people'. Although the nickname is commonly employed by lowlanders in place of Santaztarrak, it is disliked and rarely used by the majority of the Sainte-Engrâce people. In their view, the nickname has derogatory implications, e.g. that the Sainte-Engrâce people are drunkards and backward peasants who prefer to drink wine from a flask and disdain the use of a glass. I did, however, find a few men who identified themselves to lowlanders as Xahakotarrak with considerable pride. These men regarded the nickname as a compliment. As one shepherd explained, 'We are Xahakotarrak because our forefathers had the best goatskin flasks in the region, and it was they who taught the other Souletine shepherds how to drink from a *xahako* without spilling a drop!'

Within the commune itself, the Santazarrak who live in the lower community are referred to as *pekuak*, 'the lower ones', conceptually and spatially distinct from *petarrak*, the generic term for lowlanders. Santaztarrak living in the upper community are called *gaiñekuak*, 'the upper ones'.

'Upper' and 'lower' are classificatory terms which divide Sainte-Engrâce society into two categories of people; they are also spatial referents, but not to the relative elevation of the two communities. Some of the lower houses are in fact higher than Senta (600 m) and Calla (630 m). The criterion on which the classificatory distinction upper/lower is based is not elevation, but spatial proximity to the lowlands and by extension to the outside world.

The distinction between upper and lower people is best understood within the context of Sainte-Engrâce cosmological views. The world is spatially ordered by a pair of contrasted and relative terms: *pean* (down below) and *gaiñean* (up above).[1] If one were anywhere else on earth, one would be *pean* vis-à-vis Sainte-Engrâce. Conversely, those in Sainte-Engrâce are always *gaiñean* in relation to the rest of earth. Sainte-Engrâce is *pean* only in relation to Heaven, the stars, the sun, and moon.

Within the commune itself, the spatial referents remain the same (up above/down below); but the frame of reference shifts. The Caserne people, for example, are *pean* vis-à-vis the Senta people, who are *gaiñean*. But in relation to the rest of earth, Caserne is *gaiñean*; the outside world is always 'down below'.

pean (down below)	*gaiñean* (up above)
lowlands, outside world	Sainte-Engrâce
lowlands, outside world	Caserne
Caserne	Senta
Sainte-Engrâce	Heaven, stars, sun, moon

From the point of view of the Souletine people, all Basques who

---

[1] The term *pekuak* is a substantive form of *peko-*, meaning 'lower'. *Pean* and *peko-* are both derived from *pe* (bottom, base). *Gaiñean* (above, up above) is derived from the substantive *gain* (top, summit).

are not native Souletines are *Manexak*. In the dialect of Basse-Navarre, Manex is the Basque word for 'John'. The Sainte-Engrâce people claim that calling their Basque neighbours 'Johns' is no different from calling the Germans 'Fritzs'. Both nicknames have derogatory implications. The Sainte-Engrâce people are particularly disdainful of Manex Basques, whom they regard as less pure, both culturally and linguistically, than Souletine Basques. Non-Basques are classified according to their nationality or natal province. French people are *Frantsesak*. Spaniards are referred to as *Españolak*. Americans are *Amikeñak*, and people from Béarn are *Bearnesak*. But from the point of view of the Sainte-Engrâce people, all outsiders—whether Basque or not—belong to the much broader category of strangers (*arrotzak*). 'Strangers' are conceptually opposed to the category *hebenkuak*, 'the here people', to which only Sainte-Engrâce Basques who were born in the community and who reside there belong. An individual who was born and who lives outside Sainte-Engrâce, and whose parents are Santaztarrak, is not classified as either a Santaztarrak or a 'here person'; he is an *estrandjera*, which also denotes 'stranger'.

Within Soule the Sainte-Engrâce people are not always regarded favourably by their lowland neighbours. The Santaztarrak are not the only mountain people (*bortü jentiak*) in Haute-Soule about whom prejudiced and often inaccurate assessments are made by their more 'civilized' lowland neighbours; but they are the mountain Basques about whom rumours and criticisms are most commonly heard. Even some of the other mountain people in the province take a sceptical and harsh view of the Sainte-Engrâce people.

I found few Souletines who expressed an active dislike of the Sainte-Engrâce people; but on several occasions, when I acknowledged my fondness of the Santaztarrak, people studied my face, shrugged, and cautiously suggested that 'perhaps they are good people'. On the other hand, the Sainte-Engrâce people were quite possessive about my affection for them. When I returned from a household in another village, they would often ask with a trace of jealousy: 'Were those people pleasant and well-mannered? Did they give you anything to eat?' In Haute-Soule at least, the answer to the latter question is a major criterion in formulating an answer to the former one.

In lowland Soule and in eastern Basse-Navarre criticisms of the Santaztarrak take much the same form: that they are excessively proud, penurious, prone to violence, and inbred. They are reputed to fight with wine bottles, to cheat the local *fromagerie* by adding

water to their milk, and to lie to the government in order to receive
benefits for which they are ineligible. They also have a notorious
reputation for using 'bad language' as a matter of course and for
having developed a unique but shockingly obscene vocabulary for
physiological phenomena. In the lowlands I was told that all ugly
(*itsusi*), i.e. obscene, words in Souletine Basque were invented by the
Sainte-Engrâce people. The words in question, many of which I
shall discuss in Chapter XII, are not regarded as the slightest bit
itsusi by the Santaztarrak.

It would be misleading and unfair to suggest that the Sainte-
Engrâce people are generally despised and continually criticized by
their neighbours. They are not. But because they are mountain
people who keep to themselves and who stand firmly together in the
face of any opposition from the outside world, they are inevitably an
inviting target for speculation, stories, and accusations.

The Sainte-Engrâce people are proud of their cultural heritage,
their language, their cheeses, flocks of sheep, herds of cattle, and the
community in which they live. The older people are also proud of the
fact that they and their ancestors had the physical stamina and wits
to survive the uncertainties and hardships which life in the mountains
formerly brought. Young and old alike are proud of their recently
acquired prosperity.

VI

Sainte-Engrâce is now one of thirty-five communes in Soule; it is
under the political jurisdiction of the canton of Tardets in the
arrondissement of Oloron. Within the canton and province, the
commune is represented by a body of elected local officials: a mayor
and twelve councillors. Municipal elections are held once every six
years; and, unlike cantonal and national elections, they generate
considerable interest in the community. In the 1977 municipal
elections, 96·54 per cent of the electorate voted.

According to local statutes, the council must consist of nine lower
people and four upper people. Immediately after their election, the
thirteen councillors meet to decide which of them will serve as
mayor. Within living memory, every mayor has belonged to the
lower community. The council also decides which two of its members
will serve as deputy mayors; one of these must be a lower person, the
other an upper person. Although the mayor and councillors sometimes serve two or three consecutive terms, they should in principle
stand down after one term; for, ideally, people should take turns
(*aldikatzen*) filling these posts.

There is no fixed schedule according to which the council meets. Its primary duties concern the two local schools, roads, government livestock subsidies, and the mountain pastures of the commune. In principle and in practice, the mayor has no more political *indarra*, or power, than the councillors. The members of the council are said to be *bardin-bardina*, 'equal-equal', in terms of the power and authority they can exercise in community matters. There is, however, one individual who has more political *indarra* than the mayor and councillors: the town hall secretary. From at least as early as the nineteenth century, this position has been held by the Sainte-Engrâce priest.

With the exception of matters that would affect them directly, such as the extension of their road to Spain or government policies concerning sheep farmers, the majority of the Sainte-Engrâce people are uninterested in politics outside their own small community. Few people subscribe to newspapers other than those which deal exclusively with animal husbandry and farm machinery. Some of the people do, however, watch news broadcasts on television, from which they have derived some knowledge of the political problems faced by Basques in Spain.

In 1976/7 the Sainte-Engrâce people were aware of the Basque nationalist movement and of the terrorist activities of ETA (military branch); but, in my presence at least, no one ever expressed much interest in the movement.

When I returned to the commune in 1979, I found that some of the young, unmarried people had become involved in a lowland Basque nationalist movement. The majority of these young people work in the lowlands. Their interest in Basque nationalism was not, however, shared by most of their elders. A few of the adult men claimed that they are willing to support nationalists who attempt to achieve Basque independence through democratic means; but neither they nor the young people condone the terrorist activities of ETA, an organization which many of them fear.

In 1979 the majority of adults did not wish to become involved in any Basque nationalist movement. The general unwillingness to support Basque nationalism can, I think, be attributed to two main reasons. First, the people realize that they owe much of their recent economic prosperity to the French social security system and to various government subsidies, which now provide them with more than half their annual cash income. They have, therefore, an economic incentive to remain French citizens.

Second, although the Sainte-Engrâce people identify themselves as Basques (*Eskualdunak*) outside the Basque country to stress the fact that they are not French, within the Basque country they identify themselves first as Santaztarrak and second as Souletines. They have a clear and strong sense of identity not as Eskualdunak but as Basques who belong to a specific community and to a specific province. For most of them, nationalistic slogans which stress the unity of the seven Basque provinces, e.g. Zazpiak Bat, 'the seven are one', do not make much sense. They tend to regard all Manex Basque dialects as bastardized versions of the purest Basque, Souletine, and claim that they cannot, in any case, understand most of what a Manex-speaker says. The linguistic barrier which they perceive to exist reinforces their view of themselves as distinctly different from and linguistically superior to non-Souletine Basques. Like the Breton-speaking Bretons described by Hélias (1978: 340), they regard their own particular dialect as a 'private possession', something which sets them apart from other Basques and stresses their cultural purity.

VII

On the whole the Santaztarrak are finely featured, short, and stocky. Past forty years of age the women tend to be heavier than the men. Most of the people have brown or black hair, hazel eyes, and fair complexions; but a few are blonde and blue-eyed. Both sexes tend to have considerable physical strength (*indarra*), which is highly esteemed. An enormous amount of emphasis is placed upon eating, both as a vital means of increasing one's *indarra* and as a major social activity.

Neither the men nor the women continue to wear full traditional· dress. Formerly the women wore dark woollen skirts over a white petticoat. Widows wore a floor-length black cape to Mass and a shoulder-length black cape in the house. Until the first quarter of this century the men wore short black jackets and dark woollen trousers to Mass and on special occasions. In the mountains they wore hooded sheepskin capes, heavy woollen pantaloons, and wooden shoes. Only one man still makes and wears wooden shoes.

When the paved road between the lowlands and the commune was finished, traditional dress was gradually replaced by clothing bought in the Tardets shops; but it was not until the Second World War ended and war pensions were increased that people could afford such luxuries.

Men who are at least thirty years old wear black berets, which are rarely removed during the day. A few of the younger men follow the example of their elders; and red berets have become popular among boys between the ages of ten and eighteen. When they work, men wear heavy cotton trousers or loose-fitting pantaloons.

Nylon aprons are the standard attire of the women and girls; these are worn both inside and outside the house. The girls and young married women generally wear trousers beneath their aprons, whereas their elders wear skirts. Widows dress entirely in black.

The Sainte-Engrâce people are not dour peasants. With few exceptions they are jovial and garrulous. At social gatherings such as weddings, First Communion and baptismal feasts, dances, and maize-husking, they are especially noisy and boisterous. They love to eat; and among the women some of the most animated conversations concern food: how it was served, how it was prepared, and how it was judged. The men most enjoy talking about their sheep, cattle prices, farm machinery, and cheeses.

Both men and women are hard-working, and they seem to be constantly busy. They dislike and disapprove of idleness, but feel nevertheless that one should not work obsessively without pausing to rest occasionally. Among the men, the main form of amusement is *mus*, a card game similar to poker. Both men and women enjoy playing *belote* on rainy afternoons and especially on Sundays. *Belote* is similar to pinocle. Roughly half the households have televisions, which are watched almost daily by the schoolchildren but only occasionally by adults.

A few men, most of whom are young and unmarried, drink regularly in the two lower cafés. The two upper cafés, which flank the church, are crowded with local men and women after weddings, funerals, and after Mass on the major religious holidays. On these occasions they serve as important social centres, in which neighbourhood gossip and household news are exchanged by relatives and friends from different parts of the commune; but in the day to day routine these cafés are rarely used by the people. 'Who has time to sit in a café talking to others?' they ask. 'In order to live we must work, and our work is never finished!'

III. THE SEASONAL CYCLE

In attenuated form the traditional subsistence economy of rural Souletine Basque society has been best preserved in mountain communities such as Sainte-Engrâce. The people are small-scale agriculturalists and pastoralists, the majority of whom still regard sheep-raising as an essential part of their lives and as a distinctive, necessary feature of their mountain society.

I

The Sainte-Engrâce household is virtually self-sufficient in the production of food for its own needs; and the daily lives of its members are primarily devoted to subsistence activities, each of which has a well-defined place in the seasonal cycle. Table I is a summary of their distribution and of the division of labour by sex.

Spring begins in late March with the raking of the valley pastures on which the flocks graze in winter. Leaves, twigs, and dead grasses are gathered laboriously by means of hand-made wooden rakes. The 'cleaning of the fields' is thought to encourage the growth of new grass.

In April the pastures are harrowed and manured with the help of a tractor, horse, or mule. The work is generally done by husband and wife (*senharr-emazte*). These pastures, and the hay which they yield, are the only source of winter fodder for the sheep.

At present maize is the only cultivated cereal crop in the commune. Until the 1950s, wheat was raised as well. Maize is used primarily as feed for the pigs and poultry, but some households still reserve a portion of the harvest to make flour. The women grind the kernels by means of a water-driven grist mill and use the flour to make a heavy, filling bread called *pastetxa*. Formerly several other kinds of bread and a porridge were also made from this flour. An oven-baked maize bread called *mestüra* was one of the main staples in the diet until the first quarter of this century.

Virtually every house in the commune owns a share in one of the many mills scattered along the valley. Ownership of a share was established, in every case, by means of a written, notarized contract.

31

TABLE I
The Distribution of Subsistence Activities
The Division of Labour by Sex

	male and female	male	female
spring	raking and manuring valley pastures; ploughing and planting the arable fields	cheese-making in the house; lambs slaughtered	
summer	haymaking	cheese-making in mountains; agaric mushrooms gathered in the mountains	gardening
autumn	maize harvest; fern harvest	dove hunting; old ewes slaughtered	apple and nut harvest
winter		pigs slaughtered; hunting	ducks slaughtered; curing of hams and bacon; making pâté, terrine, sausages, black pudding, *confitures*

The number of houses owning shares in a mill (*eihera*) ranges from six to eight. Formerly, there was a fixed order of rotation (*üngürü*) according to which households took turns using the mill in serial succession (*aldikatzia*). Each house was assigned one day of the week, or a part of one day, when they could grind their maize. The ordering of turns for any one mill did not follow any particular pattern, e.g. according to the spatial orientation or distribution of houses or to 'first neighbour' relationships; but the order of rotation for each mill remained the same from year to year. My main interest in the ordering of *eihera* rights is that the right to use a mill was transmitted serially (*aldikatü*) from house to house in a fixed order of rotation (*üngürü*). The same two principles operate in several other spheres of economic and ritual activity—a fact that was emphasized by informants who told me about the systematic transmission of *eihera* rights. The system fell into disuse about ten years ago as the number of participating households decreased. At present, those women who continue to make maize flour may do so on any day of the week, since there are rarely more than two of them using the same mill.

In 1976/7 roughly three-quarters of the households in the commune cultivated at least one field of maize, ranging in size from 50 to 2 hectares. By 1979 more than a quarter of these households had given up raising maize because they 'had lost too many harvests owing to bad weather', and were buying it from the Tardets co-operative.

The planting of the maize is completed by the end of May and before the flocks ascend to their summer mountain pastures. The majority of the work is done by married couples; but a close male relative and/or a male 'first neighbour' is often invited to assist them. The latter is recruited from one of three households classified as an *aizoa*, or 'first neighbour'. Planting maize is regarded as neither 'first neighbour' nor 'kin work' (*aizo lan* or *askazi lan*), i.e. neither category takes precedence over the other in terms of their obligation to assist. In this particular activity the obligations of extra-domestic kin and 'first neighbours' to assist a household are judged to have an approximate equality.

The spring is an especially busy time for the men. In addition to their agricultural duties they are responsible for the herding, feeding, and milking of the sheep. Although women may assist them with the first two chores, the third is an exclusively male occupation. The women regard milking ewes—but not cows—as a filthy and disgusting task for their sex.

A shepherd can expect to have all of his lambs weaned by the end of April, when the period known as *ardi jeixten* ('ewe milking') begins. The ewes are milked twice daily: as soon as the shepherd rises in the morning, and before he eats supper in the evening. From as early as the end of January until the middle of May, most shepherds sell their milk to a *fromagerie* in Béarn. Until 1975 the milk was bought by the Roquefort Society. Households stop selling their milk at least three weeks before the flocks are due to leave the valley, so that the shepherd can make 'house cheese', *etxe-gazna*.

These cheeses are made once every three milkings. A minimum of thirty litres of milk is needed to make one house cheese of approximately three kilos in weight. The total number of cheeses made in the spring varies from four to as many as fifteen, depending upon the size of the shepherd's household and the date on which he stops selling his milk. House cheese is normally produced only for household consumption. In taste, texture, and size the house cheeses are judged to be vastly inferior to the 'mountain cheeses', *bortü-gaznak*.

II

The beginning of summer is heralded by the ascent of the flocks in late May. Their departure is especially welcomed by the shepherds who look forward to returning to the mountains and to the exclusively male social world of the herding hut.

A brief lull in the daily work of the household follows the beginning of summer transhumance. The cattle and pigs require little attention, so the shepherd can devote more time to tasks such as mending fences, chopping firewood, and repairing implements. The cattle are not moved to the mountains until late June or early July.

From the end of May until the end of September a shepherd is generally obliged to spend only two nights in the mountain hut once every ten days. A detailed account of the pastoral roles through which the shepherds progress will be given in Chapter X.

During the 'ewe milking' season in the mountains, a shepherd makes from eight to ten mountain cheeses. These hard, strong-flavoured cheeses form an important part of the diet; they are both a source of great pride to the shepherd and a means by which he may either gain or lose prestige in the community.

In late June the first of three hay harvests begins. On dry and sunny days all able members of the household cut and turn the long grass in their fenced winter pastures. When the exposed surface of the grass dries, the clumps are turned and shaken with wooden rakes until no trace of dampness remains. The second harvest takes place in late July; and if the summer has been hot and dry, a third crop can be harvested from the same pasture in early September.

In late September the flocks return to the valley; and for the duration of their eight-month stay there the daily routine of the household revolves around them. During the coldest months the sheep are moved from pasture to pasture as many as five times a day, with no pasture being used twice in one day unless all the others have been used once. The movement of the sheep is described as *ardiak khanbiatzen*, literally 'changing the ewes'. Both pastures and sheep are said to *aldikatü*, to replace or to progress serially.

The people claim that 'changing' the sheep prevents their small pastures from being cropped too closely. The veracity of that claim is arguable from our point of view, but the logic underlying it is wholly consistent with the strong emphasis placed upon the notion of serial replacement (*aldikatzia*) in Sainte-Engrâce society.[1]

III

In September and October the women gather apples, walnuts, hazelnuts, and chestnuts. Although apples are a valued supplement to the daily diet, they are also sociologically important as a form of prestation exchanged by female 'first neighbours' (*aizoak*).[2] Women between whom the latter relationship exists are expected to give each other a bag of apples whenever they visit their respective households.

'First neighbour' relationships are also characterized by dual reciprocity during the fern harvest in September. When the male head of household decides to harvest his fern, he often invites one or more of his 'first neighbours' to assist him and the members of his household. He is obliged in turn to perform the same service for those whom he recruited. The fern are cut with scythes, dried, and stacked near the barns, in which they are used as winter bedding for the livestock.

'First neighbours' are also commonly asked to assist with the sheep-shearing in late September; but many people regard shearing as 'kin work' (*askazi lan*) rather than as 'first neighbour work' (*aizo lan*) and seek the assistance of two close male relatives before asking two of their male 'first neighbours'. A man may, however, recruit one relative and one 'first neighbour'. If a 'first neighbour' is asked, he can be expected to accept the request without complaining that the work ought to be done by the shepherd's close kin; for it is widely felt that one cannot refuse to assist one's 'first neighbour', even when the task concerned is not, strictly speaking, 'first neighbour work'.

October marks the beginning of the maize harvest, an activity which is regarded as 'first neighbour work'. The recruitment of labour follows a well-defined pattern; but this cannot be fully appreciated without a knowledge of the structure of 'first neighbour' relationships. For this reason, the gathering and husking of maize will be described in Chapter V.

Autumn is also the season in which the men hunt wild boar and migratory doves. The former is always sold to restaurants in the lowlands, where the meat commands a very high price. The doves

---

[1] *Aldikatzia* will appear in a variety of contexts in this book. English translations of the term vary according to context, since there is no single English word which conveys the notion of *aldikatzia*, as this is understood by the Basques of Sainte-Engrâce.

[2] A detailed account of the 'first neighbour' relationship will be given in Chapter V.

are hung from the rafters in the kitchen for a few days and then are either eaten or preserved.

In the late autumn and early winter the old ewes (*artzarrak*) provide an additional source of meat for the household. These sheep are not taken to the mountains in summer, but remain in the valley to be fattened.

IV

In winter the primary subsistence activity is *xerrika*, 'the pursuit of the pig', to which the entire month of December is devoted. Most households keep at least two pigs, which are usually bought from a lowland pig farmer in the spring. At present only three local households raise and sell pigs within the commune.

When the 'master' (*nausi*) of a household decides to slaughter a pig, he asks at least two men to assist him. Either 'first neighbours' or close relatives may be recruited. If relatives are chosen they generally belong to the same settlement or *quartier* in which the *nausi* lives; they may be the close consanguineal or affinal kin of either the *nausi* or his wife. The recruitment of pig-killing assistants will be treated in Chapter V.

The slaughter and butchering of pigs are exclusively male tasks and can be completed in two or three hours. Since the slaughter usually takes place before sunrise, the men are often finished with their work by nine or ten o'clock in the morning. In return for their services, the men recruited by the *nausi* receive alcoholic beverages and a four- or five-course dinner.

Among the women the pig-killing season is referred to as 'the bad month' on account of the blood, the stench, and the numerous unpleasant tasks that women are required to perform. The 'woman of the house' (*etxekandere*) may be assisted by a close female relative (especially a sister, sister-in-law, daughter, or daughter-in-law). When the pig's throat is slit, the blood is collected by the *etxekandere* and is stirred rapidly to prevent it from coagulating (*kaillatürik*). Together the women clean the intestines; cook the meat; make black pudding, pâté, terrine, *confit de porc*, spiced sausages; and cure the hams and bacon with salt and red pepper. It takes them three days to complete one *xerrika*.

The food produced during *xerrika* forms a substantial part of the staple diet from one pig-killing season to the next. In addition to pork, the most important staples are vegetable soup, eggs, cheese, and bread.

With the exception of bread, coffee, salt, and sugar, all staple foods are produced by the household: pork, chicken, duck, lamb, mutton, eggs, milk, cheese, and vegetables. Every household cultivates at least one vegetable garden, in which leeks, carrots, peppers, garlic, cabbage, onions, and haricot beans are grown. At least one field of potatoes is also cultivated. Household produce is supplemented by seasonal foods such as apples, nuts, dove, trout, and occasionally hare.

V

During the past forty years the standard of living in Sainte-Engrâce has changed considerably. With the completion of the road in 1932, lowland markets became much more accessible to those wishing to sell their livestock, wool, and cheeses. Although the people were formerly reluctant to sell their cheeses, the elderly people claim that they did so during the first quarter of this century in order to receive a small cash income. Ewes' milk provided households with an additional source of income in 1933, when the Roquefort Society started buying milk from the Sainte-Engrâce shepherds.

From 1918 until the end of the Second World War, the people had access to a very limited supply of cash, the main sources of which were military pensions. Profits derived from the sale of milk, cheese, and wool were of secondary importance. Those who are now past sixty years of age describe the way of life before 1945 as a time of physical hardship and poverty when the survival of a household depended upon the assistance of one's 'first neighbours' to a much greater extent than at present.

The end of the war in 1945 marked the beginning of a financial prosperity that has increased steadily ever since. Improved means of transportation and the increased demand for ewes' milk and calves contributed to the burgeoning cash and market economy of the community; but the source of monetary wealth that has had the greatest impact upon the traditional economy is the French government. In some cases, as much as two-thirds of the cash accrued annually by a Sainte-Engrâce household comes from the government in the form of pensions, subsidies, and various social security benefits.

At present, the second largest cash income is derived from the sale of calves. In 1976/7 the market price ranged from 1,100 francs to 1,500 francs per calf. In terms of market value and labour, cattle-raising is more profitable and less time-consuming than sheep-raising—a fact which recently encouraged five households to sell their flocks and to invest solely in cattle. Other households are expected to do the same in future: either for economic gain, 'because they are lazy', and/or because they lack a shepherd for whom sheep-raising, cheese-making, and active participation in the *olha* (shepherding syndicate) are an important part of being male and a Santaztarra.[3]

[3] See Greenwood (1976) for a discussion of the various reasons why economic gains to be derived from profitable farms have been rejected by Spanish Basques in the town of Fuenterrabia.

PART TWO

IV. THE HOUSEHOLD

I N Sainte-Engrâce society, linguistic distinctions are made between the house (*etxe*), its human inhabitants (*etxenkuak*), and the property (*etxalte*) to which the house, barns, outbuildings, implements, all domestic articles, land, and livestock belong. Any shares owned in a shepherding syndicate (*olha*) or in a mill are also part of the *etxalte*.

I

For the Sainte-Engrâce people, the house is first of all a physical structure which provides shelter for its human occupants and their possessions. A Sainte-Engrâce house is never physically divided to form more than one dwelling beneath the same roof, as is sometimes done in other Basque communities (cf. Douglass 1975 : 37–8); and, in principle, it should be inhabited by only one domestic group.

Before some houses in the upper community were renovated in this century, they also gave shelter to the domestic animals owned by the heads of household. The ground floor provided a stable for the sheep, a few cows, and a horse or mule. This section of the house constituted the *ezkaratz*, a term which is now applied to the sheep barns used in winter. The *ezkaratz* was the largest room in this type of traditional dwelling; and, in most cases, the living quarters could not be reached without passing through it. A wooden staircase connected the interior of the stable to the kitchen on the first floor.

In the lower community and in some parts of the upper community, the *ezkaratz* was attached directly to the living quarters on the ground floor. In many cases the stable was built at right angles to that part of the house in which the people lived and could be entered from the kitchen or storage room. The *ezkaratz* of both types of traditional dwelling was regarded as part of the *etxe* or house.

In both halves of the commune, humans and animals continue to live in close proximity. In most lower houses the kitchen, storage room, and vestibule on the ground floor are attached to the stable. The first floor is generally divided into two or three bedrooms; and the granary occupies the entire second floor.

39

In the upper community none of the inhabited houses has a stable on its ground floor. During the past thirty years, the people have expanded their living quarters by converting the stable into a kitchen, vestibule, and storage room. Boots, an array of work clothes, and herding staffs are kept in the vestibule, from which the first floor can be reached by means of a wooden staircase. Sacks of feed for the livestock, tools, umbrellas, and most foods produced or gathered by the women of the house are kept in the storage room.

In some houses a small portion of the ground floor has been converted into a dining room, in which the best furniture, china, and tableware are kept. Since this room is unheated and is separated from the kitchen by the vestibule, it is invariably cold and musty. The room is used only on certain special occasions, such as the baptismal feast of an infant.

At present, as in the past, the kitchen is the social centre of the house. This is the room to which the members of the household return to rest between chores, to eat their four daily meals, and to exchange news at the end of the day. Men, women, and children eat together and are intermixed, not segregated according to sex or age, at table. The kitchen is also the room in which all formal and informal visits take place; and there are certainly many more of the latter during the course of the year. So long as the front door is ajar or unlocked, it is permissible for any relative, neighbour, or friend to enter the vestibule and kitchen. An open and an unlocked door indicates that at least one member of the household is within or nearby.

As the centre of domestic activity, the kitchen is the domain of the elder female head of household (*etxekandere-zaharra*), who spends most of her time near the hearth. Until roughly ten years ago, an open wood fire burned in the hearth of every kitchen from dawn until the people went to bed at night. The elder woman tended the fire and cooked food on it at least four times a day. The fire also provided warmth for the members of the house as they gathered around it to talk to one another and to any neighbours and relatives present.

An open fire is still regarded as an aesthetically pleasing sight; but in roughly 80 per cent of the houses, the fire has been replaced by a low, pot-bellied stove or gas cooker. Although people now long for the sight of an open fire, they are pleased to be rid of the smoke which formerly pervaded their kitchens.

The Sainte-Engrâce kitchen is still dominated by the wide, deep hearth and its carved wooden mantelpiece, which is always bordered by a narrow, bright red or green cloth. Highly polished copper kettles, candlesticks, and oil-lamps usually flank a small icon of the

Virgin on top of the mantelpiece. In every kitchen there is a long wooden table covered with a brightly coloured oilcloth and generally placed in the centre of the room. In most kitchens a high-backed wooden seat (*züzülü*) stands in the corner beneath the mantelpiece and can accommodate three or four adults. This seat is often more than 100 years old and is the warmest place in the house. Visitors are always offered a space on the *züzülü*.

The bedrooms in a Sainte-Engrâce house are often so tidy that they seem to be unoccupied. The furniture consists of one or two beds, a chair, a small table, and a wooden dresser in which all personal belongings are kept. A wooden crucifix, to which a sprig of 'blessed laurel' is attached, is generally hung on the wall above each bed. The house in which I lived also had a small bathroom on the first floor. Indoor toilets are no longer uncommon; but only a few houses in the commune have a shower or bathtub.

When houses in the upper community were renovated, the livestock were moved from the house into stone barns close but not attached to the living quarters of their owners. Cattle and sheep are stabled separately in these barns during the winter. In spring and autumn, they are moved to their respective stables on hillsides just below the timberline.

For as long as people can remember, pigs have been kept in their shelters outside the house. In the lower community and in most upper neighbourhoods, the pigsty, hen-house, and barns form a semicircle around the house.

II

In rural Basque society, the house is more than a physical structure; it is also a domestic establishment, in which the female head of household presides, and a socio-economic unit to which every able member contributes his or her labour and skills. In these respects, the house is, as a physical structure, indissolubly linked with the people who live in it; but the house also has certain attributes which are independent of both its inhabitants and the property (*etxalte*) to which it belongs. Some of these attributes vary from one province to another.

In Sainte-Engrâce, as in all other Basque communities, every house which was once or continues to be inhabited has a name. As in most French Basque communities, every Sainte-Engrâce house also has its own tomb in the cemetery and exclusive ownership of three ritual goods: funeral cloths, and the special basket and cloth in which 'blessed bread' was formerly carried by the female head of household.

The physical structure of a house may collapse and vanish entirely; but as a named entity, a Basque house continues to exist as long as its name is remembered by someone in the community and, in Sainte-Engrâce at least, as long as its tomb remains in the cemetery. (Some of the Sainte-Engrâce people can remember the names and locations of houses which were physically destroyed more than 100 years ago.)

In Sainte-Engrâce, the name of a house remains unchanged through successive generations of inhabitants. In a few cases, the name refers to the spatial position of the house. For example, there is a house at the extreme south-western end of the commune called Üngürütürü; the name is based on *üngürü*, rotation or circle. According to informants, the house was thus named because it is located at the point where the circle, in which Sainte-Engrâce is conceived to lie, is thought to begin.

In the majority of cases, however, houses have received the surname of their first master (*nausi*), i.e. their first male head of household. Names linking a house with a particular person are found throughout the Basque country (cf. Caro Baroja 1971: 126–31).

It is virtually impossible to trace the origins of most of the existing houses. An 1881 register and the parish records show that all but five of the ninety-nine houses existed in the nineteenth century. In other parts of the Basque country, the year in which a house was founded is commonly engraved on the lintel above the door. Only five Sainte-Engrâce houses have dated lintels; three were founded in the seventeenth century and two in the eighteenth century.

There is only one modern case in which the house-name and surname of the *nausi* have remained the same. Ownership rights to that property have passed in a direct line of descent through at least seven generations of males.

As a result of the high rate of marriages contracted within the commune over the centuries, the name of a house frequently co-incides with the surnames of persons belonging to other households. For example, there is a house called Ilharrescape whose *nausi* has the surname Elichalt. Ilharrescape is also the surname of the *nausi* in the house Etcheber.

There are five cases in which two houses have the same name. In order to distinguish between them one of the following suffixes has been appended to the name: -*gaiñe* (top), -*pe* (bottom), -*borda* (grange), -*berri* (new), or -*zaharr* (old).

All 'grange' houses are located in the lower community. These were founded by offspring who had neither inherited nor married into an upper house.[1] By means of the suffix *-borda* a lower house, e.g. Karrika-borda, is differentiated from its counterpart in the upper community, e.g. Karrika. In the nineteenth-century parish records, the suffixes *-hiry* (sc. *herri*, meaning borough) and its French equivalent *-bourg* were sometimes appended to the names of upper houses such as Karrika.

The suffixes *-gaiñe* and *-pe* may be employed to distinguish between an upper and a lower house, or between two houses in the same half of the commune according to their spatial orientation, e.g. Borthiry-gaiñe as distinct from Borthiry-pe. There is only one modern case in which the suffixes *-berri* and *-zaharr* are employed. The two houses, Espondaburu-zaharr and Espondaburu-berri, were founded by father and son respectively.

In rural Basque society, house names establish the social identity of both the house and its inhabitants. In Sainte-Engrâce, an individual is referred to by the name of his house rather than by his Christian name and surname, e.g. Jean Bidart is known as Accoceberry.[2] As is the case elsewhere in the Basque country, a person who moves from one house to another at marriage, remarriage, or adoption receives the name of his new place of residence; and his social identity changes accordingly (cf. Douglass 1975: 43).

There are several means by which members of the same house are differentiated, and two of these include the name of the house; one is based on relative age, the other on sex. The suffixes *-zaharr* (old) and *-gazte* (young) are appended to the house name to distinguish between the elder and younger male heads of household, e.g. Chilhanku-zaharra as opposed to Chilhanku-gaztea.

Female heads of household are differentiated by means of the same adjectival suffixes, but the gender suffix *-sa* is added to the house name. Chilhankusa-zaharra, the elder woman, is thus distinguished from Chilhankusa-gaztea, the younger woman. Children and unmarried adults (if the latter are not heads of household) are generally referred to by their Christian names and house name.

In addition to its name, every Sainte-Engrâce house has a plot in

---

[1] According to local tradition, the lower community existed as early as the thirteenth century, when the lower chapel of St Laurent is thought to have been built; but there is no documented evidence with which to support either claim.

[2] The practice of referring to an individual by his house name or by a combination of Christian name and house name is not unique to Basque society. Bourdieu (1962: 37) reports that in traditional Béarnais society, the house—as a moral and social entity—is thought to be embodied by the male head of household, who is often referred to by his Christian and house names, e.g. Jean of the House Timou.

the small, enclosed cemetery in Senta.[3] There is no relation between the distribution of houses in the commune and the disposition of their tombs. Stone crosses or large marble gravestones identify the house to which the space belongs. On some tombs the names of the dead are engraved beneath the house name, but the practice seems not to have become common until the twentieth century.

In Sainte-Engrâce, as in other rural Basque communities, an immutable bond exists between the living and deceased members of a house by virtue of their common residence. A Santaztarra is buried in the tomb of the house in which he resided last. Only those persons who remain in their natal house for the duration of their lives are buried in its tomb. If an individual changed residence at marriage or remarriage, he is interred in the tomb of his post-marital residence.

Although people are generally able to trace consanguineal and/or affinal ties through two generations of former *etxenkuak* (members of the house), genealogical connection is not a necessary feature of the relationship between the living and the dead of a house in Sainte-Engrâce.

The bond between the living and the dead *etxenkuak* is preserved and perpetuated by the *etxekandere*, the female head of household. In its idealized form, the household has an elder and a younger *etxekandere*. In principle either woman may fulfil the obligations to the dead of her house; but in practice these are generally fulfilled by the elder female.

The *etxekandere* is responsible for the spiritual welfare of the souls of all persons who belonged to her house from the time of its founding to the present. She is expected to pray for them at the house tomb every Sunday before Mass and on All Souls, Christmas, Easter, and Pentecost. In preparation for these religious holidays the tomb is weeded and decorated with flowers. On the Saturday preceding Palm Sunday sprigs of blessed laurel are also placed on the tomb. Until the 1960s, the *etxekandere* was also expected to pray for the souls of her house before the special Friday Mass for all souls in Purgatory (*Ostirale meza Purgatoiko arimentako*).

After having prayed for the souls of her house, the *etxekandere* may then offer prayers for the souls of her close kin at the tombs of their respective houses. This is one of the few ritual contexts in which

[3] As Douglass (1969: 73) has pointed out, the grave plots found in many French Basque communities 'have much the same properties as the church-floor sites (*sepulturiek*) in Murélaga', which are also fixed in space and linked through time to a particular house. Until recently, the *sepulturiek*—not the grave plots—were the focus of ritual activity in Murélaga. There are no *sepulturiek* in the Sainte-Engrâce church.

obligations to one's extra-domestic kin take precedence over those to one's 'first neighbours'; for the *etxekandere* in Sainte-Engrâce is not obliged to pray for the souls of her 'first neighbours' at their house tombs, as she is in some other French Basque communities, e.g. in Esterençuby and Saint Michel (Basse-Navarre).

The *etxekandere* is also the guardian of the three ritual goods owned by the house. The funeral cloths, blessed bread basket and cloth are passed on through successive generations of *etxekanderak*; they are not transferable from one house to another. Both the funeral and blessed bread cloths were made by an order of nuns in a Béarnais convent. They are white with three blue bands.

Every house has at least two small rectangular funeral cloths and one large cloth, which is suspended from the wall at the head of the deathbed. One of the small cloths is used to cover the bedside table of the deceased on which the house crucifix, an icon of the Virgin, two blessed candles, a vessel of holy water, and two bouquets are placed. The other cloth is laid on a small table in the kitchen on which the blessed candles burn for the soul of the deceased.

The blessed bread cloth differs from the funeral cloths in one respect—the initials of the *etxekandere* or of her predecessor are embroidered on one end. Formerly this cloth was placed in the special wicker basket when pieces of blessed bread were carried by the *etxekandere* from the church to the house, and from her house to that of her 'first neighbour'. The basket is circular and shallow, and has a diameter of approximately ten centimetres. Because neither the cloths nor the basket are consecrated by the priest, they do not belong to the class of 'blessed things' (*gaiza benedikatiak*).

III

As a named entity, a house can continue to exist without any human occupants or a physical structure; but as a domestic establishment and a socio-economic unit, it cannot survive without an *etxenkuak*, the people who live within it.

In its ideal form, the *etxenkuak* consist of three generations between whom the following genealogical relationships obtain: husband and wife, their son and his wife, and the unmarried children of that union.[4]

The Sainte-Engrâce Basques have a notion of family (*familia*),

---

[4] In rural Basque society as a whole, the ideal domestic group is three-generational and consists of an elder married couple, a younger married couple, and the unmarried offspring of the latter (cf. Douglass 1975: 33).

which they understand to include one's spouse, parents, siblings, and offspring; but this notion is conceptually distinct from that of *etxenkuak*. The criterion upon which the latter is based is not genealogical connection but the factor of common residence.[5]

At the level of practice consanguineal and affinal relationships generally do exist between the members of a household; but there was, until recently, one exception. During the period 1975–8, a bachelor established residence in the house of one of his 'first neighbours', with whom he has no genealogical connection. He moved in with his neighbours when the roof of his own house caved in.

Table II shows the range of relationships between *etxenkuak* as I found them in 1979. Demographic and personal factors (examples of the latter include quarrels between parents and offspring, the wish of all potential heirs and heiresses to emigrate) often prevent the developmental cycle of the domestic group from being completed; and, statistically, the composition of households varies according to the time at which it is recorded. For example, the number of three-generational households decreased considerably from 1976 until 1979 due to a high death rate among elderly heads of household.

TABLE II

The Composition of Sainte-Engrâce Households

House	Genealogical Relationships between *etxenkuak*
1.	WM, H, W, S, D, D
2.	WM, H, W, S, S, S, S, D, D, D
3.	bachelor
4.	widower, S
5.	HM, H, W, S, S, S
6.	H, W, S, D, D (outsiders)
7.	H, W, S, S
8.	HM, H, W, S
9.	WF, WM, H, W, D, D
10.	H, W, S
11.	bachelor

[5] The Basque term *familia* is rarely employed in conversation; but the French translation of it has been incorporated into Sainte-Engrâce postal addresses, e.g. Maison Harriguileheguy, Famille Etcheber. In most cases the *etxenkuak* use the surname of the younger male head of household.

TABLE II (*Continued*)

House	Genealogical Relationships between *etxenkuak*
12.	H, W, S, S, HBW
13.	widow, S, S
14.	WF, H, W, S, S
15.	H, W, S, S
16.	H, W, D
17.	WF, WM, H, W, S, D
18.	WM, H, W, S, D, WS, WD
19.	H, W, S, S, S
20.	HF, HM, H, W, S, D, D
21.	B, Z, ZS
22.	H, W (outsiders)
23.	H, W, S, D, D
24.	WF, H, W, S, D
25.	HM, H, W, S, S
26.	H, W, S
27.	WM, H, W, S
28.	WM, H, W, S, S, S, S, S
29.	H, W, S, S, S, S, D
30.	H, W, S, S, S, D
31.	HFF, HFM, HF, HM, H, W, S, D
32.	WF, WM, H, W, S, S
33.	H, W, S, D
34.	H, W, S
35.	H, W, S, D
36.	WF, widower, S
37.	H, W, S
38.	widow, S
39.	H, W, S
40.	HFZ, H, W, S, S, S
41.	widow, S
42.	B, B, B
43.	H, W
44.	widow, S, S, D, D
45.	H, W
46.	H, W, S, S
47.	widow, S, S
48.	widow, S
49.	H, W, S, S, S

TABLE II (*Continued*)

House	Genealogical Relationships between *etxenkuak*
50.	widow, S
51.	H, W, S, S, D, D
52.	HF, HM, H, W, S, D, D
53.	bachelor
54.	H, W, S, S, S
55.	bachelor
56.	HM, H, W, S, D
57.	B, B
58.	HM, H, W, S, S, D, D
59.	HF, HM, H, W, S, S
60.	H, W, S, S
61.	H, W, S, S
62.	B, B
63.	WF, WM, H, W, D
64.	widower, S, S, D, D
65.	bachelor
66.	M, S
67.	H, W
68.	bachelor
69.	HM, H, W, S, D
70.	HF, HM, H, W, S, D
71.	WM, H, W, D, D, D
72.	widower, DD
73.	widower, S, S, D
74.	widower, WMB, D
75.	HF, HM, H, W, D
76.	HM, HMZS, H, W, S
77.	HM, H, W, S, D, HB
78.	H, W
79.	HM, H, W, S, D
80.	H, W, S, D, D
81.	bachelor
82.	HM, H, W, D
83.	bachelor
84.	H, W
85.	H, W, S
86.	H, W, S, D
87.	man separated from wife

TABLE II (*Continued*)

House	Genealogical Relationships between *etxenkuak*
88.	H, W
89.	widow, S
90.	H, W, DS
91.	HM, H, W, D, SS
92.	H, W
93.	bachelor
94.	widow, S
95.	H, W, S
96.	H, W
97.	priest
98.	H, W, D, D (outsiders, schoolmaster)
99.	bachelor (outsider, schoolmaster)

The facts presented in this table were compiled by the author in 1976/7 and revised during the summer of 1979.

The fact remains, however, that the ideal composition of a domestic group has not been realized in the majority of cases cited in Table II. Only 9 of the 99 households conform to the ideal. There are, however, another 4 households in which a couple live with their daughter, her husband, and the children of that union; and in 18 households a widowed parent resides with a son or daughter, his or her spouse, and their children. That is, three generations are represented in a total of 31 households, roughly one-third of all households in the commune. Two generations are represented in 43 households; and one generation is represented in 24 households.

The composition of two households shown in Table II deserves comment. The two cases are regarded as unusual by the Sainte-Engrâce people; they are also unusual in rural French Basque society as a whole. First, there is one household in which four generations are represented (No. 31, Table II). The genealogical relationships between the members of that household are: HFF, HFM, HF, HM, H, W, S, D. The members of this household are widely regarded, and regard themselves, as being fortunate in three main respects: their property has passed through three successive generations of males; there are three, rather than two, active couples who assist one another with the routine chores inside and outside the house; and, third, relations between the couples are amicable and free of any conflict concerning the rights, interests, and obligations of any one couple.

The second unusual case is that of household 12 in Table 11. Until recently this domestic group consisted of two brothers, their respective wives, and the two unmarried sons of the younger brother. The latter died in 1978 and so is not represented in Table II. Within living memory, this is the only case in Sainte-Engrâce in which two siblings and their spouses established post-marital residence in the same house. Relations between the two couples were strained to such an extent that the women cooked on separate hearths and ate with their husbands at separate tables in the kitchen. The two couples were both pitied and criticized by many people for their inability to get along together; but, in the opinion of others, the morally most reprehensible fact was that the property had been divided equally between the brothers by their mother. Neither brother was 'master' in his own natal house. The unity of the house, as a physical, moral, and social entity, was violated not only by the division of the property, but also by the conflict between the two couples.

It is outside the scope of this book to discuss the demographic and personal factors that have contributed to the high incidence of one- and two-generational households; but one trend, which is only partially indicated in Table II, deserves mention—namely, the high rate of celibacy among men. Table II shows that eleven bachelors live alone or with an unmarried sibling; ten of these men are past thirty years of age. The Table does not show that an additional eighteen bachelors past thirty live with their parent or parents, and another eight bachelors past thirty live with a parent or parents as well as with an elder, unmarried brother.

Of the 130 Sainte-Engrâce men past thirty years of age, thirty-six are unmarried; and nearly half of these men are between the ages of forty and forty-nine. Until the 1950s, first marriages contracted by men in their thirties and forties were common; but it is now generally felt that a man who has not married by the time he reaches his early thirties is unlikely to do so if he remains in Sainte-Engrâce. There are no unmarried women in the commune past twenty-five years of age; and the few younger, unmarried women in the commune are not interested in marrying an older bachelor who is dedicated to his mountain way of life. The only other potentially eligible marriage partners in the commune—widows—are also unlikely to marry a local bachelor. Until the 1950s, bachelors often married the widow of their deceased brother. Widows, and especially those who inherited their natal house, formerly felt obliged to remarry for a variety of reasons; but the pressures underlying these reasons are no longer brought to bear upon them.

Of the 114 marriages, including those of widows and widowers, contracted by individuals represented in Table II, only 17 (15 per cent of the total) were established by a Santaztarra and an outsider. During the period 1920–78, within which all these marriages were made, 11 women and 6 men married into the community. Of these 9 came from Souletine villages; 5 came from Béarn; 2 came from a village in the Hautes-Pyrénées; and only 1 came from a Manex Basque village.

Only 16 marriages (14 per cent of the total) were contracted by persons belonging to different halves of the commune; whereas 81 marriages (71 per cent) were established by people belonging to the same half of the commune. A total of 97 marriages (85 per cent of the marriages) during this period were made between Santaztarrak. (See Table III.)

TABLE III
Marriages Contracted Between 1917 and 1978 By Persons Who Live
in the Commune at Present

Community of origin		Total number of marriages*
husband	wife	
upper	upper	18
lower	lower	63
upper	lower	6
lower	upper	10
upper	outsider	3
lower	outsider	8
outsider	upper	2
outsider	lower	4
		114

* I have included the marriages of widows and widowers in these figures, which are based on the results of my own investigations and the parish records.

Total number of marriages contracted
within the commune: 97/114
   between persons belonging to the same half
   of the commune: 81/114
   between persons belonging to different halves
   of the commune: 16/114
   between a *Santaztarra* and an outsider: 17/114

Virilocal residence was established by 60 per cent of the 114 couples; whereas only 33 per cent of the couples settled in the natal house of the wife, and only 7 per cent established neolocal residence. The high proportion of men who established post-marital residence in their natal house is in keeping with the stated preference for having a son, rather than a daughter, inherit the property.

IV

As a physical structure, a house is one of several tangible objects of which an *etxalte*, or property, consists. In Sainte-Engrâce, *etxalte* refers to the sum total of movable and immovable property in the form of barns, outbuildings, land, livestock, agricultural implements, all domestic articles, shares in a mill and in a herding hut, and the house itself.

In principle the *etxalte* should not be divided among married offspring; it may, however, be divided among unmarried offspring until one of them marries and inherits the entire property. His or her siblings are then expected to relinquish their claims to the property, in return for which they may receive a small cash compensation. Until the 1970s, this often served as a dowry for both sexes who married and settled in the community.

Both sexes are eligible to inherit the property; but there is an expressed preference for a son, through whom the house name and surname might remain the same. Ownership rights to the property are transferred to the heir or heiress by means of a written, notarized contract; in principle, this should take place about one month before his or her marriage.

Until the 1960s the contract was drawn up by the *etxenkuak* of the bride and groom and was certified by the notary in Tardets. The contract served four main purposes: it contained the will of the bride and groom and the *inter-vivos* transfer of ownership rights to the property from the elder heads of household to their young successors. Third, the contract stated the amount and kind of dowry to be paid by the in-marrying spouse; and, fourth, it ensured that the elder heads of household would be entitled to free room, board, and one-half of all cash profits. These three rights constitute the *gozamen*, usufruct, of the elder man and woman.

The rights (*dretak*) of the young heads of household are also established in their pre-marital contract. They receive ownership rights to the property, and, provided that the in-marrying spouse has contributed the dowry agreed upon, both of them are accorded *indarra*—in this context, power and authority—by the elder heads of household. The in-marrying spouse has an additional *dret*: the right to return his or her dowry to the natal household if the marriage ends in separation or divorce.[6]

The elder heads of household are legally retired when they relinquish their ownership rights to the property; but in practice they are sometimes figures of considerable power and authority.

V

In Basque a discrimination is made between male and female as heads of household and as spouses. In Souletine, the former are denoted by the terms *nausi* (master) and *etxekandere* (literally, 'the woman of the house'); the latter by the collective term of reference *senharr-emazte*, 'husband-wife'. Although these relationships may—and generally do—overlap, they are conceptually distinct from each other and should thus be treated separately.

Ideally, there are two male and two female heads of household, differentiated according to relative age. The elder male is 'the old master' (*nausi-zaharra*); the elder female is 'the old woman of the house' (*etxekandere-zaharra*). The younger male and female heads of household are *nausi-gaztea* and *etxekandere-gaztea*, in which *gazte* means 'young'. Ideally the *nausi* and *etxekandere* are also husband and wife, though in practice this is not always true of the elder heads of household.

In Sainte-Engrâce, women are not regarded—nor do they regard themselves—as the weaker sex, either morally or physically; and men do not treat them as their inferiors. As in other parts of the Basque country (cf. Douglass 1969: 107–8), a relative equality exists between the sexes which contrasts with reports for other European and Mediterranean societies where there is a marked subordination of women to men. In rural Basque society, sexual egalitarianism appears in a variety of contexts—social, economic, jural, as well as moral. In Sainte-Engrâce, the premise of equality between the sexes

---

[6] In the parish birth records, twenty-one divorces between 1939 and 1974 have been recorded by the local priest. Seventeen of these took place between 1950 and 1974. Of the twenty-one cases, sixteen divorces involved a Santaztarra and an outsider; all the outsiders had either French or Spanish surnames. In eight of the twenty-one cases, remarriage to an outsider took place; in two of these eight, the second marriage also ended in divorce. So far as I know, none of the people was ever head of a Sainte-Engrâce household. I never heard anyone criticize or condemn a Santaztarra who divorced an outsider; a less sympathetic view is taken of a Santaztarra who divorces another Santaztarra.

also appears in traditional views of certain physiological processes. (See Chapter XII.)

Male and female heads of household are said to be 'equal-equal' (*bardin-bardina*), though it is recognized that each sex has its particular spheres of activity and influence. In Sainte-Engrâce, as in other Basque communities, the qualities of the ideal *etxekandere* mirror those of the ideal male head of household. Both should be physically and emotionally strong, hard-working, and willing to co-operate with each other, as well as with the other members of the household. Considerable emphasis is also placed on strength of character. Extreme submissiveness in either sex is deplored, for it allows one sex to dominate the other.

Relationships between the adult members of a household are characterized by their mutual dependence and co-operation. Members are expected to give 'mutual assistance' (*alkharr lagüntza*) in performing the routine chores inside and outside the house. The division of labour between the sexes is flexible, in as much as many routine tasks can be performed by either sex, e.g. herding sheep when they are in the valley, milking and herding cattle, chopping and carrying firewood.

The only tasks which are widely regarded, by both sexes, as inappropriate for women are milking ewes and making cheese. Although these tasks are performed by men both in the valley and in the mountains, they are most closely associated with the exclusively male domain of the mountain herding hut (*olha*).

In a similar manner the main tasks performed in the female domain of the house—cooking, washing dishes, cleaning, and looking after children—are thought to be inappropriate for men. So long as there is a woman in his house, a man performs none of these tasks in the female domain.

From the point of view of the women, however, there is a limit to which a man can expect to be waited upon by the female members of his household. When, for example, a man ordered his wife to bring him some coffee after having refused it a few moments earlier, his wife pointed out to him that the pot of coffee was on the cooker— beside which he was sitting. The man protested loudly that she, as the young *etxekandere*, was obliged to serve him. His wife retorted that he was not treating her as his *etxekandere* but as his *neskato*, 'female servant', and continued to wash the dishes. Unwilling to accept defeat, the man then petitioned his mother. Feigning anger, she shook her fist at him and shouted: 'Me, me, me! Always me first! What a lazy, selfish man you are!' Her son laughed weakly and accepted that he had made an unfair demand, but he could not resist observing aloud that his wife and mother were bossy. 'Bossy!' his wife laughingly exclaimed, 'We're no more bossy than you are!' This remark and the laughter of the women irritated the man, who stormed out of the kitchen without having had his coffee; for he was determined not to act as his own servant in the female domain. The readiness of the women to stand up to 'the master of the house' and the manner in which they did so are characteristic forms of female behaviour in Sainte-Engrâce.

In the ideal three-generation domestic group with two married couples, the elder male head of household assists the younger man with the crops and livestock as much as his age and health permit. Because of his skill and experience as a shepherd, he is often called upon to supervise the younger man during lambing, and especially during difficult births. The advice and assistance of the elder man are generally received gratefully by his successor.

If the elder man has experienced a physical crisis, such as a heart attack, he retires from shepherding and must rest content with performing a few chores for the women inside or near the house. The younger man then represents the house in the shepherding syndicate during the period of summer transhumance.

The elder man also retires as a shepherd when his *indarra* is judged by the members of his house to be 'diminishing'. In this context, *indarra* conveys a range of meanings: physical strength, life-force, procreative power. The diminution of a man's *indarra* generally begins at fifty; but, as the people recognize, some men retain their *indarra* well past this age. At the time of my research, two elder male heads of household continued to participate in the shepherding syndicate and were widely respected and admired, by both sexes, for having retained their *indarra*. One man was sixty-four, the other seventy-five years old. The first man is widely regarded as having an unusually powerful sexual *indarra*; he has fathered thirteen children, the last of whom was born in his fifty-eighth year.

The domain of the elder *etxekandere* is the house, which is generally under her constant care and scrutiny. So long as she is physically able, the elder woman does most of the cooking, tends the garden, and looks after her young grandchildren. Considerable importance is attached to her latter function, which allows the younger woman to devote most of her time and energy to assisting her husband with chores outside the house.

Mention has already been made of the ritual duties of the *etxekandere-zaharr*; but these form only part of her role in spiritual

matters. In practice it is she—more often than the younger woman—
who fulfils mortuary obligations to their 'first neighbours' and who
formerly gave gifts of blessed bread to the church and to a particular
'first neighbour'. (See Chapters VII and VIII.)

The male heads of household play a more minor role in spiritual
matters than the two women; but there are four ritual duties which
were traditionally performed by either man. Formerly the *nausi*
called the priest to administer Extreme Unction for the 'first
neighbour' to the left of his house. In the annual procession to
Lechartzu on Corpus Christi, he carried the church cross when the
pilgrims walked across his land. Thirdly, when a member of his
house dies, the *nausi* carries the church cross in the funeral procession; and, fourthly, one of the men is expected to fulfil the 'first
neighbour' mortuary obligations of their house.

In every contemporary case the younger heads of household are
also husband and wife. Provided that there is an elder woman in the
house, they spend most of the day working side by side in the fields,
barns, and, from late September until May, herding livestock.
Great emphasis is placed upon their co-operation as partners and
their ability to organize their time and labour efficiently.

In households lacking an *etxekandere-zaharr*, the responsibilities
of the female head of household are greatly increased. She must not
only assume the role normally fulfilled by the elder woman in the
house; she is also expected to assist her husband, son, or son-in-law
with the routine chores outside the house.

If a couple has neither a *nausi/etxekandere-zaharr* nor any children
to assist them, they tend to rely more upon their 'first neighbours'
than their close relatives in the vicinity for help with tasks that are
strictly neither 'first neighbour' nor 'kin work'; for, in circumstances
such as this, it is thought to be more acceptable—morally and
socially—to place the burden of one's dependency upon one's 'first
neighbours'.

The relationship between the younger heads of household is not
simply an economic partnership; more crucially it is the procreative
union upon which the preservation and continuity of the household
depend. For analytical purposes, this aspect of the marital relationship is best treated in Chapter XII.

VI

Within the household the younger couple and their children are
expected to show respect for their elders and to take care of them in

illness and/or old age. The elder *nausi* and *etxekandere* are invariably addressed as *zü* (the respect form, second person singular personal pronoun) by their juniors in age. In principle, respect forms should also be used by a man speaking to any female member of his household: his mother, mother-in-law, wife, sister(s), daughter(s), daughter-in-law, or granddaughter. Some young men, however, now address their wives in feminine familiar forms (*hinoka*) as a matter of course; and they are criticized by some of the elderly and culturally most conservative people for being disrespectful. Their view is not shared by the wives of the men concerned, for whom *hinoka* is a means of expressing affection.

A man may use masculine familiar forms when addressing men of the same age or younger than himself, e.g. a brother, son, son-in-law, or an unmarried brother-in-law residing in his house; but it is widely considered disrespectful if he employs familiar forms when speaking to the elder *nausi*, whether the latter is his father, father-in-law, or some other elder male relative.

In principle and generally in practice, the two female heads of household address each other as *zü*; this form is also used by sisters, regardless of their marital status or place of residence. Inside and outside the household, a woman may use masculine familiar forms when she addresses her husband, son, son-in-law, or any other male relative who is her age or younger. There is, however, a tendency among women past forty to address their husbands as *zü*, unless they are irritated or are joking with their husbands; in these instances, women employ the familiar form *hi*.

There are also certain terms of relationship employed by the members of a household which convey respect. In domestic groups consisting of a younger couple and the parent(s) of the heir or heiress, the younger husband and wife address the elder heads as father (*aita*) and mother (*ama*), who generally address them by their Christian names. The elder woman may, however, address her daughter or daughter-in-law as *enea*, 'my own', if the two women have a close and affectionate relationship. I do not know of any comparable term of affection employed by a man to address his son or son-in-law.

The terms *aita* and *ama* are not employed by an individual addressing parents-in-law with whom he or she does not live; in this instance, parents-in-law are addressed either by their Christian names or, if they are elderly, as *axaita* and *axama*.

Axaita denotes both 'grandfather' and 'godfather'; *axama* means both 'grandmother' and 'godmother'. These two terms, which also convey respect, are always employed by children when addressing their paternal and maternal grandparents. The *axaita* and *axama* may not in fact be the biological grandparents of the children, e.g. they may be their great uncle and great aunt; but in most cases the elder heads of household—the *axaita* and *axama*—are in fact godparents, though never to the same child.

The traditional rules for selecting godparents are based on the principle of *aldikatzia*, which is best translated here as 'alternation'. If the first child is male, the parents are expected to ask the elder *nausi* of either the father's or mother's natal household to act as godfather and to give the child his Christian name. If the elder *nausi* of the father's household is chosen, the elder *etxekandere* of the mother's household should be asked to serve as godmother. If this is the case, the godfather of the second child should be the elder *nausi* of the mother's household and the godmother the elder *etxekandere* of the father's household. If the second child is male, he receives the Christian name of his godfather; if female, the child takes the name of her godmother. For any additional children, the same rule of alternation applies to the selection of both godparents and Christian names.

VII

Although the majority of the people strive to uphold the ideals of mutual co-operation, respect, and reciprocity within the household, they recognize that they do not always or uniformly adhere to their social norms and that, in varying degrees of intensity, conflict within households does occur occasionally. Arguments are accepted as a natural and inevitable part of having not two but four heads of household who—whether they like it or not—are permanently dependent upon each other and are in close, constant contact for the duration of their lives. Most arguments begin when one member complains that another has not done his or her fair share of the work. Accusations about being lazy, selfish, and irresponsible may be exchanged; but these are rarely taken seriously.

Lasting disputes and tensions are not taken lightly. When a dispute within a household or between close consanguineal kin belonging to different households does occur, it is characteristically concerned—either directly or indirectly—with material things.

For example, the most common sources of conflict between elder and younger heads of household include an unpaid dowry; the withholding of pensions and/or cash profits derived from the farm;

the denial of usufructory rights to the elder heads by the younger couple; the refusal of the elder couple to relinquish their ownership rights to the property; and, lastly, the failure of the latter to transmit the property intact to a single heir or heiress when they do relinquish their own ownership rights. Although irreconcilable differences in temperament and maltreatment of the elder couple are also cited as common causes of conflict, these are generally linked with the sources of conflict given above.

Traditionally, and in some cases at present, the possibility of conflict between elder and younger heads is recognized in pre-marital/inheritance settlement contracts. In these documents, it is often stipulated that if the two couples do not get along, they should separate on the grounds of incompatibility; that the property should be divided equally between them; and that the couple who establish residence elsewhere are entitled to one-half of the land, livestock, implements, domestic goods, and cash reserves of the household.

When conflict does occur within a household, it is widely regarded as the strictly private business of the domestic group and, if the dispute concerns a dowry or inheritance settlement, of those extra-domestic kin who are involved. Disputes should be concealed, as far as possible, from all other members of the community—and especially from one's 'first neighbours'. For the people, the following old saying clearly expresses this view: 'Cover the fire of the house with the ashes of the house', *etxenko suia, etxenko hautsareki tapa*. As informants explained, 'your "first neighbours" cannot help you when there's a dispute in your house, so there's no point in troubling them with your problem; and, in any case, it's not their business'. 'First neighbours' have neither the right nor any obligation to help one settle disputes within one's own household or with one's extra-domestic kin. As I shall show in later chapters, the expectations and obligations contained within the 'first neighbour' relationship—unlike those contained within kin relationships—are not concerned with issues from which conflict is likely to arise.

VIII

The ease with which the in-marrying spouse is incorporated into the post-marital residence is largely contingent upon his or her tempera-ment and the extent to which all parties are willing to conform to social expectations about their new roles and the conduct appropriate to these.

As soon as an individual moves into his new house his ties to the natal household are radically altered. He is no longer an *etxenkua* there; his obligations to the members of his natal household are drastically reduced and altered; and if he settled in another part of the commune, he may see his former *etxenkuak* only a few times a year—at a wedding or funeral, or at Mass on the major religious holidays.

Change of residence at marriage is not a single event but a process by means of which new relationships are created and existing ones reordered. During my stay in the community, I was able to observe this process in two households, in one of which I lived. In that house the *etxekandere-zaharr* and the *etxenkuak* of her son's wife had only a passing acquaintance before the wedding; and as is customary the young woman was not formally introduced to her until their engagement was announced two months before the marriage. The two houses are less than one kilometre apart; but none of the bride's *etxenkuak* had ever been in the groom's house, nor the groom's widowed mother in the bride's house until the engagement party. Because the two households belong to different neighbourhoods in the upper community, the boundaries of their respective social worlds did not overlap until the marriage took place.

If, as in this case, both spouses are Santaztarrak, at least one or a combination of the following relationships exists between them before their marriage: 'first neighbour', consanguineal and/or affinal kin, or 'the alder and the hazel' (*haltza eta ürrütxa*).[7] People are said to be 'like the alder and the hazel' if no known close affinal or consanguineal link exists between them; though, if both are Santaztarrak, they are likely to have some distant connection as kin, for, as the people themselves say, 'the Santaztarrak are all kin (*askaziak*)'.

In its broadest sense, *askaziak* denotes both consanguineal and affinal kin. The former includes one's FFF, FFM, FMF, FMM, MFF, MFM, MMF, MMM, FF, FM, MF, MM, F, M, siblings of the latter six individuals, one's own siblings, children, grandchildren,

---

[7] When asked to elaborate upon the idiom *haltza eta ürrütxa*, people gave one or both of the following responses: 'People who are like the alder and the hazel are like a French nun and a Spanish billy-goat.' 'The alder has no heart nor does it bear fruit; the hazel has a heart and bears fruit.' Secondly, people invariably recited the opening stanza of a Souletine ballad, *Bereteretchen Khantoria*, which is thought to have been composed in the fifteenth century (Colas 1923: 62–3): *Haltzak eztü bihotzik, Ez gaztamberak ezürrik; Enian uste erraiten ziela aitunen semek gezürrik*, 'The alder has no heart, nor the young cheese any bone; in my opinion the sons of Aitor do not tell lies.' (Aitor was a legendary patriarch of the Basque country.) See Sallaberry 1870: 209. A Sainte-Engrâce man offered a third explanation of *haltza eta ürrütxa*: 'You have a father, I have a father. We both have fathers but not the same father. Then what are we? Like the alder and the hazel.'

great-grandchildren, and one's first, second, and third cousins. Step-siblings are also regarded as consanguineal kin. The only affinal kin generally classified as *askaziak* are the parents and siblings of one's spouse, the spouses of one's spouse's siblings, of one's own siblings and children.

The limits of the category *askazi* are, however, subject to variation in the identification of consanguineal kin. One woman, for example, identified her FFMZD as 'a distant *askazi* of mine because we have the same blood (*ber odola*)'. The two women live at opposite ends of the commune, have seen each other only a few times, and have an age difference of nearly forty years. Although the elder woman knew that she was the first cousin of the younger woman's father's father and so has a distant *askazi* link with the younger woman, the latter had no knowledge of the genealogical relationships involved until I worked them out for her. Most people regard such genealogical exercises as pointless, given that few people in the commune are not distantly related to everyone in one way or another.

The Sainte-Engrâce people have an ambivalent attitude towards their extra-domestic close consanguineal kin. These *askaziak* have 'the same blood', a fact which links them permanently and which cannot be manipulated. Ideally their relationship should be co-operative, amicable, and free of tension. The ideal is generally realized when an individual and his extra-domestic kin assist one another in certain routine and seasonal activities—the nature of which does not readily give rise to conflict. But, as the people them-selves recognize, the most bitter and long-lasting disputes which occur in their community involve close consanguineal and affinal kin. An expectation of conflict and competition is contained within kin relationships that is strikingly absent in the two most important institutionalized relationships outside the household in Sainte-Engrâce society—namely, 'first neighbour' relationships and those which obtain between the shepherds of the *olha*.

In this small, face-to-face community, where frequency of social contact between households is largely contingent upon their spatial proximity, the people whom an individual knows best outside his own household are his 'first neighbours'. These are the persons to whom an *etxenkuak* turn first in times of crisis, for assistance in most routine activities, and for companionship. These are the persons of whom it is said, in slightly varying form, throughout the Basque country: It is better to have one good 'first neighbour' than one hundred kin (*Hobe da aizo hun bat eziez askazi ehün bat*); it is better to be on bad terms with kin who are far away and to get along well with the 'first neighbour' close by (*Hobe dela askazi hurruneki gaixki izatia, hobe dela eta khantuko aizueki untsa jitia*); 'I don't get along well with my kin, but I do with my "first neighbour"!' (*Askazieki ez untsa izanik, bena bai aizueki*!) Of all the relationships which order the social world outside the household in rural Basque society, the 'first neighbour' relationship is socially, economically, and ritually the most important.

V. 'FIRST NEIGHBOURS'

I

I N Sainte-Engrâce the word *aizo* is employed in two distinct senses: in the plural (*aizoak*) as neighbours, and in its most specific sense as 'first neighbour'. Several variations of this term appear in the literature. In Vizcaya, Guipúzcoa, Basse-Navarre, and in some villages of Navarra, 'neighbour' is expressed as *auzo*. In Basse-Navarre and Labourd, *auzo* or *hauzo* may also be employed in the sense of 'neighbourhood'. Two other variations of *auzo* as 'neighbour' are *auzoko*, used in the Guipúzcoan village of Zerain (de Goñi 1975: 376), and *auzokide* (Azkue 1969: 113). For the Vizcayan village of Murélaga, Douglass (1969: 226) glosses *auzo* as 'rural neighbourhood'.

According to Löpelmann (1968: 25), the Basque neighbourhood can be seen to consist of a group of persons bound by mutual interests and obligations and who act jointly to meet their common needs.

Echegaray (1932: 13) takes a similar view of the bonds between Basque neighbours but rightly emphasizes that what constitutes a neighbourhood varies from one village to another. It may, for example, consist of all the households within a given district, barrio, or village; but the proximity of houses is not a necessary criterion in the formation of neighbour relationships.

In Murélaga, which lies nineteen kilometres east of Guernica, the houses within an *auzo* tend to be nucleated, so that the rural neighbourhood there forms a discrete hamlet of eight to twelve dwellings located roughly in the centre of their combined holdings (Douglass 1969: 11). In that village there are four characteristic features of an *auzo*: every rural neighbourhood has a name, i.e. its own social identity; its own chapel and patron saint; its own internal political system; and, fc ᵗhly, the *auzo* acts as a corporate body in the maintenance of its own roads and public utilities (Douglass 1969: 11).

In Sainte-Engrâce the neighbourhood (*aizogoa*) has none of these distinctive features. Although the commune is divided into named settlements and rural *quartiers* the limits of a neighbourhood there

63

are defined not by these boundaries but by individual households. The *aizogoa* consists of all those households for whom one is obliged to perform certain agricultural and ritual services and from whom one is entitled to receive the same. These households, which may number from as few as three to as many as eight, are collectively referred to as *aizoak*, which in this context means 'neighbours'.

Two characteristic features of the neighbourhood in Sainte-Engrâce are its permanence (from the point of view of an individual household) and the dyadic reciprocity between households that consider themselves to be 'neighbours'.[1] A third distinctive feature is that a household may belong to more than one neighbourhood if, for example, it is obliged to assist a household which none of its other neighbours includes in their *aizogoa*. This is often the case when a household has a 'first neighbour' at some distance from the settlement to which it belongs and with which none of its other neighbours has a 'first neighbour' relationship. There is a well-defined pattern in which neighbourhoods are linked; but this will become clear only when the classification and spatial orientation of 'first neighbours' have been described.

Vicinal relationships ordered by institutionalized systems of exchange take a variety of forms in the Basque country—a fact that Basque scholars, with the exceptions of Caro Baroja (1971, 1974), Douglass (1969, 1975), and Echegaray (1932), have failed to treat. The relationship to which the most scholarly attention has been paid exists between a household and its 'first neighbour', often referred to as *le premier voisin* or *lehen auzoa* (Vinson 1882, Veyrin 1975, Webster 1901, Barandiarán 1947). The *lehen auzoa* is consistently adduced as the neighbour to whom a household turns first in times of crisis—at the birth of a child or beast, during a serious illness, at the death of one of its members—and for assistance in routine matters. A similar form of this relationship exists between a household and its *auzurrikourrena*, 'the nearest of the neighbourhood', in Murélaga (Douglass 1969). The *lehen auzoa* relationship also bears a close resemblance to the *lenbizikoatia*, literally 'the first door', in Echalar, which lies eight kilometres from the French frontier in north-western Navarra (Douglass 1975).

The 'first neighbour' relationship in Sainte-Engrâce entails many of the same obligations which exist between a household and its *lehen auzoa*, *auzurrikourrena*, or *lenbizikoatia*; but it is structurally

---

[1] Echegaray (1932: 5) identifies the bond between neighbours who reciprocally exchange goods and services as *auzotasun*. *Aizotasun* is employed in Sainte-Engrâce.

quite different from these three forms of the same social institution.[2] But for analytical purposes, as well as to add to the existing body of facts about 'first' or 'nearest' neighbours, I shall make contrastive reference only to the structural variations of *lehen auzoa* relationships that I found in Basse-Navarre and Soule. It should be borne in mind that the villages I cite are between eighteen and twenty-five kilometres from Sainte-Engrâce.

In Basse-Navarre the *auzoak* (neighbours) are generally the four or five households closest to one's own house. In the villages where I asked about 'first neighbours'—Lantabat, Esterençuby, and Saint Michel—a discrimination is made between the *auzoak* and *lehen auzoa*. In Lantabat, a household has four 'first neighbours': the first 'first neighbour' is conceptually to the left of one's own house; the second 'first neighbour' is conceived to be to the right, whereas the third and fourth 'first neighbours' are conceptually 'to the left again'. In Esterençuby, a household has only one 'first neighbour', which the people define as the first household on the side of one's house that is 'toward the church'. Webster (1901 : 12) reports that the same criterion for the classification of the 'first neighbour' is employed in Sare. In Saint Michel, the *lehen auzoa* is also the first household 'toward the church', but in that village a household may have as many as three *lehen auzoak*, among which no linguistic discrimination is made.

My investigations in seven Souletine villages revealed the following variations in the structure of 'first neighbour' relationships. In the lowland community of Ossas, which is roughly three kilometres north-west of Tardets, a household has four 'first neighbours': the first 'first neighbour' (*lehen lehen aizoa*) lies to the right of one's own house whereas the second, third, and fourth 'first neighbours' (*bigerren aizoa*, *hirugerren aizoa*, *laugerren aizoa* respectively) are conceptually to the left.

In Lacarry, a village in the Val Dextre of Haute-Soule, a household has only one 'first neighbour', *lehen aizoa*, to the right of one's house and a second 'first neighbour', *bigerren aizoa*, to the left. In Camou-Cihigue, which is roughly five kilometres due west of Tardets, a household traditionally had three 'first neighbours'. The first 'first

[2]The variety of forms which the institution of 'first' or 'nearest neighbours' takes has not received the close attention it deserves from Basque scholars. I have begun and intend to continue a comparative study of these forms and their economic, social, and ritual entailments. Such a study, which seeks to examine variations on a theme within a particular cultural area, should be not only of ethnographic but also of theoretical interest to social anthropologists.

neighbour' there was always 'in the direction of the church' (*bethi elizako gaintian*) and conceptually 'to the right' (*eskuñilat*) of one's house. The second and third 'first neighbours' were on the side of the house away from the church and conceptually 'to the left' (*eskerrilat*). In Laguinge, a tiny hamlet between Tardets and Sainte-Engrâce, and in the mountain commune of Larrau, a household has three 'first neighbours'. The *lehen lehen aizoa* is conceptually to the right, whereas the second and third *aizoak* are to the left. In Pagolle, which straddles the Basse-Navarre/Soule border, right/left distinctions are not made in the classification of one's three 'first neighbours'. In that village one's 'first neighbours' are those households whose land touches the land on which one's own house stands.

I received conflicting reports about 'first neighbour' relationships in Barcus, which lies close to the Béarn border in north-eastern Soule. A local woman told me that every household in her village has four 'first neighbours'; that the first 'first neighbour' is conceptually to the rear (*gibela*) and to the right of one's house; and that the second, third, and fourth 'first neighbours' are conceptually in front (*aitzin*) and to the left of one's house from the point of view of an individual standing in the doorway and looking outward. The retired school-master of Sainte-Engrâce, who spent several years in Barcus, told me that 'first neighbour' relationships in that village are ordered according to the proximity of fields and that Barcus 'first neighbours' are those households whose fields are contiguous.

Before I turn to the form that 'first neighbour' relationships take in Sainte-Engrâce, two facts about institutionalized vicinal relationships in the western Pyrénées deserve mention. Firstly, certain 'rights of the neighbourhood' were defined in the *fors* or *fueros*, the traditional charters of the Basque provinces. For example, the right to take fire from one's neighbour was legally established in the *fuero* of Navarre in 1237 (Echegaray 1932: 14–15). Whiteway (1901: 186) reports that in the thirteenth century *los Vesins de Baione*, the Neighbours of Bayonne, formed a distinct body over which the Episcopal Court of that town had no jurisdiction except in matrimonial matters, in cases of usury, and where 'gifts for pious purposes' were concerned.

The institution of *le premier voisin* was not, and is not at present, unique to the Basque provinces. Whiteway reports, though he does not cite specific villages, that this vicinal relationship existed in Béarn and Bigorre as well; and that 'when a Voisin (there) changed residence, or got in his harvest, he was actively aided by fellow Voisins, especially those who lived on either side of him, i.e. the

Premier on the church side, and the Contre Voisin on the other' (Whiteway 1901: 195).

The institution of 'first neighbours' still exists in Béarn. In the mountain community of Lescun, which lies roughly twenty kilometres due east of Sainte-Engrâce, a household has two *premier voisins*: one in the village nucleus and another in the rural *quartiers* to which all of the people move during the months of summer transhumance. Ideally the 'first neighbour' in the village is the household closest to one's own, whereas *premier voisins* in the 'grange' are those households whose fields are contiguous.[3]

II

In Sainte-Engrâce every household has three 'first neighbours': the *lehen lehen aizoa* is conceived to be 'to the right' (*eskuñilat*) of one's own house; the second 'first neighbour' (*bigerren aizoa*) and the third 'first neighbour' (*hirugerren aizoa*) are conceptually 'to the left' (*eskerrilat*). In daily conversation the latter two are generally referred to simply as *aizoak*, in this context 'the first neighbours'. In Souletine a second term may be used to denote the second 'first neighbour'— *altaizoa*. The root *althe-* has several meanings: 'region or locality', 'in favour of', and 'side' in the sense of taking the side of someone. *Althe* may also refer to someone who is 'a good match'. Although I found several old people who gave *altaizoa* as a synonym for *bigerren aizoa*, the term was not recognized by any person under the age of sixty.

In Sainte-Engrâce, as in some of the other Souletine communities I have mentioned, the spatial orientation of the three 'first neighbours' is conceptually defined by a bilateral asymmetry. (See Figure 1.) No two households can have the same three 'first neighbours', but every household has an *aizoa* relationship with the first 'first neighbour' of its own third 'first neighbour', with the second 'first neighbour' of its own second 'first neighbour', and with the third 'first neighbour' of its first 'first neighbour'.

'First neighbour' relationships are ordered transitively from left to right around the commune, which can be represented formally as follows:

$$a:b::b:c \supset a:c$$

[3] I wish to thank M. Pierre Fenot of the University of Paris (Nanterre) for having provided this information about 'first neighbours' in Lescun. M. Fenot has been doing field-work in Lescun during the past four years. For a discussion of 'first neighbour' relationships in another Béarnais community, see Bourdieu 1962: 85–6.

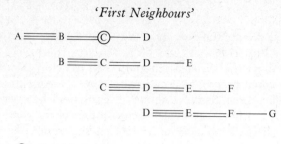

(C) : the household whose 'first neighbour'
       relationships are traced
—— : first 'first neighbour' of C
=== : second 'first neighbour' of C
≡≡≡ : third 'first neighbour' of C

Fig. 1. 'First neighbour' relationships

But as Figure 1 also shows, the *aizoa* relationship between two households that are first and second 'first neighbours' to each other
respectively is defined by dyadic reciprocity.

$$a:b \supset b:a$$

A third formal feature of the ordering of 'first neighbour' relationships can be isolated. In Figure 1 household A is a 'first neighbour'
of C, but C is not a 'first neighbour' of A. Their relationship is
asymmetric.

Unlike Murélaga, where a household may both choose and change
its 'nearest of the neighbourhood' (Douglass 1969: 154), the Sainte-
Engrâce household has neither option. Its three 'first neighbours'
are prescribed according to its spatial position in the commune
within the system of classification described.

At a community-wide level 'first neighbour' relationships form an
unbroken chain around the commune. This is an empirical fact of
which the people are clearly aware. Those who live within the same
nucleated settlement or *quartier* know exactly which households are
first and second 'first neighbours' in their own immediate social
world. They are not always certain—or correct—about the third
'first neighbour' of other households.

In the upper community, which has roughly half as many households as the lower one, people can readily identify one another's first
'first neighbour'; but they are often uncertain about the exact
ordering of *aizoa* relationships in the lower *quartiers*. The same is
true of the lower people with respect to the upper community. But
it was of considerable interest to find that people in both halves of the
commune invariably traced first 'first neighbour' relationships from
left to right in a clockwise direction around the community until

they reached the neighbourhood in which they themselves live. They visualize the commune as a circle, the centre of which is their conventional point of orientation.

In principle, 'first neighbour' relationships are immutable; but there are two circumstances in which they may be rearranged— namely, if a house is abandoned, or if a new house is built. The fact that *aizoak* relationships are altered to accommodate such changes became apparent to me when I received conflicting reports about the *aizoak* of an old widow. She claimed that the houses Ibarborda, Eyherabarren, and Esquer are her 'first neighbours'; but some of the upper people classified the first two houses and Arosteguy as her *aizoak*. The discrepancy resulted from the fact that a house within the old woman's neighbourhood was abandoned about twenty years ago and consequently her *aizoak* relationships were altered. Esquer was in fact one of her *aizoa* before this occurred; but when the house was abandoned Arosteguy became an *aizoa*. When questioned further the old widow acknowledged that Arosteguy had replaced Esquer as her first 'first neighbour', but that she continues to think of Esquer as her *lehen lehen aizoa* because that was the household to whom she gave 'blessed bread' before the ritual became obsolete.

III

In Sainte-Engrâce, relationships between a household, its three 'first neighbours', and all those whom it classifies as neighbours (*aizoak*) are ordered by dyadic reciprocity in the exchange of certain services. Two expressions convey the notion of dyadic reciprocity in this society: *alkharr lagüntza*, literally 'mutual assistance', and *ordari*, which denotes 'reciprocity', and in certain contexts 'compensation'. In Sainte-Engrâce at least, *ordari* and the verb form *ordarizkatu* are employed only in the sense of dyadic reciprocity. Another word, *aldikatzia*, conveys the notion of serial reciprocity.

In the seasonal cycle dyadic reciprocity is most apparent during the maize harvest; and the recruitment of labour follows a well-defined pattern. (See Figure 2.) On the day before he plans to harvest his crop, the younger male head of household pays a formal visit to each of his three 'first neighbours' to invite (*kümitatzeko*) them to assist him. Invitations are then extended to his neighbours, and finally to those households which lie to the right of his house and generally with whom he has a close consanguineal or affinal (*askazi*) relationship. I was able to observe this pattern during the harvests of 1976 and 1977. Extending invitations to the right is not prescribed, nor are the people themselves conscious of the fact that they do so as a general practice.

All those who are recruited to work are regarded as the *lagünak* (assistants, comrades, companions) of the household. In return for their services, the *lagünak* are paid with food and drink. The *etxekandere* prepares a four- or five-course dinner for them at noon, serves refreshments and sweets in the field, and then an 'afternoon breakfast' of bread, cheese, and wine.

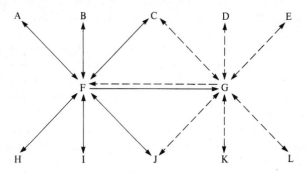

Fig. 2. Recruitment of labour during the maize harvest

The husking takes place in the barn of the host in the evening. The young male head of household circulates the goatskin wine flask among the men and women, who are not separated but intermixed. Jokes are told loudly for the benefit of all those present and are often met with uproarious laughter from both sexes. After the husking the people gather in the kitchen to eat another light snack and to continue their discussions about events within their own small social world.

Although households between whom *aizoa* relationships exist try to schedule their respective harvests on different days, a household is sometimes obliged to work for more than one of its neighbours on the same day. In order to fulfil all of their obligations, the *etxenkuak* are required to disperse (*barreatu*), which in Souletine also means 'to be in disorder'. The extent to which the dispersal of the *etxenkuak* is felt to jeopardize the social orderliness of their household was evidenced by the *etxekandere* of the house in which I lived. She was extremely distraught when we had to divide ourselves among three households on the same day. She herself worked for a neighbour who is also her *askazi* (her HFBS); the young *nausi* and *etxekandere* went to assist their second 'first neighbour'; and I was sent to a house (to the right of our house) in Senta. The elder and younger *etxekanderak* of that house are respectively the sister-in-law (HZ) and niece (ZD) of the elder woman with whom I lived.

Fern cutting and haymaking are also regarded as *aizo lana*, 'first neighbour work'. Dyadic reciprocity still orders *aizoak* relationships in these activities; but I am told that the bonds of 'mutual assistance' (*alkharr lagüntza*) were stronger in the past than at present. Formerly the entire *etxenkuak* went to the heaths of their 'first neighbours' and spent the day there working for them. During the past ten years or so it has become customary (and socially acceptable) for only the *nausi* and perhaps his wife to assist their *aizoak* in these activities. But, as in the past, the *aizoak* return the favour in kind.

One other form of 'first neighbour work'—wheat threshing (*ogi joitea*)—became obsolete during the 1940s and 1950s. Fixed groups of 'first neighbour' and neighbour households, ranging in number from five to eleven, took turns helping one another to harvest and to thresh their wheat in late July and early August. Turns to thresh and to recruit *aizoak* were ordered by two principles with which much of this book is concerned: *aldikatzia* (serial replacement) and *üngürü* (rotation). Households replaced one another serially (*aldikatü*) as hosts of the threshing party; and, at a community-wide level, turns to thresh and to recruit *aizoak* are said to have rotated (*üngüratü*) 'from left to right' (*eskerritik eskuñilat*) one year and then to have *arra-üngüratü* the following year. *Arra-üngüratü* conveys the notion of rotating backwards.[4] The Sainte-Engrâce people do not, however, say that *ogi joitea* went from right to left when it rotated backwards, though *arra-üngürü* expresses the notion of movement in a counter-clockwise direction. (See Chapter VIII.)

During *ogi joitea* turns were transmitted serially according to a fixed order of houses. For example, one year *ogi joitea* passed from house A to B to C to D, conceptually in a clockwise direction; the following year, it rotated backwards from D to C to B to A.

In some, though not all, neighbourhoods the threshing of the wheat passed 'from first neighbour to first neighbour' (*aizotik aizolat*) and, like the blessed bread ritual, crossed the river at only two points in the commune. (See Chapter VII.) People were, however, anxious to stress that when *ogi joitea* rotated in a clockwise direction it did not always follow exactly the path taken by blessed bread, though it was ordered by the same principles (*aldikatzia* and *üngürü*) which operate in the blessed bread ritual, the organization of

---

[4] Azkue (1969: 70) suggests that *arra*- is probably of foreign origin and that it is equivalent to the Latin *re*-. The original sense of *re*- in Latin is that of 'back' or 'backwards' (*OED*).

pastoral roles in the *olha,* and in the transmission of mill *(eihera)* rights.

Pig-killing *(xerrika)* is another activity in which neighbours, and especially 'first neighbours', assist one another. As in the maize harvest and planting, close relatives may be recruited as well.

The male head of household needs at least two men to act as his 'supporters' *(etxekizaleak),* those who hold the pig during the slaughter. These are commonly either the second or third 'first neighbour' and a male *askazi.* The most important role (because it requires the greatest skill) is that of the assassin *(ehailea),* the man who slits the beast's throat. One man in the upper community performs this task with his left hand—a fact which was repeatedly pointed out to me and regarded as inauspicious. At present the assassin is generally a 'first neighbour' or close relative of the pig's owner; but in the recent past the first 'first neighbour' was always invited to perform this crucial task.

During the pig-killing season, reciprocity between 'first neighbours' is also expressed in the exchange of fresh pork products. Virtually the same custom exists in Echalar, where it is called *sherri puskak,* 'the parts of the pig' (Douglass 1975: 66–7). In Sainte-Engrâce the *etxekandere* generally gives a parcel of sausages and black puddings to each of her three 'first neighbours' and expects to receive the same from them in due course. Formerly, these foods were also often given to the priest and to the schoolmasters; but these gifts were classified as *dohañik,* 'free', for which a counter-prestation was neither expected nor given. A gift for which a return prestation is expected and indeed required is called an *eskentze* or *presenta.* Gifts of this class—in addition to sausages and black puddings— include apples and nuts, reciprocally exchanged by female 'first neighbours' in the autumn.

'First neighbours' and neighbours of a household perform a variety of other services in the daily life. A man may ask a 'first neighbour' to help him chop and haul firewood, to transport and spread manure, and to prepare the soil for planting. He may ask a neighbour for the use of his tractor, and the neighbour may in turn borrow his beast of burden to do chores for which the tractor is ill-suited. If an *aizo* owns a motor car he is often asked to buy goods or to act as a taxi on market day, in return for which he is reimbursed for petrol costs.

If a household has an infant or young child requiring constant supervision, the *etxekandere* asks one of her female 'first neighbours' to look after it when she wants to go to the market or is expected to help her husband in the fields and barns. If the *aizo* also has children, the favour is returned in kind; if not, some other form of remuneration (such as vegetables, pots of jam, or cow's milk) is given.

Households are characteristically careful not to make too frequent demands upon their 'first neighbours'—especially demands which tend to disrupt the rigorously ordered routine of the household, e.g. taxiing. Favours performed on behalf of an *aizo* are rarely regarded as an imposition or a nuisance; but even when they are considered to be so, social expectations and values dictate that a household cannot refuse its 'first neighbours'.

In Sainte-Engrâce, as in other rural Basque communities where traditional forms of assistance provided by 'first neighbours' are gradually becoming obsolete, the 'first neighbour' relationship is being utilized to meet new ends. One good example of the transformations taking place within the institution was provided by the *etxekandere* of my house and our wealthy 'first neighbour', mentioned in Chapter II.

Unlike my hostess, the wealthy 'first neighbour' is not a *laborantxa* —one who works the land—though she was born and raised in the commune. She is the wife of a retired industrialist. Due to the very different socio-economic circumstances in which these two women live, most of the traditional forms of co-operation and reciprocity which characterize the 'first neighbour' relationship cannot be realized; yet the two women continue to assist each other mutually (*alkharr lagüntu*), as 'first neighbours' should. They have manipulated their relationship in an interesting way. The wealthy woman often gives my hostess expensive clothing, shoes, and bags that she herself no longer uses; in return for these items, my hostess performs a variety of domestic services for the woman, e.g. cooking for her dinner parties. On one occasion the woman asked my hostess to remove the manure left by a lorry on her drive. My hostess and I scrubbed the drive with brooms and brushes until no trace of the stains remained. The task was performed by my hostess without complaint and in a good-humoured way. We were both highly amused by the unusual nature of the 'first neighbour' assistance that we had been called upon to provide. When we finished, we were served coffee and gâteau in the kitchen.

IV

The trust, amicability, and willingness to co-operate which characterize relationships within the household are also realized in 'first neighbour' relationships. Quarrels between *aizoak* are an infrequent occurrence; and they are considered by many to be as socially disruptive as disputes within the household itself.

I know of only three cases of conflict between 'first neighbours'. Two of these involved the same household. Roughly five years ago, the younger *etxekandere* of this house owned a pig which damaged the garden of her first 'first neighbour', a bachelor. According to one version of the story, the man behaved abusively towards his neighbour and, in so doing, failed to show the respect that is due to both a 'first neighbour' and a woman. The *etxekandere* was equally abusive, whereupon the man confiscated her pig. The woman threatened to take revenge; and one night she waited for him on the road as he drank in one of the cafés. When the two 'first neighbours' met they quarrelled bitterly, and the woman thrashed the bachelor with a herding staff. He was badly injured and was taken to the house of a 'first neighbour' that he and his assailant have in common. The man has avoided and has refused to speak to his assailant ever since. He did not, however, take any legal action against her.

One year later the same woman accused the *etxekandere* of her second 'first neighbour' of allowing their hunting dog to steal eggs from her hen-house. (This was the household to which the injured bachelor had been taken to receive medical treatment.) The two women quarrelled and refused to speak to each other for about two years. Their houses lie only a few metres apart. But during that time the husband of the woman who had made the accusation continued to assist his second 'first neighbour' with their harvests and was often in their house. His children continued to play with their children. The husband was anxious to show his second 'first neighbours' that he, at least, was an *aizotiarra*, a 'first neighbour' with whom one gets along well and who fulfils his 'first neighbour' obligations.

The third case centres upon a bachelor in his late fifties who lived with his mother until her death in 1977. His attitudes and behaviour towards others contravene the values and social rules deemed so essential in this society. He reportedly disdained his mother's suggestion that he ought to find a wife; he is miserly with his money and has let it be known that he does not want to share his wealth with either a wife or an heir.

From the point of view of his neighbours, his behaviour is morally reprehensible for another reason: he is uncompromisingly antagonistic toward them; he neither seeks nor offers assistance; and he criticizes them viciously for being 'bad neighbours' (*aizo gaixtoak*) because *they* won't co-operate with him.

So far as I know, this man is the only person in the commune who has taken property disputes with his 'first neighbours' to court. Over the years he has charged all but one of his *aizoak* with some infringement of what he perceives to be his rights. Two disputes were settled in court. In one case, he accused a 'first neighbour' of letting his cattle cross his maize field and claimed damages to his crop. The *aizo* admitted that his beasts had in fact crossed the field but denied that any damage was caused. He was fined by the court, and he is still morally outraged that one of his *aizoak* should have treated him so unjustly.

When I left the community in 1977 the bachelor was in the process of taking legal action against another of his 'first neighbours' whom he charged with two offences: fouling the stream which borders their properties with waste from their lavatory, and fencing off a small strip of land which the bachelor assured me belongs to the commune. The bachelor is on speaking terms with only one of his *aizoak*. They, like the other people in the *quartier*, attribute his extraordinarily unsociable behaviour to a 'mixed head' (*bürü nahas*), i.e. mental illness.

The people take a very sober view of the bachelor and solemnly pointed out to me that in an isolated and dispersed community such as theirs a household cannot afford to have a quarrel with its 'first neighbours'. As one man observed, one's 'first neighbours' are 'closer than kin' (*askaziak hullañago beno*)—not simply spatially, but socially and in many cases affectively as well. 'If I don't get on well with my "first neighbours", who do I turn to if I lose a sheep or a cow in the hills? Who would help me with my maize and fern? And worst of all, who would look after my soul and my *etxenkuak* when I die?'

V

Like the *auzurrikourrena* in Murélaga and the *lenbizikoatia* in Echalar, 'first neighbours' in Sainte-Engrâce perform their most invaluable services at times of life crisis.

Until the 1960s, the Sainte-Engrâce women gave birth in their own houses. Although the woman's husband sometimes assisted, the role of midwife (*emagintsa*) was traditionally performed by the *etxekandere* of the second 'first neighbour'. In the event of a miscarriage or still birth, both of which are classified as an 'aborted child' (*haurr egoixtea*), she was also responsible for baptizing the infant. According to the women, baptism of an aborted child by a laywoman is permissible so long as the infant was living when it emerged from the woman's body. Unlike in Murélaga, where spiritual kinship ties may reinforce 'the nearest of the neighbourhood' relationship (Douglass 1975: 62), the *etxekandere* of the second 'first neighbour' in Sainte-Engrâce is virtually never selected as the godmother of the child at whose birth she assists.

The birth of the first child in a household (*etxeko prima* or *primia*, the first born son and daughter respectively) is a celebrated point of transition for both the young married couple and their *etxenkuak*. From the time of birth until the baptism of an infant the period known as *haurr ikhustea*, 'the child seeing', takes place. On this occasion formal invitations to see the infant are not extended by the *etxenkuak*. It is tacitly understood that all those who attended the wedding feast of the parents are welcome and expected to participate in the *haurr ikhustea*. Every household is obliged to send at least one of its *etxenkuak* to the house with the standard gift of sweet wine, biscuits, chocolate, sugar, and an article of clothing for the infant. The parcel is deposited on the sideboard and is ignored by both giver and receiver until the visit has ended. Since most couples invite an average of forty households to their wedding, the *haurr ikhustea* is a profitable custom.

In the *haurr ikhustea* an individual is formally introduced into the social world of the neighbourhood; and it is the first of five rites of passage in which his 'first neighbours' participate. The other four are the baptismal feast of the child, his First Communion feast, his wedding, and his funeral.

VI

Before the Second Vatican Council, the baptism of an infant was attended by only the godparents. The child was carried on the left arm of the godmother from its house to the church on the afternoon of the day following its birth. In her right hand the godmother carried a blessed candle, which she lit and left in the church. The godfather walked to the church on the left side of the godmother and held the infant's head in his hands.

Formerly baptism took place at the font beside the front door of the church and not in front of the altar as is done now. In principle the child should not enter the church before its baptism because it does not yet have a soul. Before the priest blessed the infant the godmother placed salt in its mouth 'in order to conserve its body' (*khorpitza konserbatzeko*). At present the priest is expected to perform this part of the ritual, but he does not always do so.

Formerly the baptismal feast was held in the house of the godmother and was attended by only the godparents, their *etxenkuak* and
the *etxenkuak* of the child. The people now explain that the 'first
neighbours' and *askaziak* were not formerly invited because households were too poor to hold large feasts.

During the past ten years or so it has become customary to invite
the three 'first neighbours' (or at least one member of each) to the
feast. Their inclusion is now felt to be obligatory, *bortxaz*, a word
which also means 'by force'. (The verb *bortxatzen* denotes 'constrain,
compel, force'.)

A failure to include these *aizoak* is considered to be a serious social
and moral offence. The extent to which this is felt became apparent
when the *etxekandere* of the house where I lived invited to their feast
only the godparents of her granddaughter, the *etxenkuak* of the child's
mother, and the priest. The date of the baptism was announced in
church, and the three *aizoak* (as well as the woman's ZD) waited
expectantly to receive their invitations. Until about a week before the
baptism, no mention was made of the feast by either the *etxekandere*
or her 'first neighbours'. The former confided to me that she knew
she was breaking convention by not asking them but defensively
pointed out that if she were to invite the 'first neighbours', she would
be obliged to ask the *askaziak* and friends of the young couple.

Her 'first neighbours' and her sister's daughter finally asked me
directly who had been invited. Some of them had concluded that
they were the only *aizoak* to have been excluded and had dared not
ask one another about the matter. Since 'first neighbours' do not
generally lie to one another, I decided that I could not be dishonest
but recited the guest list with misgivings. The sister's daughter was
extremely cross with her aunt, accused her of being niggardly (in my
presence only), and pointed out that she had invited her aunt and
cousin to the baptismal feasts of her three children. She reasoned
that her aunt therefore had a debt to pay.

The 'first neighbours' were more hurt than cross about having
been excluded. They were also more restrained in their criticisms,
which they apparently trusted would not be relayed back to my
household by me; but relations between them and my hostess—as
well as between the latter and her sister's daughter—were strained
for about a fortnight after the feast. Three other baptisms took place
during my stay in the community. In all three cases the 'first neighbours' of the household were invited to the feast.

As a child matures the feasts in his honour become progressively
larger and more expensive. At the age of twelve a child receives his

First Communion. A few weeks before the confirmation Mass, the households of all the participants issue invitations to the three 'first neighbours', the godparents of the child, to all of his close relatives (grandparents, uncles, aunts, first cousins, and siblings who have left the natal house), and to at least one of his friends (*adiskideak*). In 1977 an average of thirty-five guests was invited to each of the five feasts, three of which were held in the local hotel and two in the child's own house. Every guest is expected to give the child a gift of money of not less than 100 francs.

VII

The most festive and expensive feast is that of the wedding, which is attended by an average of a hundred guests. The 'first neighbours' and neighbours of the bride and groom, their *askaziak*, a few of their friends, and age-mates (*konskritak*) receive invitations about one month in advance.[5] 'First neighbours', friends, age-mates, and cousins of the couple are expected to give cash gifts or household items such as a linen tablecloth, lamp, or clock. Godparents, grandparents, and uncles and aunts commonly give the couple as much as 500 francs though only fifteen years ago 50 francs were considered to be a most generous gift.

Until the 1960s there were two wedding feasts. The first was held in the post-marital residence four days before the wedding. The *aizoak* of the bride and groom, their respective *etxenkuak*, and close relatives were invited. The second feast took place on the wedding day in the barn of the post-marital residence and was attended by all those invited to the wedding. At present there is only one feast (on the wedding day) and it is always held in an hotel.

As in the past a civil marriage precedes the church service. The bride is now escorted to the town hall by her 'girl companion' (*neskatila lagüna*) or maid of honour, and the groom by his 'boy companion' (*mithil lagüna*). During the past twenty years it has become customary for the young couple to ask a close friend to act in this capacity. In most cases the person selected is also a close relative, e.g. an unmarried sibling or first cousin.

[5] Friendship is an important basis of association only for children and young, unmarried people; only they, and not their elders, will classify someone as an *adiskide*, or 'friend'. *Konskritak* are people who were born in the same year and who received their First Communion together, i.e. the relationship is based on both biological and spiritual factors. Although an adult rarely has regular contact with more than two of his *konskritak*, he is characteristically sentimental about all of them. The only occasion at which *konskritak* gather together is a feast, held in an hotel in the year when they have their fiftieth birthday, the year when both sexes can expect that their procreative period will be terminated. (See Chapter XII.)

Formerly, and at least in the 1950s, the following practices were observed. The bride was escorted to the town hall and to the church by the *mithil lagüna* and the groom by the *neskatila lagüna*. Traditionally the *mithil lagüna* was the second 'first neighbour' of the groom. So far as I know, the *neskatila lagüna* of the bride was not necessarily one of her 'first neighbours'; but there was a tendency for women to ask a first cousin to the right of their house.

If the *etxenkuak* of the bride did not approve of the match, the second 'first neighbour' of the groom was also obliged to act as a mediator for him. Ordinarily the trousseau and the cash dowry of the bride were taken to the post-marital residence by her and her parents; but if her *etxenkuak* disapproved of the marriage the groom asked his *mithil lagüna* to perform this service.

One man who had to act in this capacity for his first 'first neighbour' reported that he was sent to the bride's house a few weeks before the marriage to collect her trousseau. He was given supper by the bride's parents and was dispatched to the groom's house with a large sack. Although he insisted that he did not look at the contents of the sack, he later recalled that her dowry consisted only of linens.

VIII

In the last chapter it was stated that one or a combination of the following relationships exists between Santaztarrak before their marriage: 'first neighbour', consanguineal and/or affinal kin, 'the alder and the hazel'. But no mention was made there which of these—if any—is preferred in the selection of a spouse.

People past forty say that in their youth there was a stated preference for marriage with a 'first neighbour'. They reason that this was logical since the *aizoak* are the people whom one knows best, with whom one was raised and worked from childhood until adulthood, and with whom—given the nature of expectations contained within the relationship—one is most likely to get along well. These are also households with which an alliance has already been established in a variety of social, economic, and ritual contexts. (See Chapters VII and VIII.) Furthermore, given the frequency of contact between 'first neighbours', an individual and his *etxenkuak* have ample opportunity to test the willingness of an *aizo* to co-operate and and to work hard—qualities that a spouse ought to possess.

From the point of view of the in-marrying spouse, the spatial proximity of his or her natal household is another important consideration in the selection of a marriage partner. If an individual marries out of his neighbourhood, his social and economic ties to his *ondokua*, 'womb place', are tenuous; and if he moves into the other half of the commune, these are virtually severed. But by marrying a 'first neighbour' an individual acquires a new set of social, economic, and ritual obligations to his natal household, not as one of its former *etxenkuak* but as one of its own 'first neighbours'. Marrying a 'first neighbour' also reinforces the affective bond between an individual and his natal household.

As Table III (Chapter IV) showed, the vast majority of existing marriages between Santaztarrak have been contracted by persons belonging to the same half of the commune. Of the sixty-three lower/lower marriages twenty-eight were between people who classified each other as neighbours (*aizoak*). Of the eighteen upper/upper marriages five were contracted by neighbours and seven by people who were first and second 'first neighbours' to each other before their marriage.

A close examination of marriages within the lower community reveals that fourteen of the twenty-eight were between persons belonging to the *quartier* of Athoro; and that of all the lower *quartiers* Athoro has had the highest incidence of 'first neighbour' marriages. Three of the fourteen marriages were contracted by neighbours (those who are mutually obliged to assist one another) and five by 'first neighbours'.

Although I am chiefly interested in the preference for 'first neighbour' marriage at the level of ideas, Athoro provides us with several modern cases in which the ideal has been achieved in practice, i.e. what has happened in several households is precisely what people think ought to have happened. The best example is that of the household Hustu. Over a ten-year period, Hustu provided its second and third 'first neighbours' with women and received a woman from its first 'first neighbour'. In 1939 a Hustu woman married their third 'first neighbour' and established post-marital residence in his natal house. In 1948 her brother married their first 'first neighbour' and brought her into their natal house. The following year their younger sister married their second 'first neighbour' and settled in his natal house.

Although neither the people nor I could uncover an example, the ideal exchange of marriage partners by 'first neighbours' consists of either two brothers marrying two sisters or a brother and sister marrying a sister and brother who are their 'first neighbours'. The reciprocal exchange of marriage partners by two households is called *haurr ordarizka* (literally, 'child exchange'), which, in its strictest interpretation, requires that each couple should establish post-marital residence in one of the two houses. Four cases of *haurr ordarizka* have occurred during the past eighty years; one of these involved neighbours (*aizoak*).

IX

The fifth and last rite of passage in which the three 'first neighbours' participate is at death; and it is this aspect of the 'first' or 'nearest' neighbour relationship which has been the most thoroughly documented in the literature. Because a separate chapter will be devoted to 'first neighbour' mortuary obligations I will only point out here that there are two formal relations by means of which these are ordered—dyadic and serial reciprocity.

Many of the 'first neighbour' mortuary obligations that I shall describe and analyse have been reported by other ethnographers who have worked in the Basque country; but there is one aspect of 'first neighbour' relationships in Sainte-Engrâce to which no reference has been made in the literature—namely, the ritual giving of blessed bread by the *etxekandere* to her female first 'first neighbour'. This aspect of 'first neighbour' relationships is the subject of Chapter VII.

VI. THE CHURCH, THE PRIEST, AND 'BLESSED THINGS'

I

THE traditional forms of religious experience have changed considerably within the lifetime of my eldest informants. Those who are now between sixty and ninety years old claim that 'everyone attended Mass on Sunday' in their youth, and that the church was then not simply the spiritual centre of their lives but the major social centre as well.

Until the end of the Second World War, two Masses were held on Sunday morning in both the upper church and the lower chapel; and the male and female heads of household alternated (*aldikatü*) in attending the first Mass, which was sung. If the *etxekanderak* went to the first Mass, the *nausiak* attended the second Mass. Until the 1960s, the elder *etxekandere* of the house also went to Mass every evening and to the special Friday Mass for the souls in Purgatory. She was often accompanied by her grandchildren.

At present roughly three-quarters of the population attend Mass, either in the upper church or in the lower chapel, on the major religious holidays: All Saints, Christmas, Palm Sunday, Easter, and Pentecost. With these exceptions, Mass on Sunday attracts very few people. During my stay in the commune, an average of only fifteen of the thirty-two upper households were regularly represented by their *etxekandere*; rarely more than four male heads of household attended unless it was a major holiday. The children are perhaps the most enthusiastic participants in the Mass, though most of them are too young to receive Communion; they love to sing and often join the priest in singing the Gloria in Excelsis.

An even smaller percentage of the lower people attend Mass regularly in their chapel. Only about five *etxekanderak* of the sixty-seven lower households are habitual church-goers.

The interior of the chapel presents a striking contrast to that of the richly ornamented upper church. When the chapel was built in the early 1950s, the chairs traditionally used by the women were replaced by wooden benches. Unlike the upper church the nave of the chapel is no longer divided into a men's and a women's section.

With the exception of a crucifix on the chancel wall, the chapel is devoid of any ornamentation. Even the altar is sparsely decorated. The confessional at the rear of the nave is falling apart. The stoup is sometimes dry. The upper church is in a state of disrepair as well, though some improvements to the interior of the church were made recently. An eighteenth-century wooden chandelier hangs from the ceiling in the centre of the nave. On the ceiling of the chancel the intricate murals are faded and chipped; but it is clear that the sanctuary was once very beautiful. The roman architecture of the building and the numerous art treasures within it have justly received wide acclaim.

There are twenty ornately sculptured cornices, which were made in the twelfth century. Some of these depict Biblical scenes, such as Solomon and the Queen of Sheba, the three Magi, and the Redemption. Others portray archers, centaurs, dancing maidens, and half-man, half-bird monsters. There are two splendid statues of the Virgin, one of which was carved in the sixteenth century, and a seventeenth-century statue of Sainte Madeleine. Scenes from the legend of Sainte-Engrâce are depicted on the retable behind the altar.

The church is divided into three apses at the front of which are the altar and two lateral chapels. (See Figure 3.) These are separated from the nave by a rare seventeenth-century iron grille. The nave is roughly twenty-five metres long and eighteen metres wide. A few metres in front of the altar and grille there are four rows of wooden benches on which children of both sexes and unmarried girls sit. Directly behind the benches there are six rows of high-backed wooden and cane chairs. These are the *elizako kaiderak*, 'the chairs of the church', on which the *etxekanderak* kneel to pray.

Until the 1960s the *elizako kaidera* was a necessary part of a woman's trousseau. Most of the existing chairs were made in the lowlands; and the same type of chair can be found in other Souletine and in some Béarnais churches. In Sainte-Engrâce, the broad strip across the back of the chair bears either the initials of its owner or a design. A woman leans on this strip as she kneels in prayer. With the exception of the sermon, when the women are seated facing the altar, the chairs are placed with their cane seats facing the rear of the sanctuary.

The chair of the *etxekandere* constitutes her space (*lekhü*) on the church floor. There are no marked floor sites; but every chair has a specific space in relation to the others belonging to her post-marital residence. For example, the space of the chair of Bidabe is known to

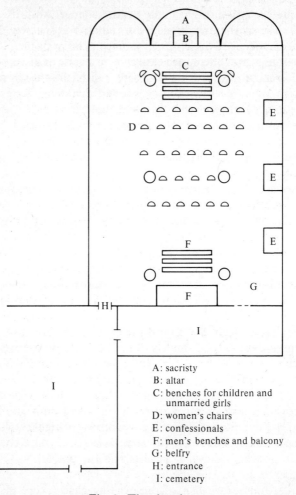

A: sacristy
B: altar
C: benches for children and
   unmarried girls
D: women's chairs
E: confessionals
F: men's benches and balcony
G: belfry
H: entrance
I: cemetery

Fig. 3. The church

be in front of the pillar opposite the chapel of the Virgin and between the chairs of the *etxekanderak* from Elichigaray and Hardoy. If the *etxekandere* of Bidabe finds that her chair has been moved—which happens occasionally—she will replace it in its proper space before the Mass. There is no apparent pattern according to which the spaces of houses (and consequently of chairs) have been allocated. The chairs are not arranged according to neighbourhoods, settlements, or *quartiers*. Although very few lower women still keep a chair in the church, those who do are not segregated from the upper women.

When I lived in the vacant house of a widow living in Saint Palais,

I was invited by her sister to occupy the chair of their mother, who was the last *etxekandere* of the house. When I moved into the house of the widow's sister, my space in the church changed accordingly. In principle I ought to have had my own chair to place beside that of the *etxekandere* of my house, for it was agreed by the woman and her *aizoak* that I was like a daughter-in-law to her. Since she and I attended Mass together and had only her chair, I was told to use the chair of her deceased sister, whose house no longer has an *etxekandere*.

Formerly the elder and younger *etxekanderak* of a house placed their chairs side by side. But now that the young married women no longer include the chair in their trousseaux, they must occupy either that of their mother or mother-in-law in her absence, or one of the old chairs that belonged to an *etxekandere* of a house now abandoned.

Before the Second World War, every lower *etxekandere* kept a chair in both the church and chapel; and I am told that the elder and younger *etxekanderak* of lower households formerly locked their chairs together with rope or wire after Mass in the church. Lower women who observed this custom explained that it reduced the likelihood of their chairs being moved by the upper women when the lower women were absent; for the latter attended Mass in the church only on the major holidays, at baptisms, weddings, funerals, and on the Sundays when it was their turn to give 'blessed bread' there rather than in the chapel. (The Singing Mass at which 'blessed bread' was given alternated between the church and the chapel.)

The men's section of the church lies directly behind and above the women's chairs and is referred to simply as 'the back of the church' (*eliza xola*). It consists of three rows of wooden benches on the church floor and a narrow wooden balcony at the western end of the sanctuary. The men do not have a 'space' in the church and may sit wherever they like on the benches.

On the southern side of the nave there are three decrepit confessionals which have not been used since the last war. The one closest to the chancel is the *Erretora*, where people formerly confessed to the parish priest. The centre confessional, the *Estrangera*, was once used by Souletine priests who travelled to the commune on Adoration to confess to its priest. The third confessional is the *Bikaria*, in which confessions were made to the vicar of the parish.

The only cemetery (*hilherria*, literally 'the village of the dead') in the commune adjoins the western end of the Senta church. It is divided into two sections, the larger of which forms a rectangle around the north-western end of the church. The Cross of the Cemetery stands in this section.

Until the end of the Second World War, the commune had both a priest (*erretora* or *apheza nausi*) and a vicar (*bikaria*) who took turns giving the High Mass (*meza handia*, 'big Mass') and the 'silent Mass' (*meza ixila*), which still alternate weekly between the church and the chapel.

Two liturgical offices were traditionally held by laymen: the sacristan and the singer of the church (*elizako khantaria*). The former is always held by the *nausi* and *etxekandere* of the house Salaber, which lies behind the south-eastern end of the church. When they assume their roles as male and female sacristan they make an oral promise to the priest that they will fulfil the ritual duties traditionally assigned to them. The male sacristan (*giltzaiña*) is the guardian of the church and the keeper of its key. He was also formerly responsible for cutting and distributing 'blessed bread' to the parishioners in the church.

In Souletine, as in some other Basque dialects, the female sacristan is called the *serora*, which also denotes a 'nun'. In Sainte-Engrâce she had until recently the curious title of 'savage sacristan' (*basa serora*), a name that is now applied pejoratively to a woman who adopts pious airs in church but who is considered to be a devil (figuratively) in her house. The duties of the female sacristan are threefold: she is obliged to lay out and care for the altar ornaments, cloths, and liturgical articles; to clean the sanctuary; and to light the altar candles.

Although either the male or female sacristan may now act as the bell-ringer, I am told that in the past this task was ideally performed by a widow or unmarried woman of Salaber. The church bell is rung on four occasions: before and after the Mass; to call the people to recite the Angelus at sunrise, noon, and sunset; to announce a death; and to calm severe winds and storms.

Unlike the office of sacristan, the church singer was a self-appointed position, assumed by the man whose singing voice had the most *indarra* (power, force). He led the men and women in song during the Mass and the processions. The last church singer died in 1956. Since no man assumed the role after his death, the office has become obsolete.

II

The form of Catholicism now practised in Sainte-Engrâce bears little resemblance to 'the old religion' (*errelijione zaharra*), as it was recalled for me by the elderly people. From their retrospective point of view, the *errelijione zaharra* had a stronger influence on their social and spiritual lives than the present religion. 'The old religion' is judged to have had more *indarra*, more power to compel the people to attend Mass regularly, to embrace their faith zealously, to participate as a community in the liturgical processions, to observe fast and abstinence, and to respect their priest, the holy sacraments, and 'the blessed things' (*gaiza benedikatiak*).

The notion of *indarra*, to which I have referred already, is of considerable conceptual complexity and of special importance in this chapter, which is primarily concerned with the uses of supernatural *indarra*. Like *mana* or honour—to give only two examples—*indarra* cannot be given any exact translation in English. The interest and significance of the concept lie in the associations it makes between different realms of meaning (cf. Pitt-Rivers 1974: 6), e.g. sacred and mundane, spiritual and physical.[1]

Supernatural *indarra* is conceptually distinct from the four main types of human *indarra*: the life-force acquired at conception; the procreative power which men and women acquire at puberty; the physical strength of the body, acquired by means of eating well and working hard; and the jural power and authority acquired by the younger heads of household through their pre-marital contract.

Inanimate objects or things may also have *indarra*. The *indarra* of wine, or the strength of its alcoholic content, is acquired during the process of fermentation. The natural elements, such as wind, rain, and thunder, have *indarra*. The *indarra* of the 'old religion' and 'the old ways' (*moda zaharrek*) is the power to constrain and to compel people to do what is expected of them by moral suasion.

Certain substances acquire their *indarra* from God through the act of blessing by the priest. These are blessed laurel (*erramü benedikatia*), blessed water (*hur benedikatia*), blessed candles (*ezko* or *tortxa benedikatiak*), and blessed bread (*ogi benedikatia*), all of which have a supernatural efficacious *indarra*. Semen also has an efficacious *indarra*, which a man acquires when he reaches puberty.

In transubstantiation the Host acquires the mystical *indarra* of God. The concept appears frequently in the Mass, and in a number of different contexts. In the Liturgy of the Eucharist *indarra* is employed in the sense of 'the fruits of the earth' (*Igantetan Elizan* 1970). The powers on high, *goiko indarrek*, bow down before God, who is implored to grant strength to the faithful by means of his succour (*indarra*) and assistance. In one Eucharistic prayer 'the power of the

[1] *Indarra* is a concept of the same order as *mana* and grace; and I am grateful to John Campbell and to Julian Pitt-Rivers for having pointed this out to me. The concept is an intriguing and perplexing one about which I intend to write at length in a separate work.

Holy Spirit' is expressed as *Ezpiritü Saintiaren indarra.* In an offertory song God is invited to 'take our heart, our good bread, clean bread, our seed of *indarra,* our life', *har, othoi, Jauna, gure bihotza, huna ogia, ogi garbia gure indarren azia, gure bizia.*

The human condition is said not to have *indarra* when it is compared with that of God. The *indarra* of God is a mystical, all-pervasive power to order and to control human events and lives, in the face of which mortals are rendered helpless. In a similar manner, laymen do not have the *indarra* of a priest, who receives his supernatural power to alter human and natural events from God.

In the 'old religion' children were taught to respect the *indarra* of God, the priest, the Host, and the 'blessed things', and they received religious instruction from their parents every night when the members of the household gathered around the hearth to recite prayers and to sing. The *etxekandere* of my house claims that she and her husband upheld this tradition with their own sons, who were born in the late 1940s and early 1950s; but it has become obsolete during the past two decades. At present the children receive virtually all of their religious education from the priest, who holds catechism classes every Wednesday morning.

The three constraints imposed upon people in the 'old religion' to which greatest importance is now attached were the fast (*barurr*), abstinence (*bijilia*), and the penance of confession. Formerly a twenty-four-hour fast was kept before Communion on the major holidays. A twelve-hour fast was observed on all other Sundays. The people also practised a twelve-hour abstinence from solid food until 1957, when the Vatican reduced the obligatory period of abstinence from twelve to three hours before Communion (Hardon 1975: 556). Although abstinence from meat on Fridays is no longer prescribed by ecclesiastical law or by the local priest, a few people continue to observe this penance. The priest has prescribed fast and abstinence on Good Friday and Ash Wednesday.

Until roughly fifteen years ago, the people were obliged to make a private confession to the priest on the first Friday of every month. During the past few years private confessions have been held only two or three times annually. In the 'old religion', confession on Good Friday was considered to be the most important one.

In 1977 the people attended Mass on Good Friday fully expecting to confess their sins individually. Although only seventeen women and three men were present, the priest announced that there would not be individual but communal confession and absolution. Having never witnessed or heard of this form of administering the sacrament of penance, the people were completely baffled, and some were outraged. On the following day I overheard several heated debates among the women about the validity of communal confession. The old *etxekanderak* charged that the priest was 'too lazy' to hear private confessions.

At Mass on Holy Sunday the priest announced that a second communal confession would be held on the following Wednesday in the chapel. The *etxekandere* of my house and I went to the chapel but neither the priest nor any other parishioners appeared. The woman was indignant about the negligence of the priest and depressed by the apathy of her fellow Catholics; but she never mentioned the incident to the priest. She explained that she had too much 'shame' (*ahalke*) to challenge the priest about his absence.

<h1 style="text-align:center">III</h1>

The decline of the 'old religion' can in part be attributed to certain changes in ecclesiastical doctrine during the 1950s and 1960s, and to an increasing religious apathy among the people themselves; but a large burden of responsibility for changes in the local form of Catholicism rests with the present priest, who assumed his duties in 1958.

Liturgical processions, which formed a fundamental part of the 'old religion', survived in the commune only so long as the priest saw fit to lead them and, from his point of view, so long as people expressed an interest in retaining them. The old people retrospectively claim that the processions played a crucial role in promoting the spiritual and social solidarity of the community; and that before the processions become obsolete the upper and lower people were not socially divided as they are today.

In both distance and time the longest of the processions were made on St Mark and Corpus Christi, when the people walked to the Three Crosses of Sainte-Engrâce, Sainte Madeleine, and St Antony at Lechartzu. The upper and lower people assembled at the old chapel of St Laurent in the lower *quartier* of Dolainty-Ükhümürrütia in mid-morning. The sacristan, who carried the church cross, led the pilgrims and was followed first by the priest and the relic and then by the men and women respectively. The journey from the chapel to Lechartzu took approximately four hours. After the benediction at the three crosses, the priest invited the pilgrims to kiss the relic. The procession then returned to the upper church, where the Litany of the Saints was offered in the evening. So far as the people can remember, this procession has not been made since the 1930s.

A second major procession on the local liturgical calendar was held on the three consecutive days preceding Ascension (*Salbatore*) and was known as the Rogation Procession. On the morning of the first day the pilgrims walked from the upper church to the Cross of Igaia (*Igaiko Kürützea*) on the south-facing ridge above Calla where the house Igaia once stood. The people were led from the church by the priest, who carried the church crucifix and was flanked by the children. The men followed in single file, and the women proceeded last. When he reached the western gate of the cemetery, the priest passed the crucifix to the *nausi* whose land the procession first crossed on its way to Calla. When the *nausi* reached the western edge of his land, he handed the crucifix to the man owning the adjacent field towards Calla and dropped back one place in line. This part of the ritual was ordered by the principle of *aldikatzia*, which is best translated here as 'serial replacement'. The crucifix was passed *en roulement* from *nausi* to *nausi* until the procession reached the Cross of Igaia.

The most intriguing aspect of this procession was the relationship 'first neighbours of the cross', *kürützean aizoak*. The 'first neighbours' of the Igaia Cross were the *etxekanderak* of the two houses whose fields flank the cross. On the morning of the first rogation, these two women were obliged to spread greenery along the path to be taken by the pilgrims from the communal spring in Calla to the cross, on which they sprinkled blessed water with sprigs of blessed laurel and placed a bouquet of flowers. The priest blessed the earth on which the cross stands with blessed water and offered a prayer 'to ask the earth to give abundant and good fruit'. The pilgrims were then led by the priest back to the church for the Mass.

On the second day of the rogation, the priest led the people to the Cross of Sainte Madeleine (*Maidalenako Kürützea*) on the south-western edge of Senta. This cross had only one 'first neighbour', the *etxekandere* of the first house toward the church from it. Her ritual duties were the same as those of the two 'first neighbours' of the Igaia Cross.

The third rogational procession went from the church to the cemetery cross (*Hilherriko Kürützea*), which is roughly five metres high and was constructed *c.* 1850 (Cuzacq 1972: 17). A crown of thorns, two nails, pincers, a hammer, a lance, and a ladder are symmetrically arranged across its arm. It too had only one 'first neighbour', the *etxekandere* of the house directly across the road from the church. After she performed her ritual duties, the priest blessed the earth and the people returned to the church for the Mass.

This three-day rogation was last performed in 1970. According to both the people and the priest himself, he abolished the practice 'because too few people attend Mass to form a procession'.

The cemetery cross was also the focal point of processions held every Sunday before Mass between St Cross on the third of May and St Cross on the fourteenth of September. The sacristan carried the church crucifix at the head of the procession and was followed first by the priest, then the men, and lastly the women. The priest offered prayers at the cross and the people sang 'Beloved Sainte-Engrâce' (*Santa Engrazi Maitea*), a song that every child was formerly obliged to learn and which recounts the history of the relic from the time of its miraculous discovery to the present. From the cross the pilgrims left the cemetery through the western gate and filed in a clockwise direction around the outer perimeter of the cemetery to re-enter it through the south-facing gate. They proceeded to the cross a second time and then returned to the church. The present priest abolished this custom in 1962.

There are several other liturgical practices considered to have been part of the 'old religion'. Before the end of the Second World War, when households raised wheat, the *etxekanderak* of the commune gleaned corn from their newly harvested fields to make their annual offering to the Virgin on the fifteenth of August. Before Mass on that day, they placed their bundles of corn (*ogi bürüxkak*) on the altar, where these were blessed by the priest. Formerly the priest's housekeeper made flour from the offerings with which she baked the unleavened bread used in the Eucharist.

Another custom which became obsolete during the Second World War took place on All Saints, when all the children in the commune set up a market in the cemetery to sell prayers for the dead. As they entered the western gate, the children recited a chant, *salmea, salmea, salmea*, which the old people glossed as *en commerce*. (The root noun *sal* conveys the notion of a sale.) Children from the same household took turns offering prayers and reciting the rosary for the souls of the dead from their own and other houses. The *etxekanderak* placed coins on top of their house tombs to invite the children to perform their ritual service. After the ceremony the children were permitted to take the coins from the tombs at which they had prayed. The woman of my house reasoned that children under twelve performed this ritual service 'because they are more pure', i.e. they have committed fewer sins, than their elders. She and her sisters participated in the ceremony during the second decade of this century.

Of all the liturgical rituals performed in the 'old religion', the one to which people now ascribe greatest importance in their social and spiritual lives was the ritual of 'blessed bread' (*ogi benedikatia*) given by the *etxekanderak* of the community. This practice was part of a twofold system of asymmetric exchange and is the subject of Chapter VII.

IV

For as long as people can remember, the priest has played a dual role in Sainte-Engrâce society. As the secretary of the town hall, he enjoys more power and authority in secular matters than do the mayor and twelve councillors. As the *nausi* of the church, he has had an undisputed authority to preserve, to modify, and to abolish traditional religious practices.

The dual role of the priest can be traced back in the parish records to the middle of the nineteenth century. (Earlier records were destroyed in a fire.) Sainte-Engrâce is the only Souletine community I have found in which the office of town hall secretary is not held by a layman.[2]

Unlike his predecessors, who reportedly conducted all their business in their house opposite the Senta church, the present priest works solely in the town hall, where he is generally available for consultation every morning from Monday until Friday. During the course of my stay, I never saw him or anyone else enter or leave his house. The people say that they have not been inside the priest's house since he took office. The shutters are tightly shut and bolted. The door never stands open; and the people speculate that the contents of the house must be mildewed. Unlike his predecessors, he has no housekeeper.

Since many of the upper people do not own motor cars and are no longer accustomed or willing to walk to Caserne, they must seek his assistance in secular matters either by waiting for him in the café, where he often eats, or by sending a message to him in the town hall. If they have a problem requiring immediate attention, they may corner him after Mass; but the latter tactic is rarely employed, since there is a great risk of being overheard.

As the town hall secretary, the priest performs a variety of tasks on behalf of the commune and its inhabitants. In matters concerning the public welfare, such as the local schools, roads, employment for the young, and pasturage rights, the priest advises and assists the

---

[2] During the 1940s, the office was in fact held briefly by a local unmarried woman when the priest was killed in a motor car accident and before his successor was appointed.

mayor and councillors. He attends meetings in the canton and province to discuss rural development schemes, tourism, and employment opportunities; registers all births, marriages, and deaths; records all deeds pertaining to the purchase and sale of land; and handles all queries about local taxes.

So far as the people are concerned, his most crucial role is as their *lagün*, their 'comrade and helper', in monetary matters, and especially those which involve government subsidy schemes. The present priest is generally regarded as the most powerful and effective secretary the commune has ever had; and it is largely through his efforts that they have obtained virtually every form of social security benefit offered by the French government. He handles all applications and queries about pensions, allowances, unemployment, and poverty benefits. He is widely praised and respected for his knowledge and expertise in such matters.

It cannot be said that the present priest is well respected as a clergyman. Jojo, as the people refer to him among themselves, is generally judged to be more interested in his secular duties than his religious ones. Although he was often censured for his refusal to preserve traditional liturgical practices, only a few of the old *etxekanderak* vehemently criticized him in my presence. Whenever she heard his name mentioned, one old woman threw up her hands and sneered bitterly, 'The priest? The priest? We have no priest!' During my stay, the only occasions at which the other women openly condemned him were after the communal confession on Good Friday and on Holy Saturday, when he distributed candles in place of burning embers, the traditional form of 'blessed fire'. So far as I know, no one challenged his breaking convention on these occasions or when he made similar changes in religious practices in the past.

One of the most striking and puzzling features of their attitude toward the priest is the acquiescence with which the older people have accepted his authority to abolish customs, such as the ritual giving of 'blessed bread', the loss of which they now sorely lament. When asked why they did not contest his decision to end the *ogi benedikatia*, 'an old backward custom', the people pointed out that they are not the *nausiak* (masters) of the church and therefore had no right to overrule their priest.[3]

[3] According to the priests of Sainte-Engrâce and Lantabat, they and their colleagues in the Basque country were encouraged by church leaders to stop the blessed bread ritual 'in order to stress to the people the supremacy of the Host over blessed bread'. Church leaders reportedly disapproved of the popularity of the blessed bread ritual in the Basque country. In some communities the people received the Host, 'the true Holy Bread', only occasionally but never failed to receive blessed bread in the church.

The submissive response of the older people to the priest's actions may in part be attributed to surviving notions about his *indarra*. From their point of view, a priest is called upon by God to act as His servant on earth. At his ordination, he receives *indarra*—a supernatural power to alter both human and natural events—from God. This is his only non-human attribute, for he is physically and emotionally human and is thought to be as susceptible to temptation, folly, and sin as any layman.

Although God is thought to have punished people in pre-Christian times, He 'no longer has the right to do so because He gave us everlasting forgiveness when Jesus Christ died for our sins; God is our Creator, not our punisher'. This view of God's compassion and inability to punish people before death is an intriguing departure from Catholic doctrine, 'in which it is a divinely revealed truth that sins bring punishments inflicted by God's sanctity and justice' (Hardon 1975: 560). The Sainte-Engrâce people with whom I discussed this matter conceded that temporal punishments are inflicted upon those who sin; but they maintained that the responsibility to punish sinners rests not with God but with their priest, who is able to do so by means of his supernatural *indarra*.

Every priest is thought to have *indarra*; but the extent to which he employs it, as well as the uses to which he puts it, are contingent upon his temperament. A priest can himself decide whether and when to use his *indarra*, which may be employed constructively or destructively. For this reason, the old people cautioned me, he is potentially dangerous, to be feared, and above all to be obeyed. In their lifetimes they have had five priests. Of these they singled out a priest called Etcheverry as the one whose *indarra* they feared and respected most. Etcheverry served in the commune during the 1930s and 1940s. He is said to have had a volatile, irascible temper and an abundance of energy. When an individual possesses these two qualities, he is said to have 'white powder' (*pholbor xuri*), which may make him difficult to live with; but if he is a priest, *pholbor xuri* renders him all the more dangerous. Etcheverry was a priest whom most people were careful not to provoke. There were, however, a few men who treated lightly both his 'white powder' and his *indarra*, for which they were duly punished.

People recalled two incidents that, to their way of thinking, verified Etcheverry's *indarra*. One of the more sceptical men of the commune once engaged a companion in an animated conversation during the Mass and at one point burst out laughing. Etcheverry reportedly stopped the service and publicly admonished him. The culprit burst out laughing a second time, whereupon the priest cursed him 'in the name of God' in the presence of the congregation. As soon as he did so, the man's mouth became disfigured and remained that way until his death.

One dictum in the 'old religion' was that no work should be done on Sunday without the permission of the priest. This custom seems to have been followed until the end of the Second World War. On one occasion during the term of Etcheverry, two 'first neighbours' reportedly planned to harvest their maize on the Sabbath. In keeping with convention one of the men sought the priest's permission before doing so; but his neighbour did not. Etcheverry is said to have been very cross about his disobedience. On Monday torrential rains fell for twenty-four hours and the man's crop was ruined. The priest had used his *indarra* to punish the man by inducing the heavy rains, which miraculously did not damage the other people's fields. Etcheverry is quoted as having reminded his hapless parishioner that 'I did my duty (*eginbidea*) but you failed to do yours. Consequently you have suffered a great loss.'

In Sainte-Engrâce, the *indarra* of the priest may also be used to exorcise an evil spirit known as the *belhargile*. Although most people now claim that this spirit was no more than a superstition, a few still contend that some of their ancestors saw it. The *belhargile* was described to me as 'a little spirit in the form of a little man, who could be seen by only certain gifted people'. If he were sighted, the person should on no account tell anyone, lest one of his beasts, *etxenkuak*, his house, or crops should be harmed. The *nausi* of the house Igaia had the ability to see the spirit and once told his *aizoa* that he had done so. That night his infant son had a tantrum and all of the furniture in his room shook violently. Realizing that he had angered the *belhargile*, the man sought the priest, who exorcised the spirit from the child's body. The *etxekandere* of my house had a similar experience with her son, who is now twenty-seven years old. When he was an infant he had violent tantrums and cried continuously. His mother took him to the priest to have the evil spirit exorcised.

By virtue of his *indarra* a priest is not only able to expel evil spirits; he is also able to compel them to do harm by giving an *eiharr meza*, literally 'a desiccation Mass'. If a 'bad type' (*ur gaixto*) wishes to inflict harm upon an enemy, he may ask the priest to give this Mass, which I was assured had no benediction and was held outside the church. As a result the victim would suffer great pain, shrivel, and die. One woman in her seventies told me that in her youth someone asked the priest to give an *eiharr meza*, but he refused to do so.

In the 'old religion' the *indarra* of the priest was relied upon to protect the fields, the house, and the livestock from harm. He was called upon to banish mice, which periodically invade the houses, barns, and fields. At present, as in the past, he offers a special Mass to protect the shepherds, their sheep and cattle on St Blaise, the third of February. According to the rules of the 'old religion', livestock should not be made to work on that day. If a man disobeys this prescription the *indarra* of the priest may be used to harm his beasts. During the term of Etcheverry the *nausi* of Behiagoity tried to harness his cattle to plough a field. One of the beasts reportedly went mad and plunged off an embankment. The loss was attributed to the priest's power.

I have heard of no cases in which the present priest used his supernatural *indarra* to punish wayward parishioners or to exorcise evil spirits. The only ways in which he employs his power from God are in the transubstantiation of the Host and the annual blessing of candles, laurel, water, and fire. The present priest will not be remembered for his supernatural *indarra*, but for his human power and authority in secular matters.

V

In Sainte-Engrâce six substances traditionally constituted the class of blessed things (*gaiza benedikatiak*): blessed ash (*hautsa benedikatia*), blessed fire (*sü benedikatia*), blessed candles (*ezko* or *tortxa benedikatiak*), blessed laurel (*erramü benedikatia*), blessed water (*hur benedikatia*), and blessed bread (*ogi benedikatia*).[4] Of these only blessed ash and blessed fire do not have an efficacious *indarra*. Blessed salt (*sel bénit*), which was distributed by the priests of some communes in Picardie on Holy Saturday (van Gennep 1947: 1256), and blessed maize (*artho benedikatia*), which is still distributed on Holy Saturday in Camou-Cihigue, are not among the class of 'blessed things' in Sainte-Engrâce.

According to both the people and to the Souletine clergy with whom I discussed the matter, the *gaiza benedikatiak* are 'for the living'. They become *benedikatia* only by means of the act of blessing performed by the priest. This in turn imbues them with *indarra* from God.

Because of their supernatural power, blessed things must be treated with respect. There are in Sainte Engrâce, as well as in many

---

[4] The adjective *benedikatia*, derived from the Latin *benedicere*, has no original equivalent in Basque.

other parts of rural France (van Gennep 1947: 1200), certain prescribed rules about their disposal. One must 'be careful' not to let them touch the ground or to come into contact with a dog or cat. Care should be taken that they are not lost or temporarily misplaced; but above all they should never be thrown away. The people and the priest, whom I questioned separately, explained that blessed things must not come into contact with 'unclean' (*zikhin*, which they gloss as *profane*) things when they are disposed of. The only means of ensuring that this does not happen is to burn them. In his discussion of *les rameaux bénits*, van Gennep (1947: 1200) records the same rule—that they must never be thrown away but burned—was widespread in rural France.

Unlike the other blessed things, blessed ash and blessed fire serve a purely symbolic function and disintegrate within a few hours of their distribution by the priest. Blessed ash is given on Ash Wednesday, the first day of Lent. Before the Mass the priest burns a bundle of blessed laurel, the ashes of which are then placed on the foreheads of his parishioners in the sign of the cross. The only interesting feature of its ritual distribution is that the *etxekandere* gives blessed ash to her second and third 'first neighbours' if they are unable to attend Mass on Ash Wednesday. The women classify this as 'a service of love' (*amodio zerbutxia*). It is not regarded as an absolute obligation (*eginbidea*), as was the ritual giving of blessed bread to the first 'first neighbour', nor is it a free (*dohañik*) service, such as providing food for the priest and schoolmasters during the pig-killing season.

At present two types of candle are blessed by the priest on Candlemas, the second of February: the *ezko* and *tortxa*. The former and traditional one is a thin coil of beeswax which, interestingly enough, the people describe as 'turning to the right' (*eskuñilat üngürü*). The *ezko* is found in both the Spanish and French Basque country. At the beginning of this century when several households kept bees, their *etxekanderak* made these candles and sold them at the church door on Candlemas. The people now buy their *ezkoa* in a Tardets shop.

The *tortxa* was introduced in the community about forty years ago. It is roughly one metre in length. Every household keeps at least four *tortxak*, which burn more rapidly than the coiled candle. One *ezko* will generally last a year or more. Both types of candle are taken to the church at Candlemas by the *etxekandere*.

Neither type of blessed candle is thought to have more *indarra* than the other; but they are now used for different purposes. The blessed *ezko* is burned by the *etxekandere* during severe rain, wind, and thunder storms, which it has the power to calm. It is also used to cure impetigo (*xingola*) and eczema. A piece is lit and rotated (*üngüratü*) by the *etxekandere* first clockwise (*eskuñilat*, to the right) nine times and then counter-clockwise (*arra-üngüratü*, 'rotated backwards') nine times over the rash as she counts from one to nine and then from nine to one.

The blessed *ezko* is regarded as a panacea, and many of the old people carry a small piece in their pocket. Nearly all the shepherds keep both blessed *ezko* and blessed laurel among their belongings or beneath their pillow in the mountain hut. Although the custom is now dying out, the blessed *ezko* is also used to bless the cattle and sheep on St Blaise. The *nausi* of the house lights the candle and singes the sign of the cross on the rump of a few of his ewes and on the crown of his cattle's heads. This is one of only two rituals involving blessed things that are performed by the *nausi*.

The blessed *tortxa* is used exclusively in mortuary rituals. At death two are placed on the bedside table of the deceased and burn continually 'to light the soul's path to God' until the funeral. The three female 'first neighbours' of the deceased are each obliged to give one blessed *tortxa* to the house, which are burned for the duration of their vigil beside the corpse. (A household also received a blessed *tortxa* from its female second 'first neighbour' when she gave her ritual gift of blessed bread.) Any blessed candles not entirely consumed before the funeral are taken to the church by either the *etxekandere* or her female first 'first neighbour'. Ideally this task should be performed by the latter woman. The candles are then burned by the priest on behalf of the soul of the deceased.

In Sainte-Engrâce, as in other Basque and many rural French communities, laurel is blessed by the priest on Palm Sunday. On the preceding Saturday the *etxekandere* cuts a bundle of laurel boughs and takes them to the church on the following morning. Before the Mass the married women extend their boughs toward the altar to receive the blessing of the priest, who asperges them with blessed water. After the Mass the newly blessed laurel is taken to the house and is divided into small bunches. The *etxekandere* collects all of the old sprigs, blessed the previous Palm Sunday, and burns them in the hearth. The new sprigs are then fastened to the crucifixes of the kitchen and bedrooms. The remaining boughs are stored upside-down in a closet or in the granary. These may be burned during the course of the year by the *etxekandere* to calm storms and in times of crisis within the house. If a member of the house dies, a sprig is used first by the priest and then by the mourners to sprinkle holy water on the corpse.

Blessed laurel is also used to make crosses (*Dona Kürützeak*) on the first day of St Cross, the third of May. These are made with freshly cut branches of hazel roughly twenty-five centimetres long and eight centimetres wide. A sprig of blessed laurel is placed vertically across the centre and secured with twine. A *Dona Kürützea* is planted in every field and pasture owned by the household. In principle the *nausi* should make these crosses. In 1977 only about half the men observed this custom. By virtue of its *indarra* the blessed laurel on the crosses protects the fields and pastures from natural disaster.

In the 'old religion' four things were blessed by the priest on Holy Saturday: water, fire, the Easter candle in the church, and bread. The *indarra* of blessed water, like that of blessed laurel, lasts only one year. After it has been blessed, the *hur benedikatia* is distributed among the *etxekanderak*, who throw the old blessed water into the garden on Easter morning. The new water is drunk before Mass on Easter to purify the body and is then sprinkled in every room.

Nearly every house has a stoup half-way down the stairs between the ground and first floors; and I am told that formerly the members of the household were careful to bless themselves with the water whenever they descended.

Before the sheep are taken up to the mountains, they are sprinkled with blessed water by the *etxekandere*; and before they begin their descent to the valley in September, the flocks are sprinkled a second time by the shepherd who made the last cheese of the season. The cheese-making shepherd is called *etxekandere*.

Until 1977 blessed fire was distributed by the priest on Holy Saturday in the traditional manner. Formerly he built a small fire on the steps of the church with sticks of wood and blessed laurel. After the benediction of the fire, the *etxekanderak* were given an ember which they carried to their houses and burned in the hearth. The fire and heat of the *sü benedikatia* are said to be 'like the love that God has for us'.

In 1977 the priest distributed long white candles among both sexes rather than the embers. An infant of a lower couple now living in Paris was baptized before the Mass that evening, and the priest explained that he had decided not to perform the traditional ritual of blessed fire 'because it would have made the whole ceremony too long'. One of his acolytes then gave candles to the men and women, who nervously asked one another what he expected them to do next. After a few moments of confusion, we filed to the front of the chancel where the priest lit our candles with his own. Although the women assumed that the candles, like the embers, should be taken back to the house, we were asked to return them to the acolyte after the Mass.

The custom of distributing the blessed bread of Easter (*Bazkoko ogi benedikatia*) on Holy Saturday became obsolete in 1962, when the priest abolished the weekly ritual giving of blessed bread by the *etxe-kanderak* of the commune. In Sainte-Engrâce, as in some parts of rural France (van Gennep 1947: 1254), the blessed bread of Easter is thought to be more powerful than that which was given on other Sundays. It has a special power lacking in ordinary blessed bread— it has the *indarra* to find and to resurrect the body of the drowned.

So far as I know, Soule is the only Basque province where Easter blessed bread is thought to have this unique power. Azkue (1935: 251) reports that in Barcus 'when one discovers that someone has drowned in a river, the blessed bread of Easter is thrown into the water where the person drowned' and 'that [the bread] makes one turn when it finds the corpse'. The Sainte-Engrâce people also claim that the bread 'makes one rotation' (*üngür bat egiten*) when it finds the body; but they add the interesting detail that it turns 'to the right', i.e. in a clockwise direction. When asked why the blessed bread of Easter has this special *indarra*, those who cared to consider the question gave an ecclesiastical exegesis: the *Bazkoko ogi benedikatia* can find and resurrect the body of the drowned because Jesus Christ was resurrected from the dead on the day that it is blessed by the priest. In the 'old religion' a piece of the bread was burned in the hearth on Easter morning by the *etxekandere* as a 'sacrifice'.

Unlike the other efficacious blessed things, the Easter and ordinary blessed bread never lose their *indarra* and therefore may be kept indefinitely. If the *etxekandere* wishes to dispose of it, she burns it in the hearth. Several of the old women have kept as many as thirty or forty pieces of both types of blessed bread; and two of them gave me a few of their precious pieces, one of which is the 'black bread' (*ogi beltza*) that was rationed during the Second World War. Although these pieces are now extremely hard, they have not mildewed. As their owners explained, blessed bread will never do so because of its *indarra* from God. The notion that blessed bread will not mildew is held in some Spanish and other French Basque communities (Azkue 1935: 250–3); it is also widely used as a cure for madness in animals, but not in Sainte-Engrâce.

The bread that was blessed on Holy Saturday and every Sunday was always bought from a lowland baker by the *etxekandere* whose turn it was to give it. Neither the bread of maize nor the bread of wheat formerly made by the women was used. The bread had to be leavened and made from wheat flour. The prescription that only bread of wheat could be blessed is consistent with the notion that the gift of *ogi benedikatia* was itself life-giving. Wheat is the grain of life; and blessed bread is the bread of life.

Until the main road was completed in 1932, orders for bread were placed with one of the local women who transported it by mule from the lowlands to the commune. The bread-giving *etxekandere* of the week was required to purchase two two-kilo loaves, the amount needed to give a small portion to everyone at Mass and to her first 'first neighbour'.

PART THREE

VII. BLESSED BREAD: A SYSTEM OF ASYMMETRIC EXCHANGE

I

THE ritual giving of blessed bread (*ogi benedikatia*) was one aspect of the institutionalized relationship between 'first neighbours', and it is for this reason that the practice was of special importance in Sainte-Engrâce society. The transmission of the gift from female *aizoa* to female *aizoa* was one ritual expression of reciprocity between their households which reaffirmed the bonds of co-operation and friendship between them; and, as I shall explain, it constituted a system of unilateral exchange defined by asymmetry.

Until 1962, when the present priest abolished the practice, the blessed bread ritual was performed every Sunday and consisted of two parts. The first part took place in the church or chapel, between which the High Mass alternated weekly. The second was performed in the houses of the bread-giving *etxekandere* and her first 'first neighbour'.

In Sainte-Engrâce, the bread-giving woman was called *elizako etxekandere*, literally 'the *etxekandere* of the church'. Although a few people claim that the bread-taker was referred to as the *neskato*, 'female servant', of the *elizako etxekandere*, the term was clearly not widely employed or regarded as an acceptable means of classification. In any other circumstances, certainly, it is an insult to refer to a woman as the *neskato* of another; the term implies that the social status of the former is inferior to that of the latter. Within the context of the blessed bread ritual, no distinction in relative status was made between givers and takers. All the *etxekanderak* of the commune who gave and received the gift of blessed bread were considered to be 'equal-equal' (*bardin-bardina*) in status.

When it was the turn of a particular *etxekandere* to give bread, she had a threefold obligation to fulfil. She was obliged to sponsor the special Mass for the souls in Purgatory on the Friday preceding the Sunday she was due to give bread. In addition to her money donation she was expected to give the priest two blessed candles, which he burned on behalf of the souls. On Sunday morning before the High Mass the *elizako etxekandere* had 'a strict obligation' (*eginbidea*) to

103

provide the priest with two two-kilo loaves of leavened wheat bread, which were blessed by him and were consequently transformed into *ogi benedikatia*. The third and last strict obligation of the *elizako etxekandere* was to give a portion of the newly blessed bread to her female first 'first neighbour' before sunset on Sunday.

The Sainte-Engrâce people claim that they, unlike some other Souletine Basques, have never made any kind of bread offering—blessed or unblessed—for the souls of the dead. In their society, *ogi benedikatia* was the only bread that was ritually given by the *etxekanderak*; and, as they repeatedly stressed, the gift of blessed bread was not 'for the dead' (*hilentako*) but 'for the living' (*bizientako*). The only surviving former priest of the commune also emphasized this point during our discussions about the ritual.

The ritual giving of blessed bread 'for the living' and the special Mass 'for the dead' are seen as opposed and complementary parts of the *ogi benedikatia* ritual. By means of the former, the *etxekanderak* of the commune are said to have brought the Sainte-Engrâce people closer together (*hullañago alkharreki*) socially and spiritually; by means of the latter, they preserved and perpetuated the bond between the living and the dead of their community. The word *alkharreki*, 'together', is derived from *alkharr*, 'mutual'. In Souletine, the verb *alkharrtu* means 'to unite, to act in concert with someone'.

In Sainte-Engrâce, the threefold obligation of the *elizako etxekandere* was transmitted serially in a clockwise direction around the commune. Only two female 'first neighbours' acted as bread-giver and bread-taker on any one Sunday; and no house had more than one giver and taker. The bread-giver of a household was its second 'first neighbour' (*bigerren aizoa*), conceptually the first household to the left of one's own; its bread-taker was the first 'first neighbour' (*lehen lehen aizoa*), the household to the right of one's own house. (See Figure 4.) If new houses were built or existing houses abandoned, 'first neighbour' and consequently bread-giver/bread-taker relationships were altered accordingly; but the direction of giving remained the same. The system was irreversible and characterized by an asymmetric ordering of givers and takers. The transmission of blessed bread from 'first neighbour' to 'first neighbour' can be formally represented as follows:

$$a \rightarrow b \rightarrow c \rightarrow a$$

I found that people who are now at least thirty years old have a very clear understanding of the principles on which this system of exchange was based: *aldikatzia* (which is best translated in this con-

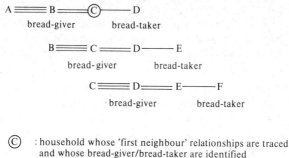

Fig. 4. Transmission of blessed bread from 'first neighbour' to 'first neighbour'

text as 'serial replacement') and *üngürü* (rotation). The transmission of blessed bread 'from first neighbour to first neighbour' (*aizotik aizolat*) is conceived as having formed an unbroken chain (*xena*) of givers and takers around the commune. At a community-wide level, the chain made a circle, or *üngürü*, which passed through the *quartiers* on one side of the valley and then through those on the opposite side in a clockwise direction. The *etxekanderak* of the upper and lower communities took turns (*aldikatü*) giving their ritual prestations, i.e. they replaced one another serially as bread-givers. The gift of bread was received 'from the left' (*eskerretik*), conceptually and generally in practice as well; and it was given 'to the right' (*eskuñilat*).

No one knows where the cycle began originally. Some people suggested that the first household ever to give blessed bread to the right was Salaber, the first house to the right of the church whose heads have always been the sacristans; others suggested that the first household was Üngürütürü, the house where 'the circle of mountains', in which the Santaztarrak live, is thought to begin.

The people are certain that the chain of givers and takers crossed the river at only two points, where giver/taker households were located on opposite sides of the river: once at the far north-western end of the commune, where the *etxekandere* of the last lower household on the east-facing side of the valley gave to the *etxekandere* of the northernmost lower house on the west-facing side; and a second time at the mouth of Khakueta, when the *etxekandere* of the northernmost upper house at the south-western end of the commune gave to the *etxekandere* of the first lower house in the east-facing *quartier* of Athoro. (Turns to thresh wheat in *ogi joitea* also crossed the river at only these two points.) When the obligation passed from north to south-east on the west-facing side of the valley, the gift was conceived as having moved 'up' (*gora*); and when the obligation passed from south-west to north on the east-facing side, the gift moved 'down' (*behera*).

The people also have a clear notion of the time it took for the gift of blessed bread 'to make one rotation' (*üngür bat egiten*) in a clock-wise direction around the commune. (This is seen as if the individual were looking outwards from the centre of the cycle.) With ninety-nine households it took the same number of Sundays for every *etxekandere* to give and to receive blessed bread once, i.e. it took roughly two years for the cycle of exchange to be completed.

Within their own neighbourhood or *quartier*, where 'first neigh-bour' relationships are known, people were able to tell me the household from which their neighbours received blessed bread and the one to which they gave it. A few of the old Calla and Senta women could recite the order of givers and takers for the entire upper community; but they were generally able to trace the chain only as far as the last upper household at the south-western end of the commune which gave to the first house in Athoro, the adjacent lower *quartier*. Most of the upper women who took part in the ritual were uncertain about the exact order of givers and takers from that point in the cycle until the obligation to give blessed bread reached the last lower household on the northern side of the valley whose *etxekandere* gave to an upper household; but in their attempts to sort out giver and taker relationships, they consistently relied upon the two rules that blessed bread moved from left to right and from 'first neighbour to first neighbour'. My own inquiries in both halves of the commune revealed that in every case the gift of blessed bread was given to the first 'first neighbour' and that, at a community-wide level, it was given in a clockwise direction from one settlement or *quartier* to another.

Although those who are now in their twenties can recall having seen the *ogi benedikatia* ritual performed in the church or chapel and in their own neighbourhood, few of them have a clear notion of the principles on which the transmission of blessed bread was based; nor do they seem to be aware of the cyclical nature of the system.

When the obligation to give blessed bread reached a household in the two-year cycle, the *etxekandere* paid the priest to offer one High Mass for the souls in Purgatory on Friday. (At present one High Mass costs 20 francs.) This Mass was generally attended by the elder *etxekanderak* of the community and their grandchildren.

Since the High Mass after which blessed bread was distributed was held alternately in the upper church and lower chapel, every second *etxekandere* of an upper household gave bread in the chapel; and likewise every second *etxekandere* of a lower household was obliged to give hers in the church. These women were often required to walk as many as five or six kilometres in order to make their ritual prestation of bread to the priest and congregation.

On Sunday morning before the High Mass began, the bread-giving *etxekandere* carried her two leavened loaves to the church or chapel in the special basket and cloth of her house. The bread was received and blessed by the priest on the altar. The newly blessed bread was then cut into small cubes by the male sacristan, who transferred the pieces from the woman's basket to that of the church.

At this point in the ritual the bread-giving woman made the first two of her four blessed bread prestations. She gave the first piece of *ogi benedikatia* to the priest and the second one to the sacristan. The gifts were classified as *emaitzak*, the generic term for 'gifts' given in the church, and were eaten before the Mass began.

Three criteria had to be met in order for a layman to receive blessed bread in the church. In principle the person had to be a confirmed member of the Church, to have kept a twelve-hour fast before the High Mass, and to have received Holy Communion that morning. By means of the fast and of ingesting the Host, the body of the recipient was purified (*purifikatu*) and therefore prepared to receive the gift from God that was imbued with his supernatural *indarra*—the gift of *ogi benedikatia*.

In Sainte-Engrâce a clear distinction is made between blessed bread and the Host (*ostia*). The former was not thought to be the body of Christ and it was never given during Holy Communion. Both kinds of bread were treated with great care and respect; but they were received by the congregation in a different manner. In 'the old religion', the Host was always received directly on the tongue of the communicant, whose teeth and hands were not permitted to touch it. Formerly it would have been unthinkable to take the Host in cupped hands, as is now done by many of the women. Several people claim that they are afraid to eat the Host 'because it is the body of Jesus Christ'.

Blessed bread was never received on the tongue; it was taken directly from the church basket with the right hand. Immediately after the High Mass the male sacristan carried the basket of blessed bread to the rear of the nave where he offered a piece to every man who had taken Communion that morning. The men in the balcony were served first from the back to the front row of benches. Recipients crossed themselves before taking a morsel with the right hand and ate the bread immediately. In some other Basque communities (see section III below) a special prayer was recited by the recipient when he took blessed bread, but the Sainte-Engrâce people claim that they have never observed this custom.

Having served all of the men in the balcony and on the church floor, the sacristan proceeded to the last row of 'the church chairs' occupied by the *etxekanderak* where he offered the bread from left to right (facing the altar). The next row was served from right to left and so on until he reached the front of the women's section. The women received the bread in the same manner as the men; but they alone were permitted to take an extra piece for any member of their household unable to attend Mass owing to illness or old age. In these circumstances the rule that the Host should be taken before blessed bread was waived.

The unmarried girls and children who had taken Communion were served last by the sacristan, who transferred the remaining portions of blessed bread to the giver's basket. Her gifts of *ogi benedikatia* to the congregation were also classified as *emaitzak*.

After the Mass the bread-giving *etxekandere* carried her blessed bread back to her house. Before the noon meal she burned one piece in the hearth as an offering to God and then gave one piece to every member of her household, whether or not they were confirmed members of the Church or had received the Host that morning. Having taken a morsel for herself she ate the bread with her *etxenkuak*. The remaining pieces of bread, protected by the special cloth and basket, were placed on the sideboard 'so that the dog would not eat them', and the crumbs were brushed carefully into the fire.

After the noon meal and before sunset, the *etxekandere* was obliged to make her fourth and most important prestation of blessed bread. On this occasion she gave to the *etxekandere* of her first 'first neighbour' (*lehen lehen aizoa*). In most cases the bread-giving woman was not accompanied by the members of her household when she went to the house of her bread-taker.

A household could not be expelled from the cycle or passed over for any reason. If a household lacked an *etxekandere*, the *nausi* acted as bread-giver. He too was classified as 'the *etxekandere* of the church' and made his ritual prestation in the same manner as a woman. The *nausi* could also act as bread-taker in the absence of an *etxekandere*.

An individual was not required to have been born in Sainte-

Engrâce or even to be a Basque in order to give and to receive blessed bread. In the upper community one house is owned by a bachelor who works as a *patissier* in Pau during the week and spends week-ends in Sainte-Engrâce. He is French and does not speak Basque. Before the ritual became obsolete, he took his turn to receive and to give blessed bread once every two years.

As soon as the bread-giving *etxekandere* crossed the threshold of her neighbour's house, she handed her basket of blessed bread to her female first 'first neighbour' and identified her gift as *gure azia*, which means 'our animal semen', 'our seed'. The possessive pronoun *gure* referred not to the *etxenkuak* of the bread-giver's house but to all of the *etxekanderak* of the commune who gave blessed bread during the two-year cycle of exchange. Only the gift of blessed bread to the female *lehen lehen aizoa* was classified as *gure azia*; and Sainte-Engrâce is the only community I have found where this form of classification was employed.

The women did not recite any prescribed prayer when they gave and received *ogi benedikatia*; but it was customary for the bread-giver to wish her neighbour good health and prosperity. The bread-giving woman was offered food and drink while they exchanged gossip and discussed local events. She was obliged to return to her own house before sunset, but none of the women could tell me why this was so. As soon as she had left, her bread-taker and the members of her household ate the blessed bread and burned the crumbs in the hearth.

Within the context of the blessed bread ritual, the word *azia* is understood in the figurative sense of 'female semen', though vegetable seed and animal semen are literal translations of the term. In all three of its senses, *azia* is conceptually opposed to *brallakia*, male and exclusively human semen. The women explained to me that they did not classify their gift of blessed bread as *gure brallakia* because 'only men have *brallakia*'; but they emphasized that their *azia*, like the *brallakia* of men, was a life-giving substance. By giving their *azia* in the form of blessed bread the *etxekanderak* of the commune are said to have given 'life' (*bizi*) to one another and to their respective households. In Sainte-Engrâce, *bizi* is a quality which all living humans, animals, and plants are thought to possess; it is also found in human semen, animal semen, and in cheeses that have been matured properly.

The Sainte-Engrâce women see nothing peculiar about their having classified this gift as 'our semen'. This became especially clear to me when I took one of them to visit her relatives in the nearby community of Larrau, where I wanted to ask about blessed bread. When the Larrau women present had finished telling us how they gave *ogi benedikatia*, they asked their Sainte-Engrâce cousin how blessed bread 'went' (*juan*), i.e. how it was transmitted, in her community. The woman obligingly gave them a detailed account and added that their gift to the first 'first neighbour' was called *gure azia*, whereupon the Larrau women burst out laughing and promptly called the men of the house into the kitchen to share the joke with them. 'So the Sainte-Engrâce women give animal semen to one another!' the *nausi* exclaimed with a grin. 'Everyone has always said that they are odd people.' The woman finally responded to their boisterous teasing with laughter and confessed that she had never before thought that *gure azia* was either an amusing or peculiar name to give to blessed bread.

When asked about the meaning of the ritual, the Sainte-Engrâce women gave a variety of explanations. They reasoned that the ritual giving of bread in the church served to bind them together socially and spiritually as a community. By giving bread *en roulement* the *etxekanderak* of the commune took a shared part in promoting the welfare of the Sainte-Engrâce people.

The ritual giving of *ogi benedikatia* to the female first 'first neighbour' was seen in a different light. Several women offered an ecclesiastical interpretation. They suggested that giving the bread to this neighbour was a re-enactment of the Last Supper in which the faithful gathered together to receive the bread given to them by God through Jesus Christ. Some of the old women felt certain that the disciples of Christ were 'first neighbours' and that the custom of giving blessed bread to one's neighbour originated during the lifetime of Christ. They reasoned that the disciples must have met in one another's houses to break bread with their Saviour 'because they didn't have churches in those days'.

One old woman suggested that blessed bread was given to the first 'first neighbour' so that the two households would be bound together by 'friendship' (*adiskidantza*). But the most common 'explanation' was a tautological one: 'We gave blessed bread to the first "first neighbour" in order to remember (*orhitzeko*) that "our semen" went from *aizoa* to *aizoa* and from the left to the right.'

II

I have made inquiries about the ritual giving of blessed bread in seven other Souletine communities: Pagolle, Lacarry, Camou-Cihigue, Larrau, Ossas, Haux, and Alçabéhéty. A comparative

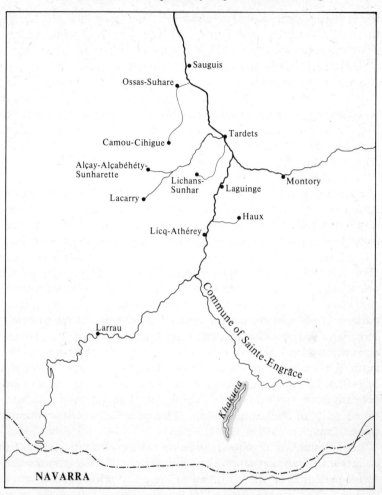

Map 3. Some Souletine villages mentioned in the text

examination of the forms that the ritual took reveals three characteristic features: first, only leavened bread of wheat was used; second,
a gift of bread was given every Sunday by an *etxekandere* of the
village, blessed by the priest, and distributed among the congregation
after the High Mass; third, the *etxekanderak* of the village replaced
one another serially (*aldikatü*) as bread-givers.

In Pagolle the obligation to give bread to the church was transmitted serially from 'first neighbour' to 'first neighbour' in a clockwise direction; but gifts of bread were not given to the priest, or to

the sacristan, or to the 'first neighbour'. The congregation received the bread from the priest after the Mass. The practice became obsolete there in about 1966, when their priest abolished it.

The *etxekanderak* of Lacarry also took turns giving bread to the church to be blessed by the priest. The obligation was transmitted serially to the right of one's own house; but the bread was not given to a neighbour. It was distributed among the congregation after the Mass and eaten in church. The weekly giving of blessed bread there ended in approximately 1946; but it was distributed on All Souls, Palm Sunday, Easter, and Pentecost until the 1950s.

Camou and Cihigue are two separate hamlets which lie less than one kilometre apart. They share the same priest but have separate churches. Interestingly enough, the *ogi benedikatia* ritual took different forms in the two communities. In Camou, which has only eight houses, the obligation to give bread is said to have been transmitted serially 'from first neighbour to first neighbour' and from left to right around the village. However, the Camou people orient themselves to the centre of their village, so that when informants listed the order of givers and takers it emerged that the general pattern of obligations to give bread followed a counter-clockwise direction. But the Camou people declined to accept this pattern, even when it was drawn out for them. They, like the Santaztarrak, argue that no ritual goods or services move in a counter-clockwise direction. In Camou, every *etxekandere* had at least six turns to give bread during the year. As in Pagolle and Lacarry they gave their bread only to the congregation. The practice was discontinued there in roughly 1967.

In Cihigue the obligation to give bread was transmitted serially in a clockwise direction around the village, but the Cihigue *etxekanderak* gave gifts of blessed bread to the priest and the sacristan, as well as to the congregation. The weekly distribution of the bread ended during the Second World War, just when they might have 'needed' the combinative effects of the ritual; but the Camou-Cihigue priest still blesses and distributes *ogi benedikatia* to the Cihigue people on Holy Saturday.

The blessed bread ritual in Larrau differed from the other forms cited in one respect: only the *etxekanderak* of houses in the rural *quartiers* of Larrau took turns giving bread to the priest, who blessed and distributed it after Mass. The *etxekanderak* of houses in the village nucleus did not act as bread-givers; but none of the Larrau women with whom I discussed the practice knew why this was so. In Larrau the obligation to give bread was transmitted serially 'from first neighbour to first neighbour' and from right to left (*eskuñitik eskerrilat*) in a counter-clockwise direction around the commune.

Unlike the Sainte-Engrâce women, the Larrau women who gave bread were not obliged to sponsor a Mass for the souls in Purgatory, to give blessed candles, or to give prestations of blessed bread to the sacristan or to a 'first neighbour'. In their community *ogi benedikatia* was given only to the priest and to the congregation. The piece given to the priest was called *buxia*, 'a small morsel', or simply *aphezaren partea*, 'the priest's portion'.

So far I have found three Souletine villages other than Sainte-Engrâce where blessed bread was ritually given by the *etxekandere* to her female first 'first neighbour': Ossas, Haux, and Alçabéhéty. In all three villages the obligation to give bread was transmitted serially from 'first neighbour' to 'first neighbour' in a clockwise direction; and, as in Sainte-Engrâce, the ritual giving of blessed bread constituted a unilateral system of exchange defined by asymmetry. In all three villages, the *etxekanderak* are said to have replaced one another serially (*aldikatü*) as bread-givers. The ritual was performed every Sunday after the Mass and became obsolete in these communities during the Second World War. In none of the villages was the gift of bread for the first 'first neighbour' classified as 'our semen'.

My own investigations have also provided evidence to suggest that these Souletine communities and Sainte-Engrâce were not the only places where gifts of blessed bread were asymmetrically exchanged by neighbours. The mother-in-law of a Souletine Basque scholar, who spends his holidays in Sainte-Engrâce, has told me that *pain bénit* was formerly given every Sunday in her natal village of Lignerolles in Normandy.[1]

The form which the ritual took there is nearly identical to that of the *ogi benedikatia* ritual in Sainte-Engrâce with one major and intriguing difference: the Lignerolles people took leavened blessed bread as the Host rather than after Holy Communion.

The obligation to give bread to the priest, the congregation, and to the *voisin* to the right of one's own house was transmitted serially in a clockwise direction around the village. (Lignerolles houses do not have 'first neighbours'.) Every household had only one bread-giver and one taker; and the female heads of household took turns

[1] I am grateful to Mme Lea Olivier for having provided me with an account of the blessed bread ritual in Lignerolles. Mme Olivier also reported that *pain bénit* is still distributed by the priest in Bivilliers, a village near Lignerolles, on the festival day of the community.

giving bread *en roulement*. After the Mass the bread-giving woman gave a portion of the *pain bénit* to her *voisin*, who 'made a *fête* by giving pieces of the bread to those who visited her house that afternoon'. The gift of bread for the *voisin* was called *le chanteau*, which in its most specific sense denotes 'the piece of bread that one sent to the person who was obliged to give blessed bread the following Sunday' (Littré 1963: 197). In Lignerolles, the bread-giver was not obliged to sponsor a Mass for the souls in Purgatory.

III

The earliest references to blessed bread with which I am acquainted are a series of seventeenth-century legal and ecclesiastical tracts concerning the right of *agotes*, a pariah group of the western Pyrénées, to receive the Host and blessed bread and the manner in which they should do so (Idoate 1973: 206–9, 228–9, 262–3).[2] According to popular tradition, the *agotes* (*les cagots*) were a race of cretins and lepers who lived along the present boundary between the French and Spanish Basque provinces and in some parts of Béarn. Fear of contamination reportedly led their fellow parishioners to oppose taking the Host and the *pan bendito* at the same time as the *agotes* (Fay 1910: 202).

I have found only a few references to blessed bread in the literature about Spanish Basques (Azkue 1935; Castillo de Lucas 1966; Donostia 1961; de Goñi 1975; Idoate 1973). Azkue (1935: 250–4) provides us with the most detailed and only comparative summary of the various attributes and powers ascribed to blessed bread. In Navarra and Guipúzcoa it is said that bread blessed on St Blaise does not mildew. In some Navarrese villages only bread blessed on the day after Candlemas will not mildew. In the Vizcayan villages of Arratia and Murélaga blessed bread was considered to be 'good for those bitten by rabid dogs'. In Anzuola (Vizcaya) 'bread is blessed on St Agatha, and a piece of it is put on the pot hook so that the house will not burn'.[3]

In the Guipúzcoan village of Zerain, blessed bread was formerly

[2] I am grateful to Jon Bilbao of the Basque Studies Program at the University of Nevada (Reno) for having found this reference for me.

[3] In many parts of the Spanish Basque country a bread called *ogisalutadore*, 'healing bread', is made on Christmas Eve. This bread is often ascribed many of the powers that *ogi benedikatia* has among French Basques: it will not mildew, and it is used to cure rabies (Barandiarán 1922: 135; Ispitzua 1922: 73–4). In the coastal town of Leikeito (Vizcaya) *ogisalutadore* is thrown into the sea to calm the waters. In Zeanuri and Elorio it is thrown into the air outside the house to calm a storm (Barandiarán 1922: 135). In these reports it is unclear whether *ogisalutadore* was ever blessed by the priest.

'given in the church and cut into pieces. After the Holy Communion an acolyte passed it on a tray first among the men, who took a piece and ate it immediately. The tray was then placed on the support of the holy water font. When the women left the church they took a piece of the bread and recited the following words: "Blessed bread, engendered in the earth, blessed on the altar, if I should die this week, my soul will be saved," *Ogie bedeinkatue, lurren endradue, aldaren bedeinkatue, ni aste ontan iltzen banitz, izan deilla nere arima salbatue*' (de Goñi 1975: 344).

Azkue (1935: 252) reports that the following prayer was recited by the people of Larraun (Navarra) before they received blessed bread in the church: 'This is the blessed bread through which the sins that I will commit all week may be forgiven.'

According to van Gennep (1947: 1254), the distribution of blessed bread every Sunday was once widespread in France; but he does not tell us who gave the bread to the church or whether the *pain bénit* was ever given to a neighbour. His accounts are almost exclusively concerned with the giving of blessed bread on Holy Thursday, Holy Saturday, and Easter.

In the Ardennes, Marne, and Meuse, the local schoolmaster made *les pains à chanter* which were blessed by the priest and distributed to all the households in the village on Holy Saturday by either the schoolmaster or his pupils. In Franche-Comté these *hosties non consacrées* were called *pains bénits* (van Gennep 1947: 1255–6). In return for his gift of blessed bread the schoolmaster generally received eggs and ham from the households he visited.

The ritual distribution of blessed bread during Holy Week took a different form in the Hautes-Alpes. Van Gennep (1946: 223–4) cites several villages in which the Last Supper was formerly re-enacted in the church on Holy Thursday. Twelve children were selected by the priest to play the part of the twelve apostles. Having washed the feet of the twelve, the priest distributed blessed bread among them.

Unlike the *ogi benedikatia* given in Sainte-Engrâce, which was exclusively 'for the living', blessed bread served as a gift for the dead in some parts of rural France. It was distributed the day after a funeral in many parishes of the Hautes-Pyrénées; the Sunday after a funeral in some villages of the Hautes-Alpes and Gers; but most frequently it was distributed after the anniversary Mass on behalf of the soul of the deceased. In the Loir-et-Cher, l'Indre, l'Indre-et-Loire, Sarthe, in Noalhat (Puy-de-Dôme), and in Massat (Ariège), the *pain bénit* was distributed the day of the burial by the mother, sister, or closest female relative of the deceased (van Gennep 1946: 753–4). The author does not make clear who received the blessed bread on these occasions.

The ritual distribution of blessed bread was not confined to Catholic France. Hertz (1928: 142) reports that *pain bénit* was formerly given to the pilgrims of five parishes in the Italian Alps who made an annual pilgrimage to the shrine of St Besse, patron saint of the region.

These sources show that the ritual giving of blessed bread took a variety of forms in many different rural European societies; but they do not provide the facts required to determine whether blessed bread was part of any system of exchange in the communities studied. This is a matter that can only be resolved by further field-work. Having found five cases—Sainte-Engrâce, Ossas, Haux, Alçabéhéty, and Lignerolles—in which there was a consistently asymmetric ordering of bread-givers and bread-takers in a closed cycle of exchange, one is led to ask whether any goods or services were similarly exchanged in the opposite direction. In Sainte-Engrâce, at least, there were two interlocking systems of unilateral exchange which moved in opposite directions.

VIII. 'FIRST NEIGHBOUR' MORTUARY OBLIGATIONS

THE aims of this chapter are two: first, to show that the asymmetry which ordered the transmission of blessed bread from 'first neighbour' to 'first neighbour' also defines the transmission of first 'first neighbour' (*lehen lehen aizoa*) mortuary obligations in Sainte-Engrâce; and second, to show that the transfer of these ritual prestations constituted two complementary cycles of unilateral exchange in which contrasted goods and services moved in opposite directions.

I

Death is not a single, private event but a process in which the survivors separate themselves from the deceased, assist his soul in its journey to Purgatory, and restore order within their own small social world. In Sainte-Engrâce society four households are directly involved in this process: the household of the deceased and its three *aizoak*—the first 'first neighbour' to the right of the bereaved household and the second and third 'first neighbours' (the *bigerren aizo* and *hirugerren aizo* respectively) to the left. Of the three the first 'first neighbour' is regarded as the most important *lagün*, companion and assistant, of both the deceased and the members of his household.[1] This is the 'first neighbour' to whom the bereaved household formerly gave blessed bread once every two years.

Death does not sever the relationship between the *etxenkuak* and deceased, for he continues to be a member of their house, but it changes the nature of their ties. In his lifetime an individual is socially, jurally, and economically bound to his *etxenkuak*. Physical death abruptly severs these ties but these are immediately replaced by an exclusively spiritual bond that will be preserved and perpetuated by the *etxekandere*. In a similar manner death alters but does not immediately destroy the relationship between an individual and

---

[1] The prominent role of the 'first' or 'nearest neighbour' (*lehen auzoa, auzurrikourrena*) during the process of death seems to be a characteristic feature of rural Basque society. Barandiarán (1947, 1949), Caro Baroja (1971), Douglass (1975), Echegaray (1932), Veyrin (1975), and Vinson (1882) are only a few of the sources in which 'first neighbour' mortuary services are discussed. But the most detailed account and only analytical treatment of mortuary obligations and funerary rituals are provided by Douglass (1969).

his three *aizoak*. The social, economic, and ritual ties that bound
them together in life are replaced by a spiritual relationship when
the individual dies; but this is terminated as soon as the *aizoak* fulfil
their mortuary obligations to the deceased and his *etxenkuak*.

The rites of separation, transition, and incorporation which follow
physical death confirm the altered relationship between the survivors
and deceased; they also serve to reaffirm the bonds of 'mutual assistance' (*alkharr lagüntza*) between the *etxenkuak* and the *aizoak* of the
deceased. At death, as in the routine matters described in Chapter V,
the relationship between a household and its three *aizoak* is defined
by dyadic reciprocity in the exchange of certain goods and services.
Within the context of death their mutual obligations to assist one
another are classified as *zorrak* (singular *zorr*), which has the meanings of debt, duty, and obligation. *Zorrak* is also used in the sense of
monetary debts, such as an unpaid dowry; in the sense of the mutual
obligations shared by the members of a household and by the
members of an *olha*; and, in the Communion Prayer, in the sense of
sins. The mortuary obligations (*zorrak*) of 'first neighbours' concern
the body and soul of the deceased and the members of his or her
household.

I I

In Sainte-Engrâce, the death of an individual is classified according
to the manner or circumstances in which death was experienced. The
generic term for death, *hil*, is applied to both humans and animals
when they are thought to have died 'quietly like a bird' and with a
modicum of suffering. If a person dies suddenly and is consequently
thought not to have suffered or experienced pain, he is said to have
had a 'cold death' (*hilhotz*). Although a cold death is considered to
be a 'good death' (*hil hun*), a clear conceptual distinction between
good and bad death is not made. The best possible death is a 'cold
death' that takes place in the person's house. The most horrible
ways of dying belong to the class of violent death, *heriotzea*.

There are two kinds of death by falling off a precipice. If the
death occurs in the mountains, it is classified as *larrütü*, which also
means 'to strip off the skin'. The term is applied to both humans and
animals. *Erortu*, 'to fall or tumble down', is employed when a person
or beast falls off a precipice in the valley. The term also means 'to
condescend, to conform to'.

Larrütü and *erortu* are forms of 'violent death'. A third kind of
death in this class is suicide, expressed by the idioms *bere büriaz*

beste egin, literally 'his other head had been done', and *bere büria eho,* 'he murdered his head'. In this context *büria* collectively denotes the head, personality, individuality of the person.

Larrütü is generally regarded as the worst possible way of dying. An individual may experience a 'cold death' by falling off a mountain precipice, but neither his body nor his soul has a *lagün,* a companion and assistant, when physical death occurs, i.e. he cannot receive the assistance of his 'first neighbours' immediately and when he needs it most.

At least six shepherds have died by *larrütü* during the past fifteen years.[2] As soon as a man is reported to be missing, at least one of his three male *aizoak* searches for him in the mountains. In the event of death, the *aizoa* is responsible for transporting the corpse back to the bereaved household. For the *etxenkuak* of the victim, *larrütü* is the most horrific form of death; for the body is inevitably dismembered and frequently decays before it is recovered.

Death by *larrütü* and *erortu* occasion all of the rituals ordinarily provided for a member of society and his *etxenkuak.* His 'first neighbours' look after his body, soul, and the members of his household. He receives a funeral Mass and is buried in his house tomb. Mass donations on behalf of his soul are given by his household, his *aizoak,* close relatives, and friends.

None of these ritual services is performed on behalf of an aborted foetus or unbaptized infant, both of which are classified as *haurr egoixtea,* literally an 'aborted child'. Neither is physically, socially, or spiritually eligible to be treated as a full member of society. Although the three *aizoak* of its household are not obliged to perform any ritual services for a *haurr egoixtea,* the female first 'first neighbour' (who was once the bread-taker of the house) formerly buried the infant in the garden of its natal household. This service was performed on behalf of the *etxenkuak* rather than for the infant.

The death of a baptized child who dies within three months of birth is treated differently. Because the infant acquired a soul by means of baptism, it is eligible to receive a funeral Mass and burial

---

[2] This figure represents only those cases that are remembered by the people. The parish records show that at least one death by *larrütü* occurred every few years during the first quarter of this century. From the point of view of an outside observer, the Sainte-Engrâce people have tended to die in extraordinary ways. I have recorded two cases of death by falling into a fire, two of death by lightning, and one by falling off a horse. During the past forty years there have been two deaths by drowning and two murders. The most unusual case is thought to have happened in the latter half of the nineteenth century: a man died by *larrütü* in the gorge of Ehüjarre when his sheep pressed him to the edge of the precipice as he distributed salt among them. All of these deaths are classified as *heriotzeak,* violent deaths.

in the house tomb, but under the age of three months it is neither physically nor socially eligible to receive the assistance of the *aizoak*. According to traditional mortuary practice, the child was placed in a coffin, opened to expose its head and shoulders. A piece of blessed candle was inserted between its folded hands by the godfather, who carried the coffin from the house to the church. The body and soul of the infant were exclusively in the care of its godparents, with whom its spiritual relationship had been established before death.

III

It is not the form of death, e.g. *larrütü*, experienced by the deceased but his physical, social, and spiritual status before death that renders him eligible or ineligible to receive a proper funeral, burial, and assistance from his 'first neighbours'. The ritual services which constitute 'first neighbour' mortuary obligations are provided by the *aizoak* only if the deceased was baptized and qualified as a physically and socially mature member of society.

The mortuary obligations of the three 'first neighbours' actually begin before physical death takes place. When an individual is judged by his *etxenkuak* and/or the Tardets doctor to be fatally ill, he is said to be *hil abantxü*, 'almost dead', and requires the assistance of both the priest and his 'first neighbours'.

During the past fifteen years or so, it has become customary for either the *nausi* or *etxekandere* of the first 'first neighbour' to call the priest for the administration of the Last Sacrament. Formerly this service was performed by the male heads of the *lehen lehen aizoa* and *bigerren aizoa* (first and second 'first neighbours'), i.e. the household 'to the right' and the first one 'to the left' of the dying person's house. The *etxekanderak* of these two houses were once his bread-taker and his bread-giver respectively.

The two men preceded the priest as they walked from the church to the house of the *hil abantxü*. In their right hand, the men carried a church bell, which they rang 'to tell the Good Lord that someone was suffering and needed His support'. In their left hand, they carried a church lantern 'to light the path for God'. The priest held the Host in its monstrance against his chest. Anyone who met the procession on the road was expected to kneel and to pray for the recovery of the 'one near death'. I am told that formerly the female sacristan tolled the bell of the upper church during the course of their journey. Those who heard the frenzied peals were expected to recite the angelus for the person whose liminal state between life and death was signalled by the bell.

At present, as in the past, the *etxekanderak* of the three 'first neighbours' are expected to take one blessed candle to their dying *aizoa*. The female first 'first neighbour' prepares his room for the arrival of the priest, lights the blessed candles, and places them on the bedside table along with the other religious articles: a funeral cloth of the house, the house crucifix, a dish of blessed water, and a sprig of blessed laurel. After the priest has administered Extreme Unction, the male and female 'first neighbours' gather to pray for their dying *aizoa* with the members of his household. Any pieces of their candles not consumed during the priest's visit become the property of the house. These may be burned later by the *etxekandere* during storms and at other times of crisis.

Neither 'the one near death' nor the deceased is 'without companions' to assist him, i.e. without 'first neighbours'. When death occurs it is automatically assumed by the bereaved household and their three 'first neighbours' that the latter will assist the soul and survivors without being asked to do so. It would be morally and socially reprehensible if the *aizoak* refused to fulfil their mortuary obligations; and it would be equally unthinkable if a household were to refuse the assistance of its 'first neighbours'.

I know of only one case, that of the bachelor judged to have a 'mixed head' cited in Chapter V, in which the mortuary services of the *aizoak* were neither offered nor sought. When his mother died in a lowland hospital, the bachelor was not assisted by his three 'first neighbours'. A vigil for the deceased was not held in his house; and the corpse was not brought back to the commune until the morning of the funeral, when it was taken directly to the church. The bachelor did not invite any of his 'first neighbours' to the meals following the funeral and Novena Mass; and they did not give any Mass donations on behalf of the soul.

Ordinarily the work of the *aizoak* begins at physical death. In principle the male first 'first neighbour' should notify the relatives of the deceased who live outside the commune. Those who are within a day's journey from the community are expected to attend the funeral. From the moment of death until the burial the three 'first neighbours' assume full responsibility for chores inside and outside the bereaved household. The three female *aizoak* do all of the domestic work; the male *aizoak* take turns tending the livestock and perform the other tasks normally allotted to the *nausi* of the house.

If the *etxenkuak* of the deceased are elderly, their 'first neighbours' may continue to assist them several weeks or even months after the funeral and burial. But in one recent case an elderly couple who had lost their unmarried son (and only child) were assisted by their close relatives rather than by their *aizoak* for six months following the funeral. Although the shifting of responsibility from the *aizoak* to close relatives is still regarded as unconventional behaviour, it may foreshadow the demise of the only surviving ritual tie between 'first neighbours', i.e. their mortuary obligations to each other.

As soon as death occurs, the female first 'first neighbour' opens all of the windows of the house so that the soul can escape. The wooden shutters are latched shut to show that the *etxenkuak* are in mourning. One of the male *aizoak* (ideally the male first 'first neighbour') paints a black band over the bright colour normally used to identify the sheep owned by the household as one other public expression of bereavement. (This practice is no longer observed by all of the households.)

Opinions vary as to the precise moment the soul leaves the body. Some people contended that the body and soul go together to meet God as soon as the corpse is buried. Others claimed that the soul leaves the body the moment death occurs.

Only one old woman ventured to elaborate upon her own notions about the fate of the soul. In her view the soul enters the body through a tiny hole on the crown of the head when an infant is baptized. This hole is invisible to human eyes. The old woman confided that before she married she was deeply worried that her soul would be split in two when she and her husband exchanged vows; and although the priest assured her that this would not happen, she is not at all certain that her soul has remained intact. She expects that her soul—or what remains of it—will escape through the hole on her head as soon as her body dies.

The soul receives assistance from the living in three ways: by means of prayer, Masses, and blessed candles. These last are provided by the *etxenkuak* and the three 'first neighbours' of the deceased. One of the first mortuary obligations of the three female *aizoak* is to give one blessed candle to the *etxekandere* of the bereaved household. These gifts are placed in the room of the deceased where they burn continuously during the two-day and two-night vigil. In principle no other form of light should be used in the house until the funeral; for only the light provided by the blessed candles has the *indarra* or power to illuminate the soul's path to God. It is the responsibility of the female first 'first neighbour' to ensure that the candles are not extinguished until the corpse leaves the house.

The *etxenkuak* of the deceased provide four blessed candles, two of which are placed on the bedside table with the house crucifix, an icon of the Virgin, two bouquets of flowers, blessed water, and a sprig of blessed laurel. The table is covered with one of the special funeral cloths owned by the house. All of these articles are laid out by the female first 'first neighbour'.

In preparation for the arrival of the priest and mourners, she washes and dresses the corpse. Sprigs of blessed laurel are placed on the chest of the body in the form of a cross. If the deceased was married, the corpse is covered with a bridal sheet. The female first 'first neighbour' is also expected to hang a special sheet, *marka mihisea*, from the wall at the head of the bed. Three crosses of blessed laurel are pinned to its upper half. This sheet and the white cloth covering the bedside table are the property of the house. Formerly the deathbed was entirely surrounded by the funeral cloths of the house. These were hung *üngürian*, in a circle, around the bed. The word *üngürü* also conveys the notion of a circle in the context of blessed bread, which made one rotation around the commune during the two-year cycle.

As soon as the female first 'first neighbour' has prepared the corpse and room, the period known as *bijita egitea*, 'making the visit', begins. The other neighbours, close relatives, and friends of the deceased gather in the kitchen to extend their sympathies to the bereaved *etxenkuak*. The female first 'first neighbour' provides the visitors with coffee and prepares meals for the *etxenkuak*. The *nausi* of the house and his male first 'first neighbour' remain seated at the kitchen table after the evening meal to greet the mourners. One of the primary tasks of the male first 'first neighbour' is to collect Mass donations. He records on a list the name of the house and the number of Masses its occupants wish to sponsor. Masses thus sponsored by 'first neighbours' of the deceased are called *obligatione mezak*, obligation Masses. The male first 'first neighbour' gives the list to the priest on the day of the funeral.

After a few moments of hushed conversation in the kitchen, the mourners are invited to pay their respects to the deceased. They join the bereaved *etxekandere* in twos and threes beside the deathbed to pray for the soul.

The vigil is kept by the three *aizoak* and a few close relatives of the deceased for approximately forty-eight hours; but its duration is ultimately decided by the priest, who may hold the funeral on the day following death. The night vigil is led by the male and female first 'first neighbour', who take turns providing companionship and praying for the deceased while the *etxenkuak* sleep.

On the second night of the vigil the corpse is carried from the bedroom into the hall by the male *aizoak* and the *nausi* of house, who place it in the coffin. Great care is taken to prevent the coffin and corpse from touching the ground. The coffin is laid on low wooden stools where it remains until the funeral. Absolute silence is maintained by the mourners from the time the body is lifted from the bed until the coffin is sealed.

On the following morning the coffin is taken to the church by the three male *aizoak* and a close friend of the deceased. Although motor cars are now used to transport the body, the pallbearers were formerly obliged to carry it on their shoulders along the most direct route leading from the house to the church. These narrow, rough tracks were called *hilbideak*, 'roads of the dead'. The tracks were also used when people walked to Mass in the church, i.e. they were not avoided.

As the coffin is carried into the church the female sacristan tolls the bell. If the deceased is male, the bell is rung once every few minutes at least twenty-four times. The death of a woman is signalled by two rapid tolls every few moments and at least twenty-four times. The bell is not rung for an infant or child who has not received First Communion. No one was able to tell me why an odd number (though repeated up to an even total) of tolls signifies the death of a man and an even number the death of a woman.[3]

The funeral procession from the house to the church and then to the cemetery is led by the *nausi* of the bereaved household. He carries the church cross, to which four blessed candles of his house are fastened.[4]

The *nausi* is followed first by the priest, his two acolytes, and then by the coffin, carried by the three male 'first neighbours' and a friend of the deceased. The male *etxenkuak*, male relatives, and friends of the deceased walk behind the coffin. They are followed by the men of the community, the female *etxenkuak*, female *aizoak*, female relatives, and lastly by the other women of the commune. Children do not attend funerals.

The coffin is placed in front of the grille separating the nave from the chancel so that the feet of the corpse point toward the altar. The female first 'first neighbour' removes the four blessed candles

[3] The associations between odd and male, even and female also occur in Murélaga. Douglass (1969: 26) reports that 'if the deceased is male, the large church bell is rung three times followed by ten seconds of continuous pealing; if female, the large bell is rung twice'.

[4] In many French Basque communities the male 'first neighbour' (*lehen auzoa*) assumes this role in the funeral procession.

from the cross, places them at the four corners of the coffin, and lights them for the soul.

The male *etxenkuak* and male *aizoak* occupy the benches directly opposite the altar on which children are normally seated. The female *etxenkuak* and female *aizoak* sit in the first row of the women's chairs, whose owners are obliged to take an abandoned or vacant chair behind them.

After the Mass the *nausi* leads the procession into the cemetery to the open grave, which was formerly dug by the male first 'first neighbour'. For at least the past fifteen years, this service has been performed by the *nausi* of the house Elichalt, which lies directly across the road from the church. He is paid a small annual sum by the commune in return for his services as grave-digger.

Prayers are offered by the priest and then the male first 'first neighbour' casts the first earth into the grave. He is later assisted by the Elichalt *nausi* and other pallbearers. The *etxenkuak* and close relatives of the deceased linger beside the grave for only a few moments; for, it is said, the pain of death is now greater for the living than for the dead. Their 'big pain' begins with the burial, when the physical and social separation of the deceased from society is ultimately expressed and finalized.

Immediately after the burial an *okasione* meal is sponsored by the bereaved household. Formerly this was held in their house; but during the past five years it has become fashionable to hold the *okasione* in one of the cafés near the church. The 'first neighbours', close relatives, and sometimes the age-mates (*konskritak*) of the deceased are invited to attend the meal by the *etxekandere* of the bereaved household. (Age-mates are often, though not necessarily, friends. Regardless of whether or not a friendship existed between the deceased and a particular age-mate, it is considered appropriate to invite the latter to the *okasione* because 'he took his First Communion at the same time as the deceased'.) The *okasione* meal consists only of soup, bread, wine, coffee, and mountain cheese, which the *nausi* of the bereaved household is expected to provide. Great emphasis is placed on the frugality of the meal not simply as an expression of respect for the dead, but also as a means of ensuring that the newly departed soul will not be jealous of the living, to whom food and drink have not been denied by death.

At the end of the meal the female first 'first neighbour' of the bereaved household leads the mourners in prayer. Formerly four prayers were offered. The first was for the soul of the deceased, the second for all the dead of his house, the third for all of his dead close relatives, and the fourth for all of his deceased *aizoak*. This was one of the few ritual occasions on which close relatives traditionally took precedence over 'first neighbours'.

In principle the Novena Mass (*Bederatzürrüna*, derived from *bederatzü*, 'nine') should be held nine days after the funeral. Anyone may attend the Mass, which is sponsored by the *etxenkuak* of the deceased. Formerly all of the blessed candles that were given to the bereaved household by the three *aizoak* were taken to the church by the female first 'first neighbour' on the morning of the Novena. During the past twenty years or so, this service has been performed by the *etxekandere* of the bereaved household.

In Sainte-Engrâce the female first 'first neighbour' in charge of the blessed candles was not named. In some Basque communities she is called *ezküandere* (or *ezkoandere*), 'the candle woman'. The Sainte-Engrâce women who recognized this term identified her as the female first 'first neighbour' in their own society; and they, like the other Souletine women with whom I discussed the ritual duties of the *ezküandere*, emphasized that this woman is 'to the right' (*eskuñilat*) of the bereaved household.

My inquiries about the *ezküandere* in Soule revealed that she is the female first 'first neighbour' in Ossas, Camou, Alçabéhéty, Haux, Barcus, and Laguinge. In the first five villages the *ezküandere* is obliged to take the blessed candles given by the *aizoak* and *etxenkuak* of the deceased to the church on the day of the funeral and to light them for the departed soul.

A detailed account of the ritual services provided by the Laguinge *ezküandere* was given to me by a former Sainte-Engrâce priest, who is a native of Laguinge. In his village, she was obliged to take the blessed candles to the church on the day of the funeral and to burn them in front of the corpse during the Mass. From that day until the Novena Mass, the *aizoak* and *etxenkuak* of the deceased went to the church every evening to pray for the soul first in the sanctuary and then at the house tomb. The Laguinge *ezküandere* placed all of the blessed candles given by the household, 'first neighbours', and close kin of the deceased on top of the grave and lit them every evening until the Novena. The basket in which she carried the candles was also used in the blessed bread ritual there.[5]

In Sainte-Engrâce the Novena Mass is followed by a second meal (*Bederatzürrün kolazione*) sponsored by the *etxenkuak* of the deceased. Only his *aizoak* and close relatives are invited. This meal

---

[5] For another account of the mortuary services performed by the Laguinge *ezküandere*, see Barandiarán 1949.

is also held in a café. The *nausi* of the bereaved household generally provides an old ewe and some of his mountain cheese for the occasion. During the past five years the meal has become increasingly expensive and extravagant. In 1977 the total cost of the *okasione* and *kolazione* meals (attended by thirty-five and twenty people respectively) was in one case 480 francs, roughly £58.

After the Novena the soul of the deceased continues to receive assistance from his *etxenkuak*, *aizoak*, close relatives, and sometimes from his age-mates. The 'obligation Masses' sponsored by his 'first neighbours' and all other honorific Masses are given by the priest during the course of the year. The name of the deceased and of the household sponsoring the Mass are read aloud in the church by the priest one week in advance.

Until the 1960s a household could choose to sponsor a High Mass, a Low Mass, or a part of one Mass on behalf of the soul. In the 1950s, the first cost 250 francs (*ancien*), the second 200 francs, and the third 150 francs. The Mass lists I have seen from the 1940s and 1950s showed that a soul generally received at least twenty High Masses, twenty-five Low Masses, and an average of twenty-five 'portions' of a Mass. The three *aizoak* of the deceased were expected to give one High Mass each, as were close relatives. Low Masses were commonly given by households who were neither 'first neighbours' nor close relatives of the deceased but who lived in the same settlement or *quartier*. Parts of one Mass were generally given by households that were socially and spatially the furthest away from that of the deceased, e.g. non-relatives living in the other half of the commune.

The *aizoak* of the deceased may give more than their one 'obligation Mass'; but their *zorrak*, or mortuary obligations, to the deceased and his survivors are formally terminated by their *obligatione meza*.

The *zorrak* of the *etxenkuak* do not end until they themselves die. They are obliged to sponsor an anniversary Mass (*Urthebürü meza*) on behalf of the soul every year on or within a few days of the date of death. On the twentieth anniversary of the death they sponsor a special Mass known as *Urthoroz*, which literally means 'yearly'.

The first anniversary Mass ends the period of formal mourning for the *etxenkuak*. After this Mass the *etxekandere* may wear colours other than black. She is now the only person for whom black mourning attire is obligatory for one year. Formerly the *nausi* of the bereaved household wore a black band on his left arm during the year of formal mourning. At present he dresses in black only for the duration of the vigil and for the funeral and Novena Masses.

Until the 1930s a bereaved *etxekandere* was obliged to wear her long black cape (*kapuxina*) in the church and a short black cape (*mantaleta*) in her house for one year; but she was expected to wear only black for a period of two years.

According to the two oldest women in the community, the period of mourning observed by an *etxekandere* was formerly determined by her genealogical relationship with the deceased. For an aunt or uncle she wore full mourning attire in the church and house for six months; for one of her children the period was extended to one year. After the death of her mother or father she remained in mourning for three years; but for her husband she was expected to wear mourning dress for the rest of her life.

IV

In Sainte-Engrâce society *aizoak* mortuary obligations are ordered dyadically, whereas those of the *lehen lehen aizoa*, or first 'first neighbour', are ordered serially. Mortuary services provided by a household and its three *aizoak* are symmetrical and reversible, in so far as the former is obliged to perform the ritual services I have described for the latter when one of their members dies. Since no two households have the same three *aizoak*, and remembering that the first 'first neighbour' lies to the right whereas the other two are to the left, *aizoak* mortuary obligations can be seen as a series of interlocking segments which make a chain around the commune. The people themselves do not in fact visualize the transmission of mortuary obligations as a circle or chain; but they have a clear understanding of the dyadic reciprocity (expressed as *ordari*) which exists between 'first neighbours' at death.

Death is a human experience from which no individual or household escapes; and any household that assists its *aizoa* at death knows that it will eventually receive the very same services from its three *aizoak* when one of its own *etxenkua* dies. In due course every household will 'take a turn' (*aldikatzen*) performing mortuary services for its three *aizoak*. For this reason, it is said, a household and its 'first neighbours' are 'equal-equal' (*bardin-bardina*) as givers and takers.

Although the services rendered by all three *aizoak* concern the body and soul of the deceased, those which are performed 'for the living' (*bizientako*) are regarded as their most vital ones. The most highly valued form of assistance they provide is the routine work that they do from the time of death until the funeral. One of their primary collective tasks is to ensure that the social and economic orderliness of the household is restored when death disrupts it.

Although the male and female first 'first neighbour' assist and provide companionship for the living, their most crucial services are for the dead. Together they lead the vigil for the soul. The male collects Mass donations, casts the first clod of earth on to the grave, which formerly he dug. But of the two the female *lehen lehen aizoa* is regarded as the more important *lagün*, companion and assistant, of the deceased. She prepares his body, bed, and room for the vigil; opens the windows so that his soul can escape; leads the mourners in prayers for his soul; and ensures that the blessed candles burn continuously. By means of these candles she provides 'light for the soul of the deceased' (*hilan arimentako argia*) as it begins its journey to Purgatory, where it and all other souls will await resurrection.

In Sainte-Engrâce society first 'first neighbour' mortuary obligations are transmitted serially from right to left in a counter-clockwise direction around the commune. Their transmission is unilateral, irreversible, and defined by an asymmetric ordering of givers and takers. The people acknowledge and emphasize the fact that the mortuary services provided by the first 'first neighbour' were the only ritual means of recompensing the household from whom one received the gift of blessed bread. In return for *ogi benedikatia*—a gift exclusively 'for the living' (*bizientako*)—the first 'first neighbour' performed ritual services 'for the dead' (*hilentako*) of its bread-giver.

Blessed bread was formerly transmitted serially to the right in a clockwise direction around the commune. First 'first neighbour' mortuary obligations are transmitted serially to the left. Before the *ogi benedikatia* ritual was abolished, two complementary cycles of exchange moved in opposite directions:

$$a \rightleftarrows b \rightleftarrows c \rightleftarrows a$$

In the last chapter reference was made to the idioms and images by means of which the people conceptualize the ritual giving of blessed bread as a system of asymmetric exchange. They visualize the passage of bread from 'first neighbour to first neighbour' as a clockwise circle.

In the case of first 'first neighbour' mortuary obligations a disparity exists between what is done at a community-wide level and how this is conceived by the people themselves. They acknowledge that certain ritual services come from the right (*eskuiñetik jiten ari dira*) by virtue of the fact that these are given by the first 'first neighbour'; but they consistently and adamantly deny that first 'first neighbour' mortuary services—or any other prestations—are given to the left. I was repeatedly told that 'only evil things go to the left'. Only two informants recognized and acknowledged that first 'first neighbour' mortuary services move, as did blessed bread, from 'first neighbour to first neighbour' but in a counter-clockwise direction (*arra-üngürian*, 'in a backwards rotation'). The other people recognized neither feature of the transmission of first 'first neighbour' mortuary obligations.

From the point of view of individual experience, the transmission of blessed bread formed an unbroken chain around the commune; but, for the individual observer (including the two informants cited above), the transmission of first 'first neighbour' mortuary obligations does not. The disparity between these two conceptualizations may be partially accounted for by the periodicity of the blessed bread ritual in contrast with the discontinuity of the exchange of mortuary services.

The ritual giving of blessed bread used to be a weekly occurrence. Although the *etxekandere* had only one turn to act as bread-giver once every two years, she knew when she would be required to perform this service, as well as where her turn fitted into the cycle. The ritual regularly reaffirmed the social and spiritual ties between 'first neighbours', as well as between the members of the community; it preserved and perpetuated social relationships.

Death is a sudden, irregular, and often unexpected event that disrupts and destroys human relationships. First 'first neighbour' mortuary services are provided sporadically in a random, disorderly fashion. The frequency with which a household gives and receives 'first neighbour' mortuary services varies greatly. Death may occur in the same household and neighbourhood several times in one year and not at all in other parts of the community. Although I know of no case, it is logically possible that a household may never be called upon to perform mortuary services for a 'first neighbour' within the lifetime of its *etxenkuak*.

Unlike the ritual giving of blessed bread, which linked 'first neighbours' in a continuous chain of givers and takers, death segments *aizoak* relationships into discrete groups of households between which mortuary services are exchanged only infrequently. First 'first neighbour' mortuary services necessarily form a cycle of asymmetric exchange moving from right to left, but only when their transmission is considered abstractly at a community-wide level of practice.

PART FOUR

IX. THE *OLHA*: A PASTORAL INSTITUTION

THE Souletine *olha* is a shepherding and cheese-making syndicate consisting of a group of shepherds who amalgamate their flocks during the months of summer transhumance and who take turns tending and milking them during that period.[1] The institution probably existed as early as the sixteenth century when the 'rights of the *cayolar*' were established by the *Coutume de Soule*. It has survived in attenuated form in mountain communities such as Sainte-Engrâce, where the ideological and social importance of sheep-raising and cheese-making has not yet been lost.

I

In Sainte-Engrâce *olha* (pl. *olhak*) has two meanings: it denotes the syndicate itself and the mountain huts jointly owned and used by the *olha* members (*olhakuak*) from mid-May until late September.

As one example of a European pastoral institution, the *olha* presents a striking contrast to the sheep-herding 'company' or *stani* of the transhumant Sarakatsani of north-western Greece (Campbell 1964). Unlike the *stani* the *olha* is a permanent corporation; it has a name, a social identity, and a formal organization in which relationships between shepherds are fixed and their pastoral roles systematically rotated; and it is an exclusively male society based upon the co-operation and amicability of its members.

Co-operation and an absence of conflict also characterize relationships between the *olhak* owned by Sainte-Engrâce households. I know of not one case in which Sainte-Engrâce *olhak* have stolen sheep from each other, have accused each other of theft, or have engaged in any major or lasting dispute.

There is, however, a certain amount of rivalry among them; for each *olha* group is enormously proud of its cheeses, combined flocks, hut, and view of the surrounding mountains which their hut affords. Among themselves the shepherds of an *olha* take great pleasure in

---

[1] The standard references to this subject are Cavaillès (1910, 1931), Lefebvre (1933), Nussy Saint-Saëns (1955), and Peillen (1965). The articles by Etchegoren (1935) and Ochkach (1935) provide colourful accounts of life in an *olha* hut. Jaury (1938) describes the experiences of an eight-year-old boy during his first trip to the *olha* with his father. These three articles were written in Basque.

extolling the virtues of their own syndicate, and I was frequently called upon to attest to these. 'Which *olha* has the most beautiful view? Ours does, does it not? And have you ever tasted cheese better than ours?'

Traditionally, and at least until the 1940s, a formal, institutionalized means of preventing conflict between the members of neighbouring *olhak* existed in Sainte-Engrâce and other communities in Haute-Soule: *xikito*, derived from the verb *xikitatu*, meaning 'to castrate'. *Xikito* was a form of ritual duelling conducted exclusively by men in the mountains; it consisted of obscene and sometimes improvised four-line verses, which always ended with the exclamation *xikito*! A call to make *xikito* was issued when shepherds from neighbouring *olhak* judged that two of their comrades were likely to fight. The adversaries were required to stand at a considerable distance from each other and to take turns shouting rhymed insults 'until their anger was spent'. One classic insult was to accuse the adversary of committing bestiality with an old sow. Opponents competed to recite or to compose increasingly obscene and insulting rhymes as the *xikito* progressed.

Xikito which aimed to prevent conflict was generally initiated when a man accused a neighbour shepherd of trespassing on the pasturage of his *olha*. I know of no case in which *xikito* was followed by a quarrel or a fight. Although this form of ritual duelling was an effective method of social control, it was most commonly initiated when shepherds merely wanted to amuse themselves; for *xikitoak* were, and still are among the men, thought to be extremely funny. Few women have ever heard *xikitoak*—since the men never played their game in the valley—and some were shocked by the obscenity of the verses when their husbands recited them in our presence.[2]

Within the Basque country, relations among pastoral syndicates of different valleys and villages have been historically neither amicable nor peaceable.[3] One of the rights accorded to *olha* members by

[2] I was told that *xikito* could, in principle, be played by the members of the same *olha* either for amusement or to prevent a fight; but no shepherd could recall having played the game with his partners for the latter reason. For examples of *xikitoak*, see Irigaray (1963: 5–8) and Peillen (1962: 27). Irigaray provides a French translation of the Basque verses.

[3] Lefebvre (1933: 190, 467) mentioned several cases of conflict between pastoral syndicates, but his accounts of the dispute between Haux and Isaba in 1511 and of the quarrels between Haux and the Roncal Valley shepherds were of special interest to me, since Haux has also had a dispute with Sainte-Engrâce shepherds.

The Bibliothèque Municipale in Pau has an interesting pamphlet written by *olhak* members in the cantons of Mauléon and Tardets in 1883. In this document the shepherds challenge the right of the Syndicate of Soule to charge them ten centimes per sheep as a pasturage tax.

the *Coutume de Soule* (1520) was that of *carnal*, which entitled them to confiscate sheep belonging to neighbouring syndicates which trespassed upon their mountain pasturage (Lefebvre 1933: 190; Nussy Saint-Saëns 1955: 66, 90). In 1977 the village of Isaba in Navarra threatened to exercise their right of *carnal* against the Sainte-Engrâce *olhak* whose cattle and sheep were found on their grazing lands. The mayor and priest of Sainte-Engrâce attended a meeting of the Isaba municipal council and promised that the trespassers would remove their beasts from the Isaba pasturage at once. The promise was fulfilled the day after the meeting.

Although the Sainte-Engrâce shepherds claim that their fore-fathers attacked trespassers from other villages with their metal-tipped wooden staffs, I have been unable to find out which villages were concerned and when the fights took place. So far as I know, the Sainte-Engrâce shepherds have been involved in only one dispute with a Souletine village in this century. In approximately 1945 the commune of Sainte-Engrâce imposed a tax of ten sous (twenty centimes) on every sheep belonging to the Haux *olha* Erainze that used the trail of the Sainte-Engrâce *olha* Sentolha in order to reach the Haux hut. (The village of Haux lies roughly eight kilometres north of the commune.) The Erainze hut is in fact within the boundaries of Sainte-Engrâce and stands less than one hundred metres away from the Sentolha hut. The two *olhak* have pastured their separate flocks on the same grazing land for at least four centuries.[4]

In 1945 the Haux *olha* took their case to the tribunal court in Saint Palais, where they argued that the tax contravened their free right, as Souletine shepherds, to gain access to their hut. At the first hearing, Sainte-Engrâce was represented by its priest Etcheverry (cited in Chapter VI) and won the case, but the dispute continued. In 1954 the Haux *olha* appealed to the authorities a second time. The court reversed its decision, and Sainte-Engrâce was required to repeal the tax. Although relations between the two groups of shepherds were almost certainly strained for a few years, there is now no trace of tension between them.

II

The 'rights of *cayolar*' accorded to *olha* members in the *Coutume de Soule* were listed in Chapter I. The members were granted *libre*

---

[4] Lefebvre (1933: 190) provides evidence to suggest that Haux owned Erainze at least as early as 1557.

jouissance (free enjoyment) and *libre parcours* (free passage) in the mountain pastures of Soule; ownership of their communal huts, corral, and the plot of land on which these stand; and the right to use timber from the forests during their stay in the mountains. These rights are still accorded to the Sainte-Engrâce shepherds by the commune, which owns both the forests and mountain pastures.

In Sainte-Engrâce the area of land on which an *olha* has the right of pasturage for its communal flocks is known as *buḻta*. According to the shepherds, the limits of their *buḻta* are not fixed in any document but are prescribed by custom. Boundaries between grazing lands are known and are nearly always respected by the syndicates. The shepherds themselves are uncertain how many hectares of pasturage their flocks use; but on the average, the *buḻta* of an *olha* extends within a radius of one kilometre from the hut.

With the exceptions of Gnabaingna, Lacourde, and Hilague, which have their huts on the eastern edge of the commune, the *olhak* are scattered across the mountains along the south-western and western borders of Sainte-Engrâce. The huts and pasturage range in elevation from 1,069 to 1,700 metres. When a shepherd travels without his sheep, he can generally reach his hut in two or three hours and is thus easily able to ascend and descend in one day if necessary. Erainze is the *olha* furthest from the community and can be reached on foot in about four hours.

The number of active *olhak* has decreased considerably during the past few decades. This can be partially accounted for by three factors: emigration, the increasing popularity of raising cattle in favour of sheep, and apathy among the young men for the profession of their fathers and forefathers. So far as I have been able to determine from conversations and parish records, nineteen *olhak* functioned during the first quarter of this century. The only detailed map of the commune, published by the Institut Géographique National, identifies thirty-two *olha* huts, e.g. Cayolar d'Ayzessaria, all but two of which I have been able to trace to one of the nineteen syndicates.

In 1976/7 Sainte-Engrâce shepherds from forty-five of the ninety-nine households actively participated in ten *olhak*, seven of which are owned exclusively by Sainte-Engrâce houses: Ayzessaria, Ligoleta, Sohotolatze, Herna, Anhaou, Lacourde, and Hilague. Although an average of eleven households own shares in these *olhak*, Ayzessaria had only eight shepherds from eight different households in 1977, and only seven shepherds in 1979; Ligoleta has six shepherds; Sohotolatze had seven in 1977 and six in 1979; Herna has four;

Anhaou has four; Lacourde is now used by only one household, as is Hilague.

Three of the active *olhak* are owned and used by Sainte-Engrâce households and outsiders. Larragorry has six Sainte-Engrâce shepherds and one Spanish Basque. Escantolha has three members from Sainte-Engrâce and one from each of the following lowland Souletine villages: Sauguis, Cihigue, Esquiule, Alçay, and Suhare.

The third syndicate is the Haux *olha* of Erainze, whose sheep were formerly taxed by Sainte-Engrâce. When the number of active shepherds in an *olha* dwindles to five, the men and their respective households have three options: they may disband, sell their sheep, but retain ownership of the *olha*; the shepherds may remain together in their *olha*, take more turns in the hut, and spend fewer days in the valley during the transhumant season; or they may retain ownership of both their flocks and shares in the *olha* and join another *olha*. They may buy shares in that syndicate, or merely establish a partnership with it by means of a written or verbal agreement. In 1975, the five remaining shepherds in the Sainte-Engrâce *olha* Sentolha decided to take the last course of action when they could no longer function by themselves. They became the partners of the Haux shepherds in Erainze. (See Chapter X, section V.)

With eighteen members and 1,380 sheep Erainze is the largest *olha* in the commune. Of the total, approximately 300 sheep are owned by the five Sainte-Engrâce shepherds. The other nine syndicates cited have an average of 375 sheep in their combined flocks.

For reasons different from those of the Sentolha shepherds, the Ligoleta men have also established a partnership with an *olha* from another Souletine village. With six active members Ligoleta is able to operate without outside assistance during the milking and cheese-making season, as well as when the ewes are *antxü*, i.e. neither carrying lambs nor giving milk. A few years ago the Ligoleta men agreed to become the partners of some Licq shepherds, whose *olha* hut lies roughly forty metres from their own, from the end of their cheese-making season in late June until the end of September.

For as long as the Ligoleta and Licq shepherds can remember, they have pastured their respective flocks on the same grazing land. I have neither heard nor read of any dispute between them. From May until late June, the Licq men pasture their flocks near their own village. As soon as the Ligoleta men have finished their milking and cheese-making season, the Licq flocks are moved to the Ligoleta pasture and are amalgamated with the Ligoleta sheep. Like Erainze, the Licq *olha* pays an annual pasturage tax of 50 francs per seven ewes to the commune of Sainte-Engrâce. From late June until late September the Licq and Ligoleta shepherds mutually assist (*alkharr lagüntzen*) and co-operate with each other. They take turns (*aldikatzen*) tending their combined flocks on a weekly basis.[5]

The Licq and Ligoleta shepherds are also '*olha* first neighbours' (*olha aizoak*). According to the elderly, retired shepherds, every *olha* formerly had three 'first neighbours'. These were the three syndicates whose huts were closest to one's own. Like 'first neighbour' relationships between households in the valley, *olha aizoak* relationships were permanent; but at least within living memory, the shepherds did not make any distinctions between first, second, and third *olha* 'first neighbours'.

At present every *olha* has only one 'first neighbour', the syndicate whose hut is closest to one's own and to whom one turns in times of crisis, e.g. when a bear attacks a flock. Like 'first neighbours' in the valley, *olha aizoak* are morally obliged to assist one another.

III

Formerly all but two of the ten *olhak* had at least two and sometimes three huts positioned at different elevations on their pasturage. The hut at the lowest altitude was known as the *peko-olha*, lower cabane. This hut was formerly used from mid-May until the snow melted in the high pastures in early June, and only the lactating ewes were taken to its grazing land. In June these ewes, the rams, one-year-old lambs, and non-lactating ewes were moved to the high pastures, where the shepherds stayed in their *gaiñeko-olha* or upper cabane. They remained there with their flocks until the end of the transhumant season in late September. (Some *olhak* formerly had a third hut, the *arteko-olha* or cabane of the ewes, which usually lay between the lower and upper huts.) At present the shepherds use only their upper cabane during their stay in the mountains.[6]

During the period of summer transhumance, the *olha* hut provides shelter for the shepherds, the space in which they make, mature, and store their cheeses, and an exclusively male social and domestic domain of which the shepherds are extremely proud.

---

[5] The manner in which they do so will be discussed in Chapter X.

[6] In 1979 a derelict 'lower cabane' of the inactive *olha* Utzipia was renovated by a group of shepherds whose households own shares in this *olha* but who, at present, participate in one of the ten active syndicates. According to the shepherds, the cabane was restored 'in case the *olhak* where we shepherd now are disbanded and we have to re-establish Utzipia'.

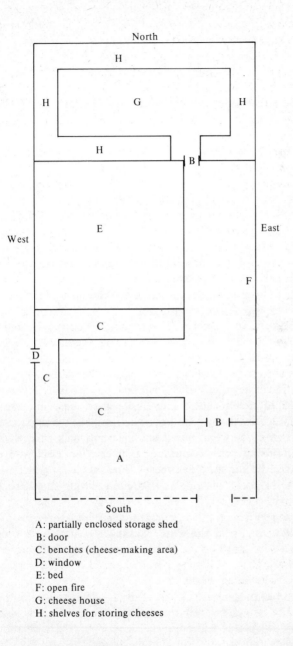

North

H

H   G   H

H

B

West   East

E

F

C

D

C

C

B

A

South

A: partially enclosed storage shed
B: door
C: benches (cheese-making area)
D: window
E: bed
F: open fire
G: cheese house
H: shelves for storing cheeses

Fig. 5. The Ligoleta hut

Like the house, the *olha* hut has a name and a social identity. The members of an *olha* are referred to and know themselves by its name, e.g. Ligoletarrak, during the transhumant season. Like the household, the hut is a social, economic, and domestic unit whose members mutually assist and co-operate with one another.

With the exceptions of Erainze and Escantolha, whose huts were completely refurbished in 1965 and 1977 respectively, the Sainte-Engrâce huts have been kept much as they were at least a century ago. They are rectangular and measure roughly five metres in length and three metres in width. (See Figure 5.) The walls are made of dry stone and the roof of wooden tiles or corrugated iron.

The hut is oriented so that the low wooden door faces south. In some huts, the door also provides the only source of natural light within the dwelling. A few huts have a partially enclosed shed on their south-facing end in which milking utensils, oil skins, herding staffs, and the shepherds' ubiquitous umbrellas are kept.

The interior of the hut is divided into two sections: the room in which the shepherds cook, eat, sleep, and make their cheeses and the *gaztantegi*, a small room on the northern end of the hut where the cheeses are matured and stored.

The interior of the hut is dank, dark, and blackened by decades of wood smoke. In the main room cooking and cheese-making utensils hang from the beams against the bare stone walls. Plates and provisions are stored on wooden shelves, which line at least one wall.

Against the eastern wall of the hut an open fire is built directly on the stone floor. Even with a favourable wind, very little smoke is drawn through a narrow slit above the fireplace which is meant to serve as a chimney. The wood smoke permeates everything and everyone in the hut, but it is tolerated as an essential element in drying and maturing the newly made cheeses. The smoke is part of the 'idea' or atmosphere (*ideia*) of the *olha* that every strong shepherd should be able to withstand.

The main room is cramped when there are only three people in it. It is largely taken up by the wide, wooden bed (*atzea*) on which the shepherds sleep. Until about fifteen years ago the bed was covered with pine boughs and fleeces; but these have been replaced by mattresses and woollen blankets.

The number of men in the hut at night varies from *olha* to *olha*; but generally two and rarely more than three shepherds share the bed on any one night. Although the *atzea* is barely wide enough to accommodate four adults, six shepherds used to sleep on it every night at the beginning of this century.

On one occasion in 1977 nine men managed to fit themselves into the bed of Ligoleta. The two shepherds in charge of the hut and flocks that night received an unexpected visit from a group of men belonging to other syndicates. (This hut is a favourite way-station for men travelling between Spanish Basque Navarra and Sainte-Engrâce.) As the shepherds later told me, they drank, played cards, and talked until dawn. But in the presence of their wives they complained that they had not had any sleep. The two shepherds who had been in charge of the hut vowed rather unconvincingly that they would never again have another fête. Their wives wryly observed that 'there is nothing they like better'.

The *gaztantegi* at the northern end of the hut is separated from the main room by a low wooden wall and door. The term consists of the noun *gaztan*, 'curdled milk', and the suffix -*tegi*, meaning house or shelter. Some shepherds refer to this room as *gaznategia*, literally 'the cheese house'.

This room is generally two metres wide and three metres long. Its walls are lined with long wooden planks on which the newly made cheeses are turned daily, dried, and matured during the summer. Although there are no windows, the room is ventilated so that both the mountain air and the smoke can easily reach the cheeses.

A small loft rests on top of the cheese house and opens on to the main room. The shepherds use this space to store implements, bags of salt, and their few belongings. At the beginning of every transhumant season every shepherd takes his own wooden box to the hut in which he keeps a few clothes, a sprig of blessed laurel, a piece of blessed candle, and a vial of blessed water. These 'blessed things' are exclusively in the care of the men only for the duration of their stay in the mountains. Like the *etxekandere* of the household the shepherds use these objects as a form of protection during severe storms and in times of crisis. They return them to the woman of the house when they descend to the valley in September.

IV

In Sainte-Engrâce membership in an *olha* is determined by two factors: ownership of a share (*partea*) or portion of a share, and residence in a Sainte-Engrâce house.

Every *olha* has a fixed number of 'complete shares' (*parte osorik*) which, I am told, was agreed upon by the original members of the syndicate according to the size and quality of their mountain pasturage. On the average the grazing land of an *olha* can accommodate a maximum of ten 'complete shares'.

In the traditional *olha*, the owner of a 'complete share' was obliged to contribute a fixed number of milking ewes to the communal flocks of the syndicate during the period of summer transhumance. This unit of sheep is known as a *txotx* (also spelled *xotx* or *tchotch*). In some parts of Soule, one *txotx* consists of a hundred milking ewes (Lhande 1926: 989). In the Sainte-Engrâce *olhak* one *txotx* equals either fifty or sixty milking ewes and two rams.[7]

In Sainte-Engrâce, as in other Souletine communities, it is possible to own a half-share or half-*txotx* (*txotxerdi*) or a quarter-share (*karta*) in an *olha*. In some Sainte-Engrâce *olhak* a half-*txotx* consists of twenty-five milking ewes; in others thirty ewes are required. A *karta*, a quarter-share or quarter-*txotx* in a syndicate, equals fifteen milking ewes. Until roughly fifteen years ago, households owning a half or quarter share were obliged to have as many *txotx* partners (*txotx lagünak*) as were necessary for them to make one 'complete share' or full *txotx* with their combined flocks.[8]

During the past few decades the traditional structure of the *olha* has changed considerably. Households owning a share or portion of a share are no longer obliged to contribute a prescribed number of milking ewes to the communal flock; nor are they even required to keep any sheep at all. During the past twenty years fifty-four households have sold their flocks, largely because they lacked a young *nausi* who was able or willing to represent the household in the *olha*. In one case an elderly man sold his flock because he had neither a son nor son-in-law to succeed him as *nausi*. But, with the exception of the man who sold his entire property, every household has retained ownership of its *olha* share(s).

Ownership of a share is legally established in a written notarized contract, which lists the rights and privileges of the owner. Every member is entitled to enjoy the three 'rights of *cayolar*', to pasture their sheep and cattle on the *buĺta* of the syndicate, and to use the hut and all communally owned property within it during the period of transhumance. Every member is also entitled to make a fixed number of cheeses from the milk yielded by the *olha* flocks. Formerly that number was determined by the size of his flock, i.e. whether he contributed a *txotx*, a half-*txotx*, or a quarter.

[7] Nussy Saint-Saëns (1955: 91) reports that the Souletine *tchotch* originally consisted of a minimum of 45 milking ewes. In Ibarre (Basse-Navarre) a *xotx* equals 60 milking ewes (Barandiarán 1955: 42). In the Souletine village of Laguinge, a *txotx* consists of 56 milking ewes, a half-*txotx* 28 ewes, and a *karta* or quarter-*txotx* 14 ewes (Barandiarán 1948: 22). For other accounts of the *txotx* system, see Cavaillès (1910) and Lefebvre (1933).

[8] The *txotx* and the relationship between *txotx* partners will be discussed in Chapter X.

In principle an *olha* share, or portion of it, should never be sold. Like the house, the share is part of the *etxalte*, the sum total of movable and immovable property that is transmitted intact through successive generations of heirs and heiresses.

In practice *olha* shares are frequently bought and sold in syndicates that have enough shepherds to tend and to milk the communal flocks; but, with one exception, households do not sell their share in the *olha* to which the first *etxenkuak* of the house belonged. In 1976 the *nausi* of one upper household sold not only the original share of his house; he sold his entire *etxalte*, i.e. all of his livestock, his land, his house, implements, and domestic articles, to a cousin in the lower community. He was both censured and pitied for his action. So far as the people are concerned, he no longer has a 'name', a social identity, even though he continues to live in the house.

I was unable to discover how much the cousin paid for the share, but the price was probably in the region of 3,000 francs. In the same year a lower household sold its share in Larragorry for 3,500 francs. In the 1950s one 'complete share' cost 1,000 francs.

The oldest contract to which I have had access was drawn up in 1848, and concerned two *olha* huts which were initially owned by the commune of Sainte-Engrâce. One hut was leased by three members of another syndicate and the parish priest for 1,800 francs (*ancien*) for a period of ten years. The second hut was leased by five shepherds in a different *olha* for 500 francs (*ancien*) and for the same duration. (The households of these eight men now claim that they jointly own these two huts; but their ownership rights were not established in the 1848 contract. The people were puzzled when I pointed this out to them and decided that there must have been a second contract dealing solely with the transfer of ownership rights from the commune to their households. We were unable to locate a second document.)

The majority of households belong to at least two *olhak*; but in any transhumant season a household participates in only one syndicate. All its sheep are incorporated into the communal flocks of one *olha*, and its elder and/or younger *nausi* acts as a shepherd for that group alone.

According to the shepherds, there are two main advantages to belonging to more than one *olha*. First, a household that has access to the mountain pasturage of more than one syndicate is better able to ensure that his own flock will have rich and ample grass and that they will be contented. Ewes are said to be as changeable as children in their likes and dislikes. A flock may graze on the same pasture for many years and 'then suddenly become restless and unhappy there'. Their milk yield is said to decrease as a result; but a 'good shepherd' moves them to another *olha* pasture before this happens. Changing syndicates 'because one's sheep are unhappy' is socially acceptable and does not give rise to any ill feelings or tensions among one's *olha* comrades. No shepherd admits to changing syndicates because he himself was unhappy; for to do so would be regarded as socially and morally unacceptable, as well as an insult to his former comrades.

The second main advantage is that additional *olha* shares increase the value of the property, or *etxalte*. Even though profits in milk and cheese are derived from only one *olha* in any given year, *olha* shares in themselves constitute a coveted form of wealth that is permanently valuable. Many households own shares in *olhak* that were disbanded in the last century. The huts of these syndicates are often derelict; in some cases no trace of them remains. But an *olha* itself 'never dies'; like a house, it continues to exist without any shepherds or sheep, without any huts or corrals, and all shares in it remain the collective, inherently valuable property of the households which own it.

In Sainte-Engrâce membership in an *olha* is not simply a matter of inheriting or purchasing a share or portion of a share; it is also determined by residence in a household. This is one other expression of the immutable bond thought to exist between an *olha* and a house.

If a man changes residence at marriage or remarriage, he is obliged to leave the *olha* of his natal or first post-marital residence and to join the *olha* in which his new household owns a share and actively participates. If his former and new places of residence belong to the same *olha*, he shepherds for the latter. Among the shepherds a preference is expressed for 'marrying within' the *olha* of one's natal household. This is the *olha* in which he learned his skills as a shepherd and in which he was initiated into the exclusive society of adult men. Marrying within the *olha* also means that a man has already established a fairly close, amicable, and co-operative relationship with his wife's father and brother(s) before his marriage —a relationship which closely parallels the one between 'first neighbours' in terms of the expectations contained within it and from which conflict is unlikely to arise.

Loyalty to the members of one's *olha* does not conflict with loyalties either to one's household or to one's 'first neighbours'. Where shepherds in an *olha* are also closely related, their loyalty as *olha* partners as well as the expectations contained within *olha* relationships tend to affect their relationship as kin in a positive way.

When *olha* partners are not only kin but also 'first neighbours', the likelihood of their forming and maintaining a positive relationship as close kin is further increased.

My own investigations revealed that several *olhak* (Lacourde, Sentolha, and Ayzessaria) originally consisted of men who were either 'first neighbours' or neighbours. Where intermarriage between *aizoak* occurred, *olha*, 'first neighbour', and kin relationships overlapped. A modern example of this is provided by one *olha*, where only two of the eight men are neither the 'first neighbour' of any partner nor closely related to the other six shepherds. Relationships between those men who are 'first neighbours', *olha* partners, and closely related are amicable, co-operative, and free of conflict in both the mountains and the valley.

V

Of the 176 men in the commune between the ages of fifteen and ninety, 117 are either retired, active, or apprentice shepherds.[9] Of the forty-five households which actively participate in the ten *olhak*, nearly half of these have a father and son or son-in-law who take turns representing their house in the syndicate. The other twenty-four households have only one active shepherd who is in most cases the young *nausi* whose father or father-in-law has retired. According to my own calculations, sixty-six adult men act as shepherds in the *olhak* for either all or half the turns in the hut that their household is obliged to take.

All these men began their careers between the ages of ten and twelve, when most of them made their first journey to the mountains with their father or grandfather. Men who are now at least twenty-five years old learned most of their shepherding skills between the ages of twelve and fifteen. They were taught how to herd, to shear, to recognize ailments and diseases in the flock, how to assist ewes during difficult births, and to skin and butcher lambs and old ewes. But their two most important rites of passage as apprentice shepherds were making their first ascent to the hut and making their first cheese.

Until roughly twenty years ago, apprentice shepherds were obliged to participate in several initiation rites in which they were harassed and humiliated by the adult members of the *olha*. So far as I know, these rites have not been documented in the literature about life in a Souletine *olha*. According to shepherds who experienced these

[9] These figures are my own.

traditional forms of humiliation, the rites served to test the good humour of the apprentice, his willingness to co-operate with fellow *olha* members, and in some cases to increase his physical strength (*indarra*).

Traditionally an apprentice shepherd was ordered by his elders to carry water from the spring to the hut several times a day. As soon as the apprentice reached the threshold of the hut, he was supposed to bless the water by saying *benedikamus*. If he failed to do so, he was ordered to throw out the water and to return to the spring for a fresh supply. (In most *olhak*, the spring is several hundred metres from the hut.) The same orders were often given even if the apprentice remembered to utter the appropriate word. Carrying water not only served to increase his physical strength; it also 'taught him how to walk in the mountains with a heavy load'.

Another traditional means of humiliating an apprentice shepherd was a prank called 'gathering the owl' (*hüntz biltzen*). During his first stay in the hut, the boy was asked by his elders if he could hear the owl on the roof, where one of the adult shepherds lay waiting with a pail of water. The apprentice was given a sack and was instructed to capture the owl. As soon as the boy emerged from the hut with his sack, the adult shepherd threw the water on him and laughingly called out 'Gather the owl! Soon you will be gathering sheep!'

The apprenticeship of a young shepherd is formally terminated when he is permitted or, in the event of death, is required to replace his father as a full-time member of the *olha*. He becomes the *lagün* (comrade, assistant, friend) of his father's *olha* partner, as well as the *lagün* of his fellow *olha* members. He also acquires a new social identity; for he is now known not simply by the name of his house, e.g. Elichabe, but also by the name of his *olha*, e.g. Ligoletarra.

His newly acquired status as a fully fledged *olha* member is formally and publicly confirmed when he attends his first annual meeting of the syndicate (*artzanide*), at which the shepherds renew their pact as friends and partners obliged to assist each other and to co-operate. Traditionally this meeting was always held on the Feast of the Annunciation (25 March); but some syndicates now postpone theirs until April.

The pact is always renewed before the ascent of the flocks in late May, and the meeting always takes place on a Sunday either in a Sainte-Engrâce café or in one of the lowland hotels. (The Erainze meeting is held in Haux, because the Haux shepherds are the *nausiak*, 'masters', of the syndicate.)

At this meeting the shepherds jointly decide when they will burn

1. A view of 'the circle of mountains'

2. A house in the lower community

3. The church in Senta

4. A man carrying hay to the loft of his barn

5. A Sainte-Engrâce widow

6. The sacristan, who distributed blessed bread in the church, and his wife

7. A shepherd tending the flock of his *olha* in summer

8. A shepherd making house cheese

the old grass on their mountain pasturage and when they will prepare the hut and corral for the forthcoming transhumant season. (These tasks are generally performed by all the shepherds in late April.) The members also decide which domestic articles and cheese-making implements in the hut need to be replaced or repaired, how many nails for repairing the corral and how much salt they will need for the forthcoming season, and which of them will assume responsibility for purchasing these. Those who bought goods for the *olha* the previous year present their list of expenses. The total cost is divided equally among the members, who reimburse as necessary their *txotx* partners in cash.

Two other monetary transactions take place during the meeting. In the *olhak* which still make cheese and have at least four active members, the first cheese made in the hut is sold in the lowlands by the shepherd who made it; and at the *artzanide* meeting the profit derived from the sale is divided equally among the *olha* members. This cheese is known as the *majeko gazna*, literally 'the chief cheese'. The division of the profit is seen as a ritual expression of the equality of the shepherds as individuals, the amicable relations between them, and their solidarity as a group. Since the first cheese is rarely more than four kilos in weight, the profit is generally about 160 francs, so that in an *olha* with eight members every shepherd would receive 20 francs from the *majeko gazna*.

The money that the shepherds receive for the 'chief cheese' is almost immediately passed by them to the treasurer, who is in charge of the cash reserves of the *olha* and responsible for renewing the fire insurance policy held by the syndicate on their hut. (This office is no longer rotated but is held by the same man year after year.)

When these matters have been dealt with the shepherds review their plans for the forthcoming season. The total number of milking ewes, rams, and lambs in their combined flocks is calculated; and the members jointly decide whether they have too many or too few rams. If additional rams are required, they decide whose turn it is to contribute one.

A tentative date for the ascent of the flocks is generally set. Although the order in which shepherds take turns (*aldikatzen*) tending and milking the flock is fixed, this is reviewed annually so that every man will know exactly when and how many times he is due to be in the hut. The first two shepherds are reminded of their obligation to provide mattresses and blankets for the *olha* bed.

For the five *olhak* which still make mountain cheese and have at least four active members, the most important decision concerns the number of turns each shepherd will take; for this determines the number of cheeses that he will make. This decision is partly based on the date at which the shepherds expect their ewes to stop lactating, and partly on the individual preferences of the shepherds—namely whether they wish to sell their ewes' milk until the end of May, postpone their ascent and make only four or five mountain cheeses for the year, or to stop selling milk in late April or early May, make their ascent as soon as the snow melts, and produce between eight and ten cheeses in the hut.[10]

When the shepherds jointly decide how many turns each man will take in the hut, they make their agreement orally (*aho-mihiz*, literally 'by word of mouth'). In principle every man is obliged to fulfil the terms of this verbal contract; but should even one shepherd later decide that he does not wish to take the full number of turns agreed upon for the milking and cheese-making season, his colleagues do not have 'the right' (*dreta*) to continue taking turns and making mountain cheeses without his permission, even though he may have returned his sheep to the valley before the end of the season.

Permission to make as many cheeses as possible before the lactation period ends is not, however, granted in every case. In 1977 the members of one *olha* faced this very problem. At their annual meeting in the spring, the seven shepherds had decided that the first two men to stay in the hut would take five turns tending and milking the flock and making cheese and that the other five members would take four turns. (The first two men are permitted to take an extra turn because the first two cheeses they make are not kept by them. The first is sold on behalf of the *olha*, and the second is generally given to the guard of the forest.) Approximately half-way through the cheese-making season in the mountains, two of the seven shepherds told their co-partners that they did not want to take their third and fourth turns in the hut. They added that they were content to make only four rather than eight cheeses (the number decided upon), because their respective households do not eat much cheese; that they wanted to keep their respective flocks in the mountains but that they did not want their colleagues to make cheese in their absence. Their attempt to excuse themselves from their duties on the grounds that their

[10] The annual meeting of the *olhakuak* functions in a manner similar to that of the *Alprechnung* (alp reckoning) held in Kippel in the canton of Valais, south-western Switzerland. The alp associations described by Friedl (1974: 54–5) resemble the *olha* in several ways. For example, the members of these associations have 'use rights' not unlike the 'rights of *cayolar*'; and, like *olha* members, they take turns tending their beasts according to a system of rotation. For an account of an intriguing and entirely different form of pastoralism and transhumance in western Europe, see Freeman (1979: 1–4) on the Pasiegos of the Montes de Pas in the province of Santander.

households 'do not eat much cheese' was scoffed at by their co-partners. The claim was known to be untrue and was regarded as a shabby attempt to conceal the truth—namely, that the two men had had their fill of the rain and cold weather in the mountains that summer. Although the other shepherds and their wives complained bitterly among themselves that they were being denied four precious mountain cheeses and would therefore have to buy vastly inferior cows'-milk cheese in Tardets, they refused to entertain the possibility that they might continue to make mountain cheese without the permission of their two dissenting colleagues. Since the latter did not want any more cheese to be made that year, the seven shepherds decided jointly that the milk of their combined flocks could not be used by any *olha* member. During the last two weeks of the lactation period, five shepherds took turns milking the ewes; but the milk was not collected. The jets of milk from the ewes' teats were squirted directly onto the ground.

If a shepherd announces at the annual meeting in spring that he does not want to take any turns in the *olha* during the entire transhumant season but that he does want to graze his sheep on the *olha* pasturage, he is obliged to pay his colleagues to tend and to milk his flock. The fee is generally about 15 francs per ewe. In 1978 a Ligoleta shepherd paid a total of 825 francs for his fifty-five sheep, rather than take his turn in the hut. His colleagues were not cross with him, though they were required to spend more time in the hut due to his absence. He took all of his turns in the *olha* during the 1979 season.

VI

During the transhumant season the women are invited to the hut on only one occasion. When the flocks ascend in May the shepherds are sometimes accompanied by their wives and/or unmarried daughters, who are responsible for herding the pigs of the household. The women and pigs precede the sheep and men on the trails. The pigs stay in the mountains only for the duration of the milking season, when they are fed the whey which remains after the cheese and soft curds have been removed from the milk. Although whey is recognized to be an inexpensive means of fattening the beasts, very few households still observe this practice. The women now argue that their pigs are weakened by the arduous journey; and the men claim that they are glad to be rid of them, since they are a nuisance to herd and to keep track of.

For the shepherds the ascent of the flocks in late May is a festive occasion that marks the beginning of a season of hard work, physical discomfort, and lively male camaraderie.

The manner in which the flocks are herded to the mountain pastures varies from *olha* to *olha*, depending on how close the members' houses are to one another. Those who live in the same half of the commune generally combine their sheep before the ascent and make the journey together. But if the houses of the *olhakuak* are scattered across the commune, the shepherds tend to make the journey by themselves or with partners living in the same settlement or *quartier*.

In 1977 I assisted three different *olhak* during their ascent, and each syndicate organized the event in a slightly different manner. The shepherds of one group arrived punctually at the appointed place of departure at 8 a.m., and we reached the hut together four and a half hours later as planned.

The second syndicate I assisted was not at all well organized. Although its shepherds are older and more experienced than the first group were, they were also more apathetic and generally less interested in the collective welfare of the syndicate. Two hours after the appointed time of departure only four of the eight members and their flocks had arrived at the departure point in Calla.

The *etxekandere* of the house in front of which we were assembled strolled over to her husband's flock with her hands and forearms thrust beneath her apron. When she saw that the shepherds were not looking, she quickly drew out what she had taken such pains to conceal—a vial of blessed water and a sprig of blessed laurel. She hastily cast some water across the backs of the sheep and blushed when she saw me watching her. She knew that I had seen other women blessing their husband's flock before the ascent but felt certain that her husband and his partners would have laughed at her for being superstitious had they seen her doing so. I wondered about the grounds of her claim since all the men took their own blessed water, blessed candle, and blessed laurel to the hut.

The first two *olhak* with whom I made the journey had 369 and 346 sheep respectively. The third *olha*, Erainze, had a total of 1,380, more than three-quarters of which belong to the Haux shepherds. The five Sainte-Engrâce members of Erainze took their flocks up separately; but the Haux flocks, which had travelled roughly ten kilometres from their Haux pastures to the upper community, were divided into two groups.

The progress of every flock is closely watched (and with intense interest) by the people whose houses they pass; but because of their size the Haux flocks generated more than the usual amount of excitement when they passed through the valley and disappeared into the forest. The first flock had left Haux at 2 a.m. and reached the upper community at 7 a.m. The second flock arrived about an hour later. The ascent took just over five hours. When I reached the hut with some Haux shepherds, the Sainte-Engrâce men were ready to make their descent. Unlike the Sainte-Engrâce shepherds in the other *olhak*, they do not remain in their hut to socialize; nor do they make mountain cheese or rotate roles in the traditional manner.

In all the *olhak* except Erainze, Lacourde, and Hilague (the latter two have only one active member), the ascent is a major social event. When the flocks reach the hut at mid-day, the shepherds and women gather in the *olha*. The first shepherd who is due to stay in the hut lights the fire, and his partner may make some hot broth for the group. The goatskin wine gourd is passed round, and everyone settles down on the bench or bed to eat ham, sausages, bread, and cheese.

Having eaten and drunk, the men kick off their boots and wrestle playfully for a space on the bed; but sleep is virtually impossible because of the commotion which ensues. Their conversations turn at once to the flocks, the cheeses that they will make, and to their encounters with bears.

If any women are present, they are completely ignored. If the men decide that they want soup for dinner, they make it themselves. Women do not perform any domestic tasks in the hut.

On one occasion two women and a twelve-year-old girl made the ascent with me and the shepherds. For the first few hours, the two women sat huddled on the bench complaining about the smoke, cold, and filthiness of the hut, while the men played pranks.

When one of the five men in the bed began to snore, he was pricked with a large pin and swore loudly. The other shepherds roared with laughter. The culprit was thus encouraged to play other tricks. Red pepper was thrown on the fire, and all the men in the bed rushed outside the hut coughing and spluttering.

At 4.30 p.m. the shepherds had their afternoon breakfast of bread, cheese, and wine and set out to herd the flocks into the flimsy corral beside the hut. The sheep were divided into two groups: the lactating ewes in one, and the non-lactating ewes, lambs, and rams in the other.

As the flock was driven toward the corral, the women and shepherds formed two lines on either side of the gate. Only the lactating ewes were permitted to enter the corral. According to the shepherds, the adult ewes know to which group they belong after this first cutting.

The lambs, which have made their first ascent and are thus inexperienced in such matters, do not learn where they belong until the flock has been divided several times.

The first cutting is done with considerable skill and speed. The lactating ewes are, for a shepherd, easily recognized by the red, blue, or green paint on their foreheads. These marks are placed on the ewes by the shepherds before the ascent.

When all the lactating ewes have been squeezed into the corral, the shepherds milk them; and then all but two of the shepherds and all the women prepare for their descent to the valley. The only two shepherds who remain in the hut are those who occupy positions one and two in the fixed order of rotation by means of which the *olha* members take turns in the hut. These two men make the first two cheeses of the transhumant season. In Sainte-Engrâce, as in many other Souletine communities, the shepherd whose turn it is to make cheese is called *etxekandere*, 'the woman of the house'.

X. ROTATION AND SERIAL REPLACEMENT IN THE *OLHA*: PAST AND PRESENT

THE aims of this chapter are to describe the hierarchical roles traditionally performed by *olha* members; to analyse the manner in which these were systematically allocated; to trace transformations in the structuring of *olha* relationships that have taken place since 1900; and finally to show that relationships within the *olha*, in both their traditional and their present forms, are ordered by means of two principles: *üngürü* (rotation) and *aldikatzia*, which in this context is best translated as 'serial replacement'.

I

In their traditional form, relationships among *olha* members were systematically organized so that every shepherd who contributed a full *txotx* (fifty or sixty milking ewes and two rams) to the communal flock spent exactly the same number of days in the hut and made exactly the same number of cheeses in summer as did his comrades. The system was characterized by two features: the rotation of individual shepherds between their houses in the valley and the hut in the mountains, and the serial replacement of shepherds as they progressed through six hierarchical roles within the hut during the milking and cheese-making season (*ardi-jeixten*).

In Sainte-Engrâce, *olha* members took turns performing the six traditional roles until the beginning of this century. Six shepherds lived and worked together in the hut for the duration of the *ardi-jeixten*. Each man had a specific, named role to perform for a period of twenty-four hours. The six roles were ordered hierarchically according to their relative importance. From the most inferior role to the most prestigious one, these roles were as follows: the *neskato*, 'female servant', the *axurzain*, 'guardian of the lambs', the *antxüzain*, 'guardian of the non-lactating ewes', the *artzain-mithil*, 'servant shepherd', the *artzain-nausi*, 'master shepherd', and the *etxekandere*, 'woman of the house'. The shepherds employed these six named roles as terms of reference. So far as I know, they were not used as terms of address.

In their mountain huts, the shepherds re-created the socio-
151

domestic and ideologically female domain of the house. In the carefully balanced division of labour, feminine roles were played by shepherds working within the hut, whereas masculine roles were played by those who worked outside the hut among the sheep.

Outside the hut the master shepherd, his servant shepherd, and the guardian of the non-lactating ewes worked together tending and herding the main flock. Of the six shepherds only the guardian of the lambs worked alone.

Even as the house is the domain of the female *etxekandere* in the valley, the hut was—and still is—the domain of a male *etxekandere* playing an ideologically 'feminine' role. He cooked and served all of the meals, tidied the bed of pine boughs and fleeces, swept the floor, lit and stoked the fire in the open hearth. In his hut the male 'woman of the house' performed all the domestic tasks for which his female *etxenkuak* were exclusively responsible in the valley. Although considerable importance was attached to the domestic skills of the male *etxekandere*, his most crucial tasks concerned the 'mountain cheese' (*bortü gazna*) which he and his comrades made during the milking season. He was not only the cheese-maker of the day; he was also responsible for looking after the cheeses made by himself and his fellow shepherds earlier in the season. As the shepherds still observe, newly made cheeses are like new-born infants; they need to be cared for and assisted (*soiñatu*) during the early stages of life.[1]

Within the hut the *etxekandere* was aided by his 'female servant' (*neskato*), who assumed responsibility for menial domestic chores such as washing the milking and cooking utensils, carrying water from the spring and the ewes' milk from the corral to the hut, sweeping the ashes from the hearth, and feeding any pigs that were brought to the hut by the women.

At night the six men slept together on the hard wooden bed, which was placed against the wall of the cheese house and the western wall of the hut. The master shepherd slept on the outer edge since he was the first man to rise in the morning. I am told that the *etxekandere* slept beside him, but I do not know whether the other four shepherds were positioned in any prescribed order.

Shortly before dawn the master shepherd set out at once to waken the main flock. The *etxekandere* lit the fire and roused the other shepherds. The servant shepherd joined the master shepherd and

---

[1] The ideological connections between cheeses and infants will be explored in Chapters XI and XII. The verbs *soiñatu* and *lagüntu*, both of which mean 'to assist', are employed in different contexts. Infants, elderly people, and cheeses are *soiñatu*. 'First neighbours' and shepherds *lagüntzen* each other.

helped him drive the main flock toward the corral, where the *etxekandere*, his 'female servant', and the guardian of the lambs separated the lactating and non-lactating ewes. As soon as this was done, the guardian of the lambs set out to waken his flock and to take the lambs to their morning grazing land. The other five shepherds remained in the corral and milked the ewes. According to the old shepherds, they were often responsible for milking 500 or 600 ewes.

When the milking was finished, the master shepherd, his servant, and the guardian of the non-lactating ewes took the main flock to their morning pasture. The 'female servant' carried the vats of warm ewes' milk to the hut, where he strained it through a piece of fine muslin. The *etxekandere* built up the fire and prepared to make his second cheese. (His first cheese had been made the previous evening.)[2]

Having made his cheese, the *etxekandere* squeezed out the whey and rubbed the cheese with coarse salt. The new cheese was then placed on the lowest shelf in the *gaztantegi* on the northern end of the hut. All the other cheeses in this room were then turned and salted by the *etxekandere*. (These two tasks are an essential part of 'assisting' young cheeses.)

While his 'female servant' replenished their supplies of water and firewood, the *etxekandere* made six pieces of unleavened cornmeal bread (*pastetxa*) for their first meal of the day. The four shepherds tending the flocks returned to the hut one by one to eat their meagre morning meal. Water, ewes' milk, and occasionally whey were drunk.

The *etxekandere* prepared the main meal of the day at noon. In the latter half of the nineteenth century this meal generally consisted only of a thick porridge of ewes' milk and cornmeal bread. This was often followed by the soft, curd cheese called *zümbera*, which some shepherds and their families still eat. Although no one admitted to the practice, since whey is no longer thought to be fit for human consumption, I was told that 'good shepherds' formerly ate the whey from their cheeses as well. Whey was thought to increase the *indarra* or physical strength of a shepherd. Some shepherds also contend that their forefathers ate whey in order to increase the *indarra* of their semen.[3]

When the four shepherds returned to the hut for their dinner, they moved the two flocks to the pastures surrounding their dwelling. In the past, as at present, the noon meal was a jovial occasion at which

---

[2] A detailed account of cheese-making will be given in Chapter XI.
[3] Some shepherds now argue that only *zümbera* has *indarra* and that whey is *indarr-gabe*, 'without force'.

pranks were played and stories exchanged. In the early afternoon the four shepherds returned to their respective flocks. The two 'female' shepherds remained in the hut to wash the utensils and to complete any domestic chores begun that morning. During the brief lull between the noon meal and the second milking, these two men often searched for edible agaric mushrooms (*buxeuak* in Souletine, *mousserons* in French), of which the people are still very fond. In the past, as at present, the shepherd who had the time to look for the prized *buxeuak* was jokingly referred to as the *hor-üzkü*, literally 'the dog's arse'.

At 4 p.m. the main flock was driven from their afternoon grazing area to the corral for the second milking, in which all six shepherds participated. At this point, the shepherds were all advanced by one stage in the hierarchy of roles. The 'female servant' became the guardian of the lambs. The guardian of the lambs became the guardian of the non-lactating ewes. The guardian of the non-lactating ewes became the servant shepherd. The servant shepherd became the master shepherd, and the master shepherd became the cheese-making *etxekandere*. The retiring *etxekandere*, having made his two mountain cheeses, waited in the hut for the arrival of the new 'female servant' or *neskato*, i.e. the seventh shepherd in the syndicate, before he descended to his house in the valley. The new 'female servant' was expected to reach the hut before sunset, since he had domestic chores to perform for the new *etxekandere*.

In the Sainte-Engrâce dialect, the verb *aldikatü* describes the manner in which the shepherds progressed through the six hierarchical roles. The word (or its noun form *aldikatzia*) has appeared in earlier chapters, where it has been variously translated as 'to take turns', 'to alternate', 'to replace serially', depending upon the context in which it was employed. Translating the word has presented certain difficulties, since the Basque notion of *aldikatzia* covers two different concepts in English; alternation, as 'the action of two things succeeding each other by turns', and serial replacement. Within the context of traditional *olha* hierarchical roles, there is no reciprocal movement such as would constitute an alternation, i.e. the guardian of the lambs becomes the 'female servant' but does not then become guardian of the lambs again.

In the early evening the new *etxekandere* made his first of two mountain cheeses and then prepared cornmeal bread and perhaps some onion and garlic soup for the men. As he did so, his comrades bedded down the main flock and the lambs for the night. At sunrise the following morning, the cycle of herding, milking, and cheese-making began again; and every evening the retiring *etxekandere* descended and the new *neskato* ascended.

During the milking season, every *etxekandere* was obliged to record the amount of milk yielded by the communal flock before he made his cheese. For every kilogram of milk one notch was cut into a small stick, which was itself called *txotx*. Shepherds who are now in their eighties recalled having observed this practice in their youth.

In keeping with local tradition, all milking and cheese-making ceased on Sainte-Madeleine (22 July). On or shortly before this day, all the *olha* members gathered in the hut for the *olha-barreia*, the 'dispersion' of the *olha*.[4] The primary purpose of this ritual meeting was to ensure that no member received more or less mountain cheese than his comrades.

In some *olhak* the shepherds counted the number of notches on their sticks in order to determine which of them had received less milk and consequently had made smaller cheeses than their companions. As the old shepherds now observe, the comparison of sticks and counting of notches were ritual gestures; for years of experience have taught them that the first and last cheese-makers of the season are at an extreme disadvantage. During the first few days of the cheese-making season, the ewes are exhausted as a result of their arduous journey and consequently give less than their normal amount of milk. The daily yield also decreases during the last few days of the season as the number of non-lactating ewes increases. The weight of the first and last two cheeses is often one kilo less than that of the other cheeses, which now weigh eight or nine kilos.

The first and last cheese-makers were compensated for their losses in one of two ways. In some *olhak* the other members gave them equal portions of their own mountain cheeses. In other syndicates all the cheeses were weighed and divided equally among the shepherds with a *txotx* of ewes. Men with only a half-*txotx* (twenty-five or thirty milking ewes) received exactly half as many cheeses as those with a full *txotx*.

After the *olha-barreia* and the cessation of the cheese-making season, the flocks descended to the valley for the shearing. On the following day they returned to their mountain pasturage, and the 'sterile, non-lactating' (*antxü*) season began. From the time of this second ascent until the end of September, the *olha* members continued to rotate (*üngüratü*) up and down the mountains; but they did so in pairs, constituted by neighbouring roles such as *etxekandere/*

---

[4] See Peillen and Peillen (1965) for another account of the *olha-barreya* (*barreia*) and the traditional organization of roles within the hut.

master shepherd, rather than singly. For the duration of the *antxü* season, there were only two shepherds in the hut on any given day or night.

II

The concepts of *aldikatzia* (in the sense of serial replacement) and *üngürü* (rotation) are crucial to an understanding of the *olha* as a system, and of the ordering of relationships within that system.[5]

The word *üngürü* is employed in the sense of rotation; but it also denotes the circumference of a place or object, a circuit, a circle. The verb form *üngüratü* means to surround, to encompass, to encircle, to rotate, as well as to recite the rosary.

During the period of summer transhumance, the shepherds are said to be 'in the *olha* rotation' (*olhan üngüria*). Like the gift of blessed bread, shepherds are conceived as moving up and down (*gora-behera*) and from left to right (*eskerretik eskuñilat*) as they ascend and descend; they rotate in a clockwise direction. In the traditional *olha* system, the shepherd who became the 'female servant' ascended (*gora igan*) the mountains to the right (*eskuñilat*), whereas the shepherd who finished his duties as *etxekandere* descended to the left (*eskerrilat eraitsi beheralat*). In the rotation of both blessed bread and shepherds, up is associated with movement to the right and down with movement to the left. In both cases the people visualize movement from left to right as if they were looking outwards from the centre of the cycle.

Like the *etxekanderak* in the valley who replaced one another serially as givers of blessed bread, the shepherds replaced one another serially as they progressed through the cycle of hierarchical roles. The order in which they did so, as well as the order in which they rotated up and down the mountains, was fixed according to the households that they represented. For example, the shepherd from the house Arospide has always been preceded by the one from Motolibarr and followed by the shepherd from Soccorots.

The fixed order in which shepherds progressed through the hierarchical roles in the hut and rotated up and down the mountains determined which of the *olha* members would act as the first cheese-making *etxekandere* of the transhumant season. In Sainte-Engrâce this role was, and still is, regarded as the most privileged of all. In the traditional *olha* system, the shepherd who served as the first

[5] The general importance of these two principles in Sainte-Engrâce society is a subject for Chapter XIII, in which a summary of their various uses will be provided.

Year I		Year II
shepherds	order of rotation	shepherds
A	first *etxekandere* of the season	B
B	second	C
C	third	D
D	fourth	E
E	fifth	F
F	sixth	G
G	seventh	H
H	eighth	I
I	ninth	J
J	tenth	A

Fig. 6. Traditional order of rotation in the *olha*

etxekandere one year was last in line the following year. As Figure 6 shows, each shepherd moved up one place in the fixed order of rotation every year. With ten members and ten *txotx* in the *olha*, each man was accorded the privilege of being first *etxekandere* of the season once every ten years. The shepherds have a clear notion of the time it took for the cycle to be completed in their syndicate.

Figure 7 is a diagrammatic representation of serial replacement with ten shepherds progressing through the six traditional hierarchical roles. For analytical purposes, I have assumed that each of the shepherds contributed a full *txotx* (fifty or sixty milking ewes) to the communal flock.

With ten *txotx* contributed by ten shepherds, every man spent six days in the hut and then four days in his house before ascending again. During the course of the cheese-making season (approximately sixty-seven days), shepherds C to J inclusive in Figure 7 had six turns to be *etxekandere* and each made a total of twelve cheeses. Shepherds A and B took a seventh turn as *etxekandere* at the very end of the milking season. These men were permitted to make a thirteenth cheese since neither one kept his first cheese of the season. Shepherd A made 'the chief cheese' (*majeko gazna*) that was later sold by him in the lowlands and from which every shepherd received an equal share of the profit. The second cheese of the season, made by shepherd B, was given either to the priest or to the guard of the forest.

In Figures 6 and 7 it was assumed that each shepherd had one full *txotx*. Although the majority of Sainte-Engrâce households formerly

roles	days										
	1	2	3	4	5	6	7	8	9	10	11
	shepherds										
etxekandere	A	B	C	D	E	F_1	G	H	I	J	A
artzain-nausi	B	C	D	E	F_1	G	H	I	J	A	B
artzain-mithil	C	D	E	F_1	G	H	I	J	A	B	C
antxüzain	D	E	F_1	G	H	I	J	A	B	C	D
axurzain	E	F_1	G	H	I	J	A	B	C	D	E
neskato	F_1	G	H	I	J	A	B	C	D	E	F_2

F_1 and F_2 are *txotx* partners

Fig. 7. Serial replacement with ten shepherds and six hierarchical roles

made a full *txotx* by themselves, some had only enough milking ewes to make a half-*txotx* (*txotx-erdi*), i.e. twenty-five or thirty ewes. In the traditional *olha* system every household with a half-*txotx* had a *txotx* partner (*txotx-lagün*) who also had only a half-*txotx*. Together the two households 'made *txotx*' (*txotx-egin*). In principle it was also possible to have two *txotx* partners, each of whom had a quarter-*txotx*, fifteen milking ewes; but I am told that households always had enough ewes to make at least a half-*txotx*.

The number of turns in the hut taken by a shepherd was determined by the number of milking ewes he contributed to the communal flock. A man with a full *txotx* was obliged to take the total number of possible turns (ten in Figure 7); but a shepherd with only a half-*txotx* took half that total number, e.g. three turns in Figure 7, and consequently made half as many cheeses as the man with a full *txotx*.

The order in which *txotx* partners rotated up and down the mountains was also fixed. Let us assume that two partners are represented by F in Figure 7. The first *txotx-lagün* (F_1) spent days 1 to 6 in the hut, beginning his turn as *neskato* and ending his stay as *etxekandere*. On the eleventh day his *txotx* partner (F_2) ascended to serve as *neskato* and also stayed in the hut six days. Four days passed between their respective six-day turns in the mountains; but these men spent fourteen rather than four days in the valley between turns.

In principle the *txotx-lagün* relationship was permanent. In practice a household with a half-*txotx* could change *txotx* partners, but this was done only when one's partner sold his half-share in the syndicate and moved to another group.

III

At the annual meeting of the *olha* in spring, *txotx* partners renewed their verbal agreement to contribute exactly twenty-five or thirty milking ewes to the communal flock. If one man had fewer than the required number, he was obliged either to buy or to lease the number of ewes he lacked in order to make his half-*txotx*. If his partner had more ewes than required, the shepherd generally bought or leased the beasts from him; but he could, if he wished, buy or rent the sheep from any other shepherd in the commune.

A shepherd generally leased the ewes if he expected that his own flock would soon provide him with enough female lambs to make his half-*txotx*. But if he lost many of his adult ewes as a result of a natural disaster (such as lightning) or disease that he was unable to check, the shepherd generally bought the ewes he lacked.

If a shepherd bought or leased the ewes from his *txotx* partner, the two men jointly decided upon the terms of the transaction and made an oral (*aho-mihiz*) agreement to abide by these. They agreed on a price or fee as well as the number of years the buyer/leaser could take to reimburse his partner. During that period the buyer/leaser— and not the owner of the beasts—was 'master' (*nausi*) of the ewes. If the shepherd leased the ewes, he paid his partner in cheese or cash for the *gozua* (the profit in wool, milk, and lambs derived from a ewe) yielded by the sheep.

If the shepherd bought or rented the ewes from someone else, he was obliged to follow the same procedure. An oral agreement was made; and if the beasts were leased, the shepherd was required to pay their owner for the *gozua* in the manner described.

Households can buy a full or half-share (*txotx* or *txotx-erdi* in sheep) from a household belonging to another *olha*. In the past it was also possible to lease a full or half-*txotx* for a certain period of time, agreed upon by the two households involved. Although the shepherds told me that their fathers and grandfathers were free to decide upon the duration of the lease, they repeatedly gave examples of leases that were held for periods of three, six, or nine years. Whether a man leased the sheep from his partner or from another shepherd, the final outcome was the same if he held a nine-year lease. At the end of the period, the leaser became the owner of the beasts; for it was reasoned that he had paid for them in cheese and cash.

IV

When asked why their predecessors took such pains to contribute an exact number of milking ewes, the shepherds now reason that the prescribed rules for 'making *txotx*' were based upon a notion that was fundamental to the traditional *olha* system—namely, that the members of the *olha* are 'equal-equal' (*bardin-bardina*) as givers and takers of milk from the communal flock, in the same manner as the *etxekanderak* of houses in the valley were 'equal-equal' as givers and takers of blessed bread.

Shepherds who 'made *txotx*' were also 'equal-equal' in status; for although the six roles were ordered hierarchically, relationships among individual shepherds were organized in such a manner that hierarchy in the *olha* could not exist. The systematic rotation of shepherds up and down the mountains and the serial transmission of hierarchical roles within the hut resulted in a set of consistently intransitive relationships among shepherds.

With six roles a minimum of ten shepherds with ten *txotx* was needed for the system to work. As Figure 7 shows, A is superior to F, his 'female servant', on day 1; F is superior to A, his 'female servant', on day 6; but A is not superior to the other shepherds (G, H, I, J) to whom F is superior during his stay in the hut. In the same manner, F is not superior to the shepherds to whom A is superior (B, C, D, E).

With six roles and more than ten shepherds in the syndicate, the following proposition applies: A is superior to F, his 'female servant', but is not superior to the five shepherds to whom F is superior during his turn as *etxekandere* (shepherds G, H, I, J, K in Figure 8). When the number of shepherds participating in the *olha* dropped below ten, the number of hierarchical roles was reduced accordingly so that the members would remain 'equal-equal' in status.

roles	days												
	1	2	3	4	5	6	7	8	9	10	11	12	13
	shepherds												
etxekandere	A	B	C	D	E	F	G	H	I	J	K	L	A
artzain-nausi	B	C	D	E	F	G	H	I	J	K	L	A	B
artzain-mithil	C	D	E	F	G	H	I	J	K	L	A	B	C
antxüzain	D	E	F	G	H	I	J	K	L	A	B	C	D
axurzain	E	F	G	H	I	J	K	L	A	B	C	D	E
neskato	F	G	H	I	J	K	L	A	B	C	D	E	F

Fig. 8. Serial replacement with twelve shepherds and six hierarchical roles

After Sainte-Madeleine, which marked the end of the milking and cheese-making season, the *olha* members rotated up and down the mountains in pairs. The order in which pairs of shepherds ascended and descended corresponded to the order in which they became *etxekandere*. The shepherds in Figure 6 were divided into the following pairs: AB, CD, EF, GH, IJ. During the non-lactating (*antxü*) season, each pair was obliged to spend six days in the hut on two separate occasions. Each pair spent twenty-four days in their houses between their first and second turns.

During the *antxü* period, two roles were alternated daily: *etxekandere* and *artzain-nausi*, 'the woman of the house' and the 'master shepherd'. The *etxekandere* assumed responsibility for all domestic work in the hut; whereas the *artzain-nausi* tended and herded the flocks.

V

Shepherds who are now in their eighties and nineties began their careers just as the traditional organization of the *olha* started to change. Many of them recalled having seen six shepherds in the hut during their apprenticeships; but by the turn of the century the six traditional hierarchical roles had been reduced to five in every syndicate. According to the old shepherds, there were neither enough shepherds nor enough sheep for the traditional system to operate. The first of the six roles to become redundant was the *antxüzain*, guardian of the non-lactating ewes.

From approximately 1900 until the 1930s, five roles were alternated daily in the huts of the Sainte-Engrâce *olhak*: the female servant, the guardian of the lambs, the servant shepherd, the master shepherd, and the *etxekandere*. As the shepherds who participated in the five-role system have realized, these five roles had to be circulated among a minimum of eight men in order to ensure that their status remained 'equal-equal'. With eight shepherds and eight full *txotx*, A was superior to E when the former served as *etxekandere* in Figure 8; E was superior to A during his turn as cheese-maker. But A was not superior to the other three shepherds (F, G, H) to whom E was superior as *etxekandere*, nor was E superior to the three (B, C, D) to whom A was superior.

With more than eight shepherds progressing through the five roles, the following proposition held: A was superior to E but was not superior to any of those to whom E was superior when he served as *etxekandere*. (See Figure 9.)

With eight shepherds representing eight *txotx* and progressing

roles	days									
	1	2	3	4	5	6	7	8	9	10
	shepherds									
etxekandere	A	B	C	D	E	F	G	H	I	A
artzain-nausi	B	C	D	E	F	G	H	I	A	B
artzain-mithil	C	D	E	F	G	H	I	A	B	C
axurzain	D	E	F	G	H	I	A	B	C	D
neskato	E	F	G	H	I	A	B	C	D	E

Fig. 9. Serial replacement with nine shepherds and five hierarchical roles

through five roles, each man spent five days in the hut and then three days in his house before ascending again during the milking season. Shepherds with only a half-*txotx* spent five days in the hut and eleven days in their houses. During the *antxü* period, the eight men rotated between the hut and valley in pairs.

In the 1940s the number of roles was reduced to four in most *olhak*. During the milking and cheese-making season, a minimum of six shepherds took turns playing the following roles: *neskato* (female servant), *artzain-mithil* (servant shepherd), *artzain-nausi* (master shepherd), and *etxekandere*. Although only six shepherds were required, nearly all the *olhak* had eight active members in the 1940s and 1950s. As in all the other examples given, the principle of serial replacement (*aldikatzia*) ordered relationships among the members. With eight shepherds progressing through four roles, each man spent four days in the hut and four days in his house between turns. A shepherd with a half-*txotx* spent four days in the hut and twelve days in his house.

In Sentolha the four hierarchical roles were circulated daily during the cheese-making season until 1975, when the number of active members decreased from six (the minimum needed to maintain 'equal-equal' relationships with four hierarchical roles) to five and the men jointly decided to disband. One other option available to them—but which they did not favour—would have been to reduce the number of roles circulated among them to three or to two; but in doing so, they would have been unable to maintain 'equal-equal' relationships. (With three hierarchical roles, this can be achieved only if there are exactly four shepherds.)

In all the other *olhak* the number of hierarchical roles was reduced to three in the 1960s. During this period, these *olhak* had more than four active members, i.e. with three roles they were unable to organize their relationships in such a manner that a hierarchy could not exist. Furthermore, for the first time, not all the syndicates retained the same three roles. Seven of the *olhak* classified their three men in the hut as female servant, master shepherd, and *etxekandere*; but in two syndicates the 'female' classificatory names were dropped. The cheese-making shepherd was referred to as the master shepherd (*artzain-nausi*). The second man to ascend was classified as *artzaiña*, the generic term for shepherd; and the third man was called *axurzain*, guardian of the lambs. The men who belong to these *olhak* were unable to tell me why they suddenly dispensed with the two 'female' terms of reference. The cheese-making master shepherd performed all of the tasks traditionally assigned to the *etxekandere* and his female servant: he did all the domestic chores in the hut, cooked the food, washed the utensils, made cheese, and cared for the cheeses made earlier in the season. Like the *etxekandere* in the traditional *olha*, the master shepherd played an exclusively feminine role.

With the exceptions of Erainze, Lacourde, and Hilague (only one household is regularly active in each of the latter two), the *olhak* now have only two men in their huts on any given day during the cheese-making season; but even with only two shepherds relationships among *olha* members are still ordered by the principle of *aldikatzia*. The order in which shepherds ascend to become *etxekandere* is fixed according to households, as it was in the past; but, for reasons unknown to me and the shepherds, the order has been reversed. In the traditional order of rotation represented in Figure 6, the man who served as first *etxekandere* of the season one year dropped back into last place the following year. In the present system, the first *etxekandere* of the season one year occupies position 2 in the cycle the following year, when the last shepherd in line becomes first *etxekandere*.

Although the number of shepherds in the hut was reduced to two in the 1970s, four of the six traditional roles have been retained in most syndicates. One man serves as both *etxekandere* and master shepherd (*artzain-nausi*) while his partner serves as his female servant (*neskato*) and servant shepherd (*artzain-mithil*).

Although the principles ordering the system and relationships within the system have remained the same, the manner in which shepherds rotate up and down the mountains now differs slightly from one *olha* to another. In *olhak* such as Ayzessaria, members ascend and descend singly, as was done in the traditional system; but in Ligoleta, shepherds now rotate between the valley and the hut in pairs during the cheese-making season.

roles	days								
	1	2	3	4	5	6	7	8	9
	shepherds								
etxekandere/artzain-nausi	A	B	C	D	E	F	G	H	A
neskato/artzain-mithil	B	C	D	E	F	G	H	A	B

Fig. 10. Serial replacement in Ayzessaria

In *olhak* whose members rotate one by one, relationships among individual shepherds are ordered by serial replacement. In these syndicates, as in the traditional *olha*, shepherds do not alternate in performing their pastoral roles during the cheese-making season. (See Figure 10.)

In Ayzessaria, as in the other syndicates, all of the active members ascend to their hut on the first day of the transhumant season; but only two remain there on the first night—the first two *etxekanderak* of the year. With the milk yielded by the flock after their journey, the first *etxekandere*, i.e. the man who occupies position 1 in the fixed order of rotation, makes the first cheese, which he later sells on behalf of his *olha*. The shepherd who occupies position 2 acts as his female servant within the hut; he washes the milking utensils, carries water from the spring to the hut, and chops firewood. But, as in the past, it is the *etxekandere* who cooks and serves their meal.

On the morning of the second day the two men rise at 6 a.m. and set out in the darkness to round up the sheep for the first milking of the day. Both men milk, and then the *etxekandere* prepares a breakfast of eggs, bacon or ham, bread, and wine. After having eaten, he descends to the valley; and his female servant/shepherd servant becomes the second *etxekandere*/master shepherd of the season.

As master shepherd, he is expected to take the flock to one edge of his *olha* pasturage and to stay with the sheep as they gradually move back toward the hut. One of his primary responsibilities is to ensure that they do not graze too close to any of the numerous precipices and gorges or suddenly head for the trail leading to the valley below. The oldest and most experienced ewes in the flock know exactly where the trail lies; and during a cold, wet summer they turn instinctively toward the valley and must be watched closely. In 1977 approximately sixty adult ewes from one *olha* evaded the unwary eye of their master shepherd on two separate occasions in August and were found waiting at the gates of their respective barns.

For some Ayzessaria shepherds who recall the hard work and constant, lively male camaraderie of the traditional *olha*, life in the hut now seems lonely and boring. The master shepherd guides the flock back to the hut at midday, prepares and eats his dinner by himself, and then moves the flock to another corner of the pasturage.

In the middle of the afternoon, the monotony is broken by the arrival of the third shepherd, who assumes the role of 'female' and 'male servant'. He and the *etxekandere*/master shepherd drive the flock toward the corral, cut the lactating ewes from the other sheep, and milk them. The *etxekandere* makes his second cheese, and then the two men move the sheep to another part of the grazing land and remain there until sunset.

In the evening the sheep gather around the hut. The *etxekandere* prepares supper, and the two men spend the next few hours sitting beside the fire chatting, smoking, and drinking wine from their goatskin flasks. On some occasions they may leave the hut after the *etxekandere* has made his cheese and walk to the bar in Spanish Basque Navarra which lies approximately four kilometres from the Ayzessaria hut. Shepherds from different *olhak* often call in at one another's hut when they pass between the bar and their own respective huts; and it seems to me that the joviality of these gatherings recaptures some sense of the former way of life enjoyed by men during the period of summer transhumance.[6]

On the morning of the third day, the two men drive the lactating ewes into the corral and milk them. After breakfast the retiring *etxekandere*/master shepherd descends to the valley and is replaced by the third shepherd in the manner described.

In Ayzessaria, as in all of the other *olhak*, shepherds who change pastoral roles, either by retiring to the valley or by assuming a new role in the hut, are said to *aldikatü*. As I have explained, the Basque concept of *aldikatzia* covers both alternation and serial replacement, as these are understood in English. In Sainte-Engrâce, persons who alternate in performing roles or providing services and those who serially replace one another are all said to *aldikatü*.[7]

---

[6] These boisterous gatherings are a common occurrence. If a day passes in the hut and no visitors arrive, the shepherds complain about the lonely life they lead. Although visitors are given ample amounts of wine (and return the favour in kind), they are not fed. On one occasion when we saw two Licq shepherds approaching the hut, the *etxekandere* of the evening suddenly hid all the food we had been eating. We sat around the fire and waited silently for our guests. I cannot explain the extraordinary behaviour of the *etxekandere*; but I have seen women act in a similar manner when unexpected visitors arrived at the end of a meal.

[7] *Aldikatü*, in the sense of 'to alternate', is conceptually distinct from *ordarizkatu*, 'to reciprocate, to exchange reciprocally, to compensate, to recompense', though persons

In Ayzessaria, as in the traditional *olha*, relationships among shepherds are ordered by serial replacement (*aldikatzia*) and are asymmetric. But in the *olha* Ligoleta, an interesting structural transformation has taken place. During the cheese-making season, Ligoleta shepherds rotate between the valley and their hut in pairs. The relationship between partners in a given pair is ordered by alternation; but relationships between pairs are ordered by serial replacement. (See Figure 11.)

During the cheese-making season, each of the three pairs of Ligoleta shepherds spends two consecutive nights in the hut every turn. These pairs are formed according to the position of the shepherds' households in the fixed order of rotation, i.e. the composition of these pairs changes annually as shepherds occupying positions 1 through 5 drop back one place in the fixed order of rotation and the shepherd occupying position 6 one year assumes position 1 the following year. In 1977 two pairs of shepherds also claimed that they rotated together that year because they are *txotx* partners. Even though shepherds are no longer obliged to contribute a fixed number of milking ewes to the flock, as were *txotx* partners in the traditional *olha* system, these Ligoleta men have retained the *txotx-lagünak* relationship but have altered its nature. Rather than taking separate turns in the hut, as was done in the past, Ligoleta *txotx* partners now take their turns together. It will be interesting to see how the Ligoleta shepherds reorganize themselves when one of them retires and has no son or son-in-law to replace him.

Like the Ayzessaria shepherd, the Ligoleta shepherd who makes cheese and who is in charge of domestic activities within the hut is referred to as *etxekandere*; outside the hut he plays a masculine role as master shepherd (*artzain-nausi*). Inside the hut his partner acts as female servant (*neskato*); outside the hut he plays a masculine role as servant shepherd (*artzain-mithil*).

As Figure 11 shows, the shepherds within a given pair alternate (*aldikatü*) in performing the roles *etxekandere/artzain-nausi* and *neskato/artzain-mithil*; whereas pairs of shepherds replace one another serially (*aldikatü*).

For at least the past five years the milking and cheese-making season in the mountains has averaged only four or five weeks; it is roughly half as long as it was during the first quarter of this century. This can be attributed partly to the increasing interest among the

and households who *ordarizkatzen* may in fact alternate in providing goods, services, and, in the case of *haurr-ordarizka*, marriage partners. *Ordarizkatu* is never used in the context of *olha* roles and relationships.

roles	days						
	1	2	3	4	5	6	7
	shepherds						
etxekandere/artzain-nausi	A	B	C	D	E	F	A
neskato/artzain-mithil	B	A	D	C	F	E	B

Fig. 11. Alternation and serial replacement in Ligoleta

shepherds to sell their milk for high profits and for a longer period of time; but the men also claim that their milking season is shorter because the ewes come into heat, lamb, and stop lactating earlier than they did in the past.

In 1977 the cheese-making season of Ligoleta lasted thirty-one days. Ligoleta shepherds spend two days in their hut and then four days in their houses between turns during the milking and cheese-making period. In 1977 the first two shepherds to ascend took six turns, and the other members took five. On their sixth turn the first two men made one cheese each, so that by the end of the season they had made a total of twelve cheeses. The two cheeses made on the last day of the milking/cheese-making season compensated the first two shepherds for the cheeses they made for the *olha* and the guard of the forest. All other shepherds made ten cheeses each.

When the milking season ends in Ligoleta, the Licq sheep are amalgamated with those of Ligoleta, and the two *olhak* take turns tending their combined flock on a weekly basis. During the first week of the non-lactating period, the Ligoleta shepherds rotate up and down the mountains one by one. Each man spends two days and two nights in the hut by himself. During the second week, the Licq men are in charge of the hut and flock.

Now that the milking and cheese-making season ends some time between 18 and 25 June, the non-lactating period generally lasts about twelve weeks, seven of which the Ligoleta shepherds spend in the hut. (The Licq flock generally returns to the valley one or two weeks before that of Ligoleta.) In that seven-week period most of the Ligoleta shepherds take five two-day turns in the hut before their combined flock descends in late September. Unlike the cheese-making season, which is not terminated until every member has made the same number of cheeses, the non-lactating period may end before all the shepherds have taken their five turns. The date of descent depends solely upon the weather and the first snowfall.

In 1978, when snow remained in the mountains until mid-June,

Ligoleta and several other *olhak* were unable to make mountain cheese. Much to their dismay, they had to keep their flocks in the valley during the milking season and to rest content with making cheese in their houses. The flocks were, however, taken up to the *olhak* in late June for the non-lactating period. In Ligoleta, positions in the fixed order of rotation were assumed in the usual way during this period and as if the shepherds had been rotating during the cheese-making season. Since no one had been able to make mountain cheese in 1978, positions in the fixed order for 1978 remained the same in Ligoleta during the 1979 season, so that the shepherd who ought to have been first *etxekandere* in 1978 would not lose his turn.

In 1979 a Sohotolatze shepherd kept his sheep in the valley during the entire transhumant season and did not participate in his *olha*. At their annual meeting three of his colleagues also decided to keep their flocks in the valley, but only for the duration of the milking season; they wanted to sell their milk rather than make mountain cheese. There were, however, two Sohotolatze shepherds who wanted to pasture their flocks in the mountains for the entire transhumant season and to make mountain cheese. Their colleagues granted permission for them to do so at the annual meeting. During the cheese-making season, these two shepherds took turns tending and milking their combined flocks and making mountain cheese. Each man spent two days in the *olha* and then two days in the valley between turns. When the non-lactating period began, the other three active members took their flocks up to the *olha*. The five shepherds assumed their positions for the 1979 season in the fixed order of rotation and took turns tending the flock until the sheep descended in mid-September. Each of the five men spent two days in the hut and then eight days in the valley between turns. The system was not allowed to break down during either the cheese-making or the non-lactating season.

In 1979 an early snowstorm in mid-September forced all but two households to return their flocks to the valley. In the *olha* Anhaou, two shepherds managed to keep their sheep in the mountains in spite of the snow, which melted after a few days. According to the unwritten law of the *olha*, shepherds must continue to take turns in the hut even if the flock of only one member remains in the mountains. Although two of the four Anhaou shepherds had taken their own sheep back down to the valley when the snowstorm began, they were obliged to continue to take their turns in the hut until the flocks of their two colleagues descended to the valley in late September. They took their turns without complaint.

VI

In syndicates such as Ligoleta, Ayzessaria, and Sohotolatze, the shepherds manipulated the traditional structure of *olha* relationships as the number of members decreased and have managed to survive as permanent corporations in which pastoral roles are systematically ordered. But in the three *olhak* which no longer make mountain cheese, the *olha,* as a system, has begun to break down. In these syndicates no distinction is made between a milking and a non-lactating season; none of the traditional pastoral roles within the hut is recognized or performed; on any given day, there is only one shepherd in the huts of these three *olhak.* But the principle of rotation still orders the manner in which the members of these syndicates ascend and descend.

The *olha* Erainze serves as a good example. In this syndicate the order in which shepherds take their turns depends upon the number of sheep that they own. The order is decided upon at their annual meeting in the spring. According to the size of their flocks, the members are assigned certain days when they are obliged to be in the hut. Since the five Sainte-Engrâce households in Erainze have much smaller flocks than the average Haux household, they are consequently required to spend less time in the hut than their Haux comrades. For example, two Haux men with flocks of more than 120 sheep were obliged to spend a total of nine days in the hut during the summer of 1977. The Sainte-Engrâce shepherds spent only five or six days there. Those obliged to spend six days in the hut took two turns consisting of three consecutive days. The days on which these turns were taken were decided upon at the annual meeting of the syndicate. Although Erainze now bears little resemblance to the traditional *olha,* the rotation of its members is nevertheless systematically ordered.

From the point of view of the other Sainte-Engrâce shepherds, syndicates such as Erainze have lost their primary reason for existing: they no longer make mountain cheese. When the Erainze men take their flocks to the mountains, the ewes are already *antxü,* sterile, neither lactating nor carrying lambs. In Erainze no distinction is made between a lactating (*ardi-jeixten*) and non-lactating (*antxü*) period. The shepherd in charge of the flock is responsible only for herding and caring for them; and he does so without any *lagünak,* comrades and assistants.

The division of the transhumant season into the lactating and non-lactating periods is an ideologically important one. In the traditional *olha*, the point of transition separating the two was the *olha-barreia*, the ritual dispersal of the cheeses on Sainte-Madeleine. The verb form *barreiü* means not only 'to disperse' but also 'to be disordered'.

With the cessation of milking and cheese-making in the mountains, the cycle of ovine fertility, productivity, male sociability, and (as I shall explain) male procreativity ends. In some *olhak* the termination of this period is still dramatically expressed by the descent of the flocks to the valley for the shearing. When the flocks ascend again, the period of sterility, unproductivity, and as the shepherds often complain, the time of loneliness begins.

XI. SHEPHERDING AND CHEESE-MAKING

I

TOWARDS his ewes and lambs a shepherd must have the patience (*pazientzia*) of a woman towards her children. According to the men of Sainte-Engrâce, sheep actively seek affection and require attention from their master. Like some children, sheep are fickle; they may develop a sudden, strong dislike for a particular pasture and refuse to graze there. As autumn draws near in the mountains, the ewes may seem settled and content one moment and then rush toward the trail leading to the valley below. Ewes may also behave in a fickle manner with regard to rams; one year the beasts may accept a particular ram, and then reject him in the next rutting season.

In Sainte-Engrâce, ewes are considered to be intelligent beasts by virtue of their *asmia*, instinct. They know when a storm or snow shower is imminent and will seek shelter of their own accord. They know instinctively where the trail to the valley, their winter pastures, and the barns lie. By virtue of their *asmia*, ewes also know when a stranger is present and will resist his attempts to milk them.

Sainte-Engrâce shepherds are characteristically indulgent toward their ewes, especially during the lambing season. When the beasts are roused in the morning and bedded down at night, their master often spends an hour or so talking to them and stroking their backs and heads. A 'good shepherd' always gives his animals a pinch of salt as a treat when he has finished milking them.

Even as the ewes know their master, he in turn knows every one of them, generally by name. Sheep are usually named according to distinctive physical features, such as a black spot on the forehead or the shape of the horns. The shepherds claim that their intimate knowledge of their own flock—as well as of the flocks of their *olha* partners—enables them to see at once when and which ewes have gone astray.

The most common and prized breed is the *bürü-xuri*, 'white head', which is unique to Soule. The pure 'white head' is closely related to the slightly larger Béarnais sheep. Both breeds are raised primarily for their milk and are readily recognizable by their large roman noses and protruding wide-set eyes. A pure *bürü-xuri* is entirely white, has large floppy ears and long, slim legs. Its body is considerably longer than that of any British breed. Both sexes are horned. The fleece of a 'white head' is coarse and averages three to four centimetres in length before shearing. An adult ewe yields approximately two kilos of wool per year; but because of its texture, the wool brings a low price on the market. In 1977 the shepherds received only 3 fr 50 per kilo from the Saint Palais buyers who visit the commune every September.

Four breeds have been crossed with the native *bürü-xuri*; the Béarnais, *manexa* (a black-faced sheep common to Basse-Navarre), *anglesa* ('English' sheep), and the merino. The first two are well suited to the mountain terrain and climate of the region. When the four breeds are crossed with the 'white head', their offspring are referred to as 'bastards' (*bastartak*). The Béarnais 'bastard' is regarded as the best milker of the cross-breeds. The short-legged stocky merinos are not milked. They were introduced into the community a few years ago by two shepherds who wished to improve the quality of meat and wool yielded by their flocks. In 1977 two *olhak* had at least two merino rams in their communal flock. The offspring of these rams are sold as lambs.

With the exception of one or two rams, the flock owned by a household consists entirely of ewes, the generic term for which is *ardiak*. In addition to being identified by name, the ewes are classified by their master according to two criteria which tend to coincide: the number of teeth and the number of seasons a beast has spent in the mountains.

From its birth until its first ascent a female lamb is referred to as an *axuri*. The term *ürrüxa*, 'female', distinguishes it from a male lamb (*aharia*). After its first descent a female *axuri* becomes a *bildotxa*. When the beast has made its second ascent, has two teeth, and has had its first lamb, it is classified as a *lehentxa* or, less commonly, as a *bihortzak*, literally 'two teeth'. When the ewe has made its third ascent it becomes a *lauhortzak*, 'four teeth'. A ewe with six teeth that has made its fourth ascent is a *seihortzak*. When the beast has ascended to the mountain pasturage a fifth time, it is classified as an *artzarra*, an 'old ewe'. An *artzarra* generally continues to lamb and to be taken to the hut until it is seven or eight years old. Some shepherds have *artzarrak* that are ten years old, but these are regarded as exceptional animals in a commendatory sense and are prized on account of the volume of milk they yield. An old ewe is usually slaughtered or sold after its eighth season in the mountains.

When a ewe is carrying a lamb, it is classified as an *ernaria*. The word *ernai*, 'pregnant', is applied solely to animals. A pregnant woman is *izorra*. A ewe that is neither carrying a lamb nor giving milk is referred to as an *antxüa* (or *antzüa*). The adjective *antxü* means 'sterile, temporarily incapable of producing offspring and/or milk'; and it is applied exclusively to female livestock in Sainte-Engrâce. An infertile woman is classified as *dehota*.

There are only two terms for male sheep in the local dialect. An *aharia* is a male lamb or young ram. An adult ram, i.e. one which has made its second ascent, is called *marrua*. So far as I know, there is no term for a ram that successfully induces pregnancy in a ewe; but the word *xixkla* is applied to both rams and men who fail to make a fertile female pregnant after repeated intercourse.

The cycle of ovine productivity begins with the rutting season when the ewes come in heat (*ardi-arkhara*). This period generally begins in mid-July and often lasts until September. In most *olha* flocks there is one ram per twenty-five to thirty ewes. Rutting takes place in the mountains and coincides with the *antxü* or sterile, non-lactating period.

The first signs of pregnancy appear two months after mating. Ewes rarely remain *antxü* after the rutting season; but if this occurs, the shepherd is often teasingly asked whether the fault rests with a *xixkla* ram or *xixkla* master, i.e. the virility of the shepherd is jokingly contested.

The period of gestation lasts five months. During this time, the ewes are watched closely by the shepherd, who knows virtually to the day when each ewe is due to give birth. The first lambs are born in early November. Although a man has no control over the mating of his beasts, his expertise as a shepherd is judged by the number of lambs his ewes bear in that month. In some households the lambing season does not end until late January or early February.

Unless the winter is unusually mild, the ewes are rarely released from their barn if they are carrying or suckling lambs. Ewes that have given birth are segregated from the others in an enclosed stall and are fed the best hay in order to increase the quantity of their milk.

During the lambing season, a shepherd may spend several nights watching and assisting his ewes. Although the shepherds are highly skilled midwives, they refuse to perform a caesarean section. If this is required, the ewe is taken to the veterinary surgeon in Mauléon. The shepherds claim that they are not squeamish about the blood expelled at birth by a ewe; but the very idea of opening the womb of a living animal is repugnant to them, and they cannot bear to see a ewe suffer. (On one occasion in 1977 the men were deeply grieved and horrified when a woman pulled out the entrails of a ewe as well as the lamb. Her husband was in hospital at the time, and her son knows nothing about sheep. She ought to have asked a male 'first neighbour' to take charge of her ewes during the lambing season.)

One of the first tasks of a shepherd is to train a new-born lamb to recognize its mother and to suckle. Ewes that reject their offspring are placed in a small stall, and a shepherd may spend hours coaxing it to accept its young. The same gentle treatment is given to a ewe that is 'asked' to suckle an orphan lamb in addition to its own. A foster mother is also found for a twin that has been rejected by its own mother.

Lambs of both sexes are evaluated at birth according to their strength, physical appearance, and liveliness. Only one or two of the male lambs are kept if the shepherd needs to replace one of his adult rams. Most shepherds choose males that are either pure *bürü-xuri* or Béarnais 'bastards'. All other male lambs and females judged to be weak and/or ugly are sold. The largest and most profitable market takes place just before Christmas, when prices range from 12 to 15 francs per kilo. The lambs are weighed before the bargaining begins. Live weights range from eleven to fifteen kilos. The majority of the men take their stock to the Tardets market. Some use the one in Mauléon, where prices are sometimes higher. Nearly all the buyers are Basques, and they attend both markets.

Prices at the Easter market are considerably lower than those at the Christmas one. January lambs sold in March or April may bring only 9 francs per kilo. Most households prefer to set aside late lambs for their own use.

Female lambs judged to be both strong and beautiful are kept in the barn for about six weeks after birth. They are weaned when they are two to three months old; and the shepherd clips the wool from their mothers' tails (*ilhe markisatzen*) in preparation for the milking time (*jeixt denbora*) in the valley. The date on which this season begins varies greatly from household to household, depending upon the month when the bulk of the lambs were born. Shepherds whose lambs were born in early November may start to milk at Christmas; but most men do not do so until mid-January.

At present most of the milk yielded from January until April is sold. According to the elderly men and women, the shepherds first sold their milk in approximately 1923. For a period of roughly ten years, their milk was bought and then resold by a Licq *ramasseur*. In 1933 the Roquefort Society arranged to buy the Sainte-Engrâce milk through an enterprising local woman who later became postmistress of the commune. She acted as the *ramasseuse* until the beginning of the Second World War, when the German occupation severely restricted the movements of the Sainte-Engrâce people. After the war, the Society re-established its commercial ties with the community and maintained these until 1976, when the shepherds decided to sell their milk to a Béarnais *fromagerie* which offered a higher price. This *fromagerie* sends a refrigerated lorry to the commune once every two days from January until mid-April. During the first three months of this period, they paid the shepherds 3 fr. 45 per litre. From late March until April, they offered only 3 fr. 25 per litre, but this was generally regarded as a very good price.

Since this *fromagerie* does not collect the milk every day, as the Roquefort Society did, the shepherds had two options: to purchase an electrically powered cooler in which they could store their milk, or to convert all their milk into cheese. In the upper community, many shepherds decided to purchase a cooler with their *txotx* partner. In some cases, two shepherds who are 'first neighbours' but belong to different *olhak* jointly purchased the device. Those partners living in the same settlement or neighbourhood agreed to move their cooler from one house to the other half-way through the milking season, so that they could take turns paying for the electricity. Partners whose houses are some distance apart generally leave the cooler in one house and later divide the cost of running it. One lower household decided that they could not easily afford a cooler, which costs several hundred francs. All their milk is made into 'house cheese' during the milking time in the valley. They sell roughly half their cheeses to the local hotel and to a wholesale buyer in Mauléon. One other lower household also converts all its milk into cheese. This household, which is now the sole active member of the *olha* Lacourde, has the largest flock (170 sheep) in the commune and makes well over a hundred cheeses every year. Roughly three-quarters of their cheeses are sold to Sainte-Engrâce households whose men do not make cheese or cannot make enough cheese to meet their own needs.

From January until April the ewes are milked twice daily by their shepherd: when he first rises in the morning and in the evening before supper. The milk is filtered through a cloth and is stored in the cooler. The *fromagerie* collects the milk after three milkings. The number of litres is recorded by the lorry driver in the shepherd's special booklet.

Shepherds who sell their milk to the *fromagerie* are bound by a written agreement not to add anything to the pure ewes' milk; but there have been a few cases in which either water or cows' milk was added and subsequently discovered by the *fromagerie*. Two men were fined and warned not to repeat their offence. One man was caught a second time, and the firm threatened never to buy his milk again. A heavier fine was imposed, and the culprit has been watched closely by the *ramasseur* ever since.

The milk yield increases steadily as the weather improves and the ewes are able to graze outdoors. In 1977 a shepherd with 76 ewes averaged only 12 litres per 3 milkings in January. The volume increased to 16 litres the following month. In March he received an average of 23 litres per 3 milkings; and in April this increased to 26 litres. Another shepherd, who has 70 ewes, had an average yield of 47 litres per 3 milkings. For shepherds who sell their milk during the four-month period, total profits range from 4,000 to 7,000 francs.

II

The Sainte-Engrâce shepherds make two kinds of hard ewes'-milk cheese: house cheese (*etxe gazna*) and mountain cheese (*bortü gazna*). The latter is thought to be infinitely superior to the former. They also make a soft, smooth curd cheese (*zümbera*) which resembles *fromage frais* in texture; but *zümbera* is not classified as cheese (*gazna*).[1]

House cheese is made in the kitchen of the shepherd's house during the milking season in the valley. In principle, house cheese-making is an exclusively male occupation that is performed by individual shepherds rather than by *olha* members; but two lower women (whose households do not sell any milk) occasionally make house cheese when their husbands are particularly busy with the livestock and/or agricultural work.

Unlike the mountain cheese-making season, which is rigorously ordered by the *olha* members, the house cheese-making season begins and ends at different times in Sainte-Engrâce households. A shepherd decides for himself when he will stop selling his milk and how much house cheese he will make. His decision is largely based upon the needs of his *etxenkuak*, which should take precedence over the attractive monetary profits that ewes' milk now brings. A shepherd with several children, a wife, and an elderly couple to feed generally makes his first house cheese in January and sells the milk every third or fourth time the *ramasseur* visits the commune. But if the winter is severe and the milk yield low, most shepherds do not

---

[1] I am interested not only in the making but also the meaning of cheese in Sainte-Engrâce society. Neither subject has received the full attention of ethnographers working in European societies.

make house cheese until late April or early May. The total number of house cheeses made by individual shepherds usually ranges from ten to twenty-five. (The household belonging to Lacourde is an exceptional case.) The members of the *olha* Erainze generally make twice as many house cheeses as the other shepherds since their syndicate no longer makes mountain cheese.

According to the shepherds, a minimum of six or seven litres of milk is needed to make one kilo of house cheese. The milk yielded by the ewes in the valley is regarded as 'thin' in comparison to milk given in the mountains. The shepherds reason that the alpine grass is much richer than that of the valley and consequently that mountain milk has a much higher fat content.

House cheeses are made from pure ewes' milk produced by the flock of the shepherd's household. The cheese is made once every three milkings; it is not marked with the special symbol of the household that is imprinted on every mountain cheese that a man makes.

House cheese-making is regarded as a household enterprise. If the ewes have not given enough milk to make a cheese after the third milking, a shepherd must risk making a small cheese (less than two kilos in weight) that will probably spoil before it has fully matured.

On one occasion in 1977 a shepherd broke convention by asking one of his 'first neighbours' to give him a few litres of milk for his cheese. The neighbour complied but harshly criticized the man for having failed to feed his own ewes properly and for having compensated his own loss in milk at the expense of his *aizoa*. The request for milk was sanctioned by gossip in the man's own neighbourhood for a few days.

On another occasion a shepherd asked a fellow *olha* member if he wanted to be his partner during the house cheese-making season. This too was regarded as extraordinary and unconventional behaviour. The shepherd argued that if they pooled their milk toward the end of the house cheese-making season they could both sell their milk later in the spring, increase their cash profits, and still make several house cheeses for their respective *etxenkuak*. The other shepherd rejected the proposal. In the valley, *olha* members are expected to fend for themselves as cheese-makers.

Mountain cheese is made in the hut from late May until mid- or late June. Unlike house cheese-making, mountain cheese-making is a collective enterprise which requires the full co-operation of all member shepherds. The milk yielded by the combined flocks of the *olha* is distributed equally among the members in the form of cheese.

At present two mountain cheeses are made every day in the hut during the 'milking time' (*jeixt denbora*): the first is made after the morning milking, the second after the late afternoon milking. The shepherds claim that only five litres of milk are needed to make one kilo of mountain cheese; but in practice they are able to use about seven litres per kilo.

In the mountains a ewe gives approximately half a litre per milking. An *olha* flock of 230 ewes yields roughly 57 litres at each milking. With this volume a shepherd can expect to make an eight- or nine-kilo cheese.

The total number of cheeses made in the hut varies from *olha* to *olha*. In 1977 one syndicate made 62 mountain cheeses, whereas another made only 32. Most men can expect to make 8 to 10 cheeses per season; but, as I explained previously, this depends largely upon the willingness of syndicate members to take their total number of turns in the hut.

The shepherds know well that mountain cheese brings a high price in the markets of south-western France; but, in 1976 and 1977, only two shepherds were interested in selling their *bortü gazna* at the cheese fair in Tardets which is held every August. Both men are members of Ligoleta. In 1977 each of them sold two mountain cheeses at the fair and received 37 francs per kilo. They were very pleased with their profits until they learned that pure ewes'-milk cheese was selling for 40 francs (roughly £4·50) in some supermarkets at that time.

The fair attracts a few Béarnais shepherds, but the majority of participants are Souletine Basques, among whom the cheese bartering generates considerable competition. In 1979 eight Sainte-Engrâce shepherds took cheeses to the fair. Four of them sold some of their house cheeses (none of them makes mountain cheese); one of them had both house and mountain cheeses; whereas the other three, all of whom belong to Ligoleta, took only mountain cheeses to the fair. In that year house cheese was sold for 40 francs per kilo; mountain cheese brought 45 francs per kilo.

In the main plaza of Tardets, the shepherds arranged their cheeses on one of the long wooden tables set up for the occasion. The Sainte-Engrâce men offering mountain cheese displayed them with considerable pride. To give potential buyers some idea of the quality of their *bortü gaznak*, they also exhibited a small portion of a mountain cheese taken from a cheese that their households were in the process of consuming. Prospective customers were invited to taste this cheese but were not allowed to buy it. The Sainte-Engrâce shepherds also refused to divide into portions any of their mountain cheeses that were for sale. They were determined to sell the latter *osorik*, 'intact', even though few customers that day wanted to purchase an eight- or nine-kilo cheese. The very idea of cutting up and dispersing a mountain cheese among several buyers was an anathema to them. As one shepherd argued, 'my mountain cheese would die if I sold it bit by bit'.

No mention was made of the possibility that a house cheese might die if not sold intact; and the Sainte-Engrâce shepherds with house cheeses at the fair were content to cut them up and to sell them in portions. Most of the house cheeses were sold; the majority of mountain cheeses were transported intact back to Sainte-Engrâce after the fair.

Mountain cheese is more than an important staple in the diet; in Sainte-Engrâce, it is also an object by which a man is judged as a shepherd and as a provider for his household. Within the neighbour-hood or *quartier* the social status of a man depends largely upon the quality of his mountain cheeses. Among the shepherds a mountain cheese is also one means of evaluating the sexual prowess of a man. A shepherd who knows how to make good *bortü gazna* is reckoned to be skilled at both causing and preventing the pregnancy of his wife.

A shepherd and his wife are extremely proud of his mountain cheeses. Unlike his house cheeses, to which the attention of visitors is never drawn, his mountain cheese is an object to be displayed and unabashedly admired by its maker. Mountain cheeses generate as much competition among the shepherds as do new-born infants among the women of this society. Even within the privacy of his household, a man rarely admits that another's cheese is better and more beautiful than his own. In much the same way, mothers and grandmothers are reluctant to compare their infant unfavourably to the offspring of another woman in the community.

Within the neighbourhood, competition among cheese-making shepherds is most intense during the autumn maize harvest. As I have explained in Chapter V, maize-husking is a major social event for *aizoak* and more distant neighbours; and it was, until 1978, one of the few occasions at which large groups of people gathered in one another's households. Since a man works for as many as five or six different households during the harvest, he has ample opportunity to judge the cheeses made by his fellow shepherds. (These men will enjoy the same opportunity when they work for him.)

When the men are fed by the host household, they expect to be served mountain cheese, not house cheese and certainly not cows'-

milk cheese. Since mountain cheese needs to be matured at least
five months, only the first cheese made that summer is ready to be
eaten.

During the harvest of 1976 one shepherd ignored conventional
expectations and attempted to serve his workers house cheese. A
piece of *etxe gazna* was placed on the table by the *etxekandere* and
was duly ignored by the shepherds. In spite of repeated petitions
from the hostess to 'take some cheese', the men merely sat with their
elbows on the table, opening and closing the pocket knives with
which they pare the rind. Finally one man queried in a loud, mocking
voice. 'Do the shepherds of this *olha* milk their ewes into the ground,
or do they make mountain cheese?' The other shepherds laughed
uproariously; their host squirmed uneasily on the bench and told his
wife to bring some mountain cheese. During the course of their stay,
the shepherds ate all of the mountain cheese that had been offered.
This is rarely done, since everyone knows how precious the cheese
is. But on that one occasion, the men were deliberately greedy in
order to punish the stinginess of their host.

When mountain cheese is served during the maize harvest, the
men engage in lively debates about its merits and faults. The cheese
is passed from shepherd to shepherd and is studied closely by each.
A cheese is judged by its colour, texture, taste, and rind. A good cheese
should have a 'white heart' (*bihotz xuri*). The heart is the interior of
the cheese. Between the heart and rind (*axal*) there should be a very
narrow dark line, which is said to form if the shepherd has cared for,
assisted (*soiñatu*) the cheese well. The texture of the cheese should be
dry and hard but not crumbly. A cheese with these qualities has
'bone' (*ezürra*), formed by the rennet. In taste a good mountain
cheese should be *azkarr*, which seems best translated as 'strong, full-
bodied'. (A full-bodied red wine is also *azkarr*.) If too much rennet
was used or if the milk was too hot when the rennet was added, the
cheese will be *borthitz*. This word is glossed by Lhande (1926: 180)
as *violent, fort, vigoureux*; but the people were not entirely satisfied
with these French terms since, for them, they can also be applied to
foods described as *azkarr* and *mingar* (which is itself best described
as the taste of hot red peppers). In their vocabulary of taste, *borthitz*
is applied to acidic foods such as tomatoes, to garlic, salt-cured ham,
and green peppers. House cheeses are much more commonly judged
to be *borthitz* than is mountain cheese.

Close attention is also paid to the texture and hardness of the rind.
The word *axal*, covering rind, crust, bark, peel, epidermis, is distinct
from *larrü*, the 'skin' which covers humans and animals. If the rind

has not been salted well enough, it remains slightly moist and has a gummy texture; and the heart of the cheese may well rot before maturation is complete. A soft, moist rind also results from the shepherd's failure to care for and to assist (*soiñatu*) the cheese by turning it at least once a day. The rind of a good cheese is hard, rather rough in texture, dry, and unblemished by holes and cracks. These last two faults are said to occur when the shepherd has amassed the substance (*materia*) of the milk too quickly in making his cheese.

A house cheese should be aged at least two months and a mountain cheese five months. If either cheese is eaten before it is mature, it is said to be green. A cheese which has been allowed to mature properly but in which too little rennet was used is judged to be 'dead' literally as well as in taste.

The faults that shepherds find in one another's mountain cheeses are mostly attributed to the manner in which the cheese was made, rather than to the place in which it was stored. But the men are also competitive about the relative merits of the cheese houses of their respective huts. Each cheese-making syndicate contends that its cheese house has the best *ideia* or atmosphere in which to mature cheese.

For most of the shepherds it would be an anathema to make cheese from cows' milk or from cow and ewes' milk, which are often mixed by neighbouring Basque and Béarnais shepherds. Only one Sainte-Engrâce shepherd, who was a rather unreliable informant, claimed to have mixed his milk for cheese-making. The people say that their cattle do not yield enough milk for cheeses; and they are convinced that even a small amount of cows' milk will adversely affect the rind, bone, and flavour of a ewes'-milk cheese. The elderly shepherds often cited Béarnais cheese as an example. One old man made the interesting observation that Béarnais mountain cheese formerly had a sweet (*ezti*) flavour because the huts there were covered with earth. The humid atmosphere reportedly had a profound effect upon the maturation process.

Most shepherds also have a low opinion of pure cows'-milk cheese; but in 1977, the *fromagerie* to which they sell their milk managed to sell some cows'-milk cheese to several households by offering it at a reduced price. The cheese was similar in flavour and texture to Camembert. Although the locals extolled the virtues of the price (13–15 francs per kilo), they did nothing but criticize the cheese itself, which was judged to be too soft and thin in flavour; but the most serious faults of the cheese were that it had no rind and consequently a 'short life' (*bizi laburr*). Several shepherds refused to eat it.

The relative merits and faults of Cheddar cheeses which I gave as gifts were also widely discussed. The English Cheddar was praised for its hard bone and long life; but the shepherds were sceptical about its cloth rind, which was not regarded as an *axal* at all. Some people found the cheese *borthitz*, too yellow in colour, and fit only to melt on cornmeal bread.

Since some shepherds cannot (or will not by choice) produce enough house and mountain cheese to last the entire year, they must buy cheese either from the lower household already mentioned or from a *fromagerie* in the lowlands. In 1977 several households tried the pure ewes'-milk cheese made by the Montory *fromagerie*. The Montory cheese has a flavour distinctly different from the Sainte-Engrâce mountain cheese. It was not well liked because it has a plasticized rind, rubbery texture, and a rather sweet flavour. As one elderly shepherd advised me, 'machines don't know how much rennet to put into the milk'.

III

In Sainte-Engrâce, house and mountain cheese are made in exactly the same way; but the shepherds exercise much greater care in both the making and maturation of their *bortü gaznak*. It is also clear that they enjoy making mountain cheese much more than house cheese. The physical and social atmosphere of the hut is thought to be more conducive to cheese-making than the house.

It takes approximately two hours to make one cheese and the soft curd by-product *zümbera*. The volume of milk used to make a house cheese ranges from eighteen to thirty-five litres. A mountain cheese is made from fifty to fifty-eight litres.

First, the shepherd strains the milk to remove any dirt. At present nearly all the men use a muslin cloth for this purpose. A few shepherds continue to employ the traditional method and use nettles. According to the elderly men, nettles 'washed' and 'purified' (*xahatü*) the milk more effectively than cloth.

In the mountains the milk is strained into metal containers (*khotxiak*) which have a capacity of roughly thirty litres. These containers are carried to the hut where the milk is poured into a large copper kettle (*bertza*), which holds a maximum of sixty litres. Formerly the shepherds carved their *khotxiak*, as well as a variety of other wooden utensils, from beech.

The kettle is placed on a gas ring or is suspended above an open fire from a wooden cross-beam. The shepherd starts stirring the milk immediately with his right forearm or a long wooden whisk (*tortilla*). The milk must be warmed evenly and gradually. All the shepherds whom I watched stirred in a clockwise direction.

The most crucial point of the entire process takes place during the first 'heating of the milk' (*ezne beroazi*). When the milk becomes almost too hot to touch, the shepherd adds his rennet (*presüra*). Unlike some shepherds, the Sainte-Engrâce men to not use thermometers to gauge the correct temperature. If the day or evening is cold, the shepherd soaks his arm in warm water before heating the milk, the temperature of which he may otherwise misjudge.

At present all the men buy their own bottle of rennet from either the chemist or the agricultural co-operative in Tardets. Until roughly ten years ago, they used the fourth stomach (*gatzagi*) of an unweaned male lamb. The mass of curdled milk in the stomach of unweaned lambs and calves contains the enzyme rennin, which converts the caseinogen of the milk into soluble casein (the principle albuminous constituent of milk). The soluble casein then unites with the lime salts in the milk, and curds begin to form. (*Encyclopaedia Britannica* 1955. See 'Nutrition'.) According to the shepherds, the rennet of the *gatzagi* had more *indarra* or force than the rennet they now purchase; and some men claim that the rennet sold by the co-operative has more *indarra* than that sold by the chemist.

In the traditional method of producing rennet, the *gatzagi* was hung to dry above the hearth in the kitchen and then wrapped in a cloth. The dried piece of stomach was sometimes softened in salt water before it was placed in the milk. Shepherds say that they used the same piece during the entire cheese-making season. In the hut each shepherd kept his *gatzagi* in his own special box along with his blessed candle, blessed laurel, and blessed water.

At present some men mix the rennet with a few tablespoons of water before adding it to the hot milk; but those who continue to embrace the 'old customs' of the *olha* prefer to use 'pure rennet'. Approximately one teaspoonful of rennet is used to make between five and eight kilos of cheese. Knowing exactly how much *presüra* to use and when to add it to the milk are the two most important skills of the cheese-maker.

When the rennet has been added, the shepherd stirs the milk rapidly and removes the kettle from the fire. A clean white cloth, draped over a wooden stick, is then placed on top of the kettle. Although Peillen and Peillen (1965: 55) report that it takes only thirty minutes for the milk to curdle properly, the Sainte-Engrâce shepherds allow at least one hour.

During that period, the *kaillatia* or curdled milk forms. The verb form *kaillatü* (also spelled *khallatu*) means to curdle, clot, congeal, coagulate. Lhande (1926: 577, 594) contends that this word applies only to milk; but in Sainte-Engrâce I heard people use the term to describe dried mucus, hailstones, and pig's blood that formed clots after the beast's throat was cut.[2] Although the people consistently employed the noun *kaillatia* when referring to the thick mass of curdled milk, they corrected me whenever I described the action of the rennet upon the milk as *kaillatü* or *kaillatürik* (-*ik* is a pluperfect suffix that the Sainte-Engrâce people commonly add to a transitive verb). They employ the verb forms *gatzatü* and *gatzatürik*.

According to Lhande (1926: 343) *gatza* conveys the general idea of coagulation and is derived from the Latin root *cas*, as in *cāseus*, 'cheese'. He glosses the verb *gatzatü* as 'to coagulate, curdle, harden, lose sensibility, to be conceived in the womb of the mother'. The Sainte-Engrâce people translated *gatzatü* as *cailler*, not as *coaguler*, *se durcir*, or *concevoir*; but, as I shall explain presently, a woman who has conceived is said to have been curdled.

When the milk has become *gatzatürik* or curdled, the shepherd draws the sign of the cross on the surface of the curdled milk (*kaillatia*) with the forefinger of his right hand. Those who continue to observe the 'old customs' invite any other shepherds in the hut to taste the *kaillatia*, which the cheese-maker lifts from the kettle in cupped hands.[3]

The kettle is then placed on the fire again. The shepherd stirs the curdled milk rapidly in a clockwise direction with his right forearm. As the liquid gathers heat, he must 'break up well' (*untsa xeheki*) the small lumps with his hands and fingers until the *kaillatia* is completely smooth. If the curd has not been broken up thoroughly, hard kernels form in the interior of the cheese.

It takes roughly twenty minutes for the curd to reach a temperature of about 40 °C. If the curd is allowed to become too hot, the cheese will have a rough texture. When the milk reaches the correct temperature, the kettle is removed from the fire, and the shepherd plunges both forearms into the hot curdled milk. During this second heating, the 'substance' or 'material' (*materia*) of the milk settles as a thick sediment on the bottom of the kettle. The cheese-maker gradually amasses or gathers (*biltzen*) this substance into a round cake. If he does this too quickly, holes and cracks will form in the cheese and

---

[2] The blood of the pig is also said to be *gatzatürik*. Human blood is never said to be *kaillatürik*; it, too, is said to *gatzatü*.

[3] For another account of this custom, see Peillen and Peillen (1965: 55).

rotting will result. As it was often said to me, the shepherd must also have the patience of a woman towards her children when he amasses his cheese.

Since this stage of the process occurs beneath the surface of the milk, I was unable to see exactly how the cheese is amassed. After about eight minutes, the shepherd suddenly pulls a steaming, wet, white cheese from the kettle. On one occasion when I watched a shepherd do so, he held the newly made cheese at arm's length and proudly exclaimed, 'my little baby!' (*ene nini txipi!*) The full import of that remark will become clear when I explain the local notion of conception.

Until about forty years ago, the shepherds broke up the curd and amassed (*xeheki eta bildü*) their cheeses twice in the large copper *bertza* in the manner described. The newly made cheese was then transferred to a smaller copper kettle (*beskua*) where the 'substance' was broken up and amassed a second time. Shepherds who employed this traditional method claimed that the flavour of the cheese was not improved, but that the bone of the cheese was strengthened.

When the cheese is removed from the kettle, it is placed on a circular wooden board (*zorzia*) into which a circular groove and small hole have been carved on the outer rim. A shepherd makes his own *zorzia* during his apprenticeship. Pine and spruce pine are the woods most commonly used.

The newly made cheese contains a considerable amount of whey (*xirikota*) which must be removed from the 'substance'. A pliant wooden mould (*axala*), generally made of beech, is fitted around the cheese and is tightened with a rope. The *axala* enables the shepherd to squeeze (*tinkatzen*) the cheese and thus to remove the whey. The verb *tinkatzen* is also employed in the sense of 'hugging'.

All mountain cheeses are squeezed with an *axala*. A circular metal container with perforated sides and base is sometimes used to squeeze house cheese.

In order to remove as much whey as possible, the shepherd pricks the upper surface of the cheese with a thin metal rod (*zizpitia*). The rope connected to the *axala* is drawn tighter, and the pricking continues until the whey ceases to flow into the groove of the *zorzia*. Black puddings are also punctured or pricked (*txistatzen*) when they are boiled by the women in the valley; so too is the vagina *txistatu* by the penis during intercourse.

The pricking of the cheese (*gazna txistatzia*) takes about ten minutes. If it is a mountain cheese, the shepherd then places his 'mark' on the upper surface by pressing a small piece of wood or metal which is the symbol of his house. No two houses have the same symbol, which is used year after year. Some symbols are the first letter of the house name, e.g. A for the house Arosteguy. Others are an image, such as a cross, the word for which is part of the house name, e.g. the house Kürütxaga has the symbol of the cross, *kürütxea*. A rectangle is the symbol of another house. The shepherds claim that they mark their mountain cheeses with their symbol so that they can readily identify their own cheeses at the end of the summer, when all cheeses are moved to the valley; but, in light of the conceptual links between making mountain cheese and 'making babies', it seems to me that the use of these symbols cannot be fully explained by such practical considerations. House cheeses are not marked.

When the house symbol has been imprinted on the cheese, the shepherd removes the *axala* and rubs the upper surface of the cheese with handfuls of coarse salt. The cheese remains on the *zorzia* for about six hours, and then the lower surface and sides of the cheese are also rubbed with salt. The cheese is then placed on a wooden shelf in the storage room of the hut or house.

In addition to the practice of amassing the cheese twice, two other traditional steps in the cheese-making process have become obsolete and deserve mention. Having gathered the cheese a second time in the kettle, the shepherd formerly 'scratched' and 'pricked' (*xixkatu*, as distinct from *txistatu*) the surface of the wooden board with his fingernails before placing the cheese on it. The elderly shepherds now reason that this step served to 'break up' the substance of the cheese a third time; but I do not understand how this was achieved, since the surface of the *zorzia* is smooth.

Having scratched the *zorzia*, the shepherd squeezed the cheese with the *axala* in the manner I have described and then turned the cheese in front of the fire to warm all of its surfaces. This practice (*hegitatzia*) is said to have strengthened the bone of the cheese; it is an especially interesting custom because new-born infants were also *hegitatü*, turned and warmed in front of the fire, by the midwife until about twenty years ago. The bones of the infant were also thought to be strengthened by means of this practice.

Only 10 per cent of the milk used to make cheese is converted into curd by the rennet; 90 per cent of the volume is whey. Having made his cheese, the shepherd heats the remaining liquid a third time so that the small amount of curd contained in the whey will rise to the surface. This curd is called *zümbera* in Sainte-Engrâce. As the liquid begins to boil, the *zümbera* bubbles and breaks on the surface, and is quickly gathered with a spoon. This soft curd may be kept for two days before it sours; it is eaten with sugar or in sweet coffee. As was done in the past, some shepherds salt their *zümbera*, wrap it in a cloth, and hang it to dry. When treated in this manner, the curd may be preserved for several months.

The majority of the people regard *zümbera* as an inferior, bitter food that 'only poor people eat'. But I was told that this curd is considered to be a delicacy in some villages of Navarra, and especially in Isaba. For the Sainte-Engrâce shepherds, *zümbera* has become a valuable trading item. The owner of the hostel/bar in Navarra where the shepherds buy wine and Ricard is very keen to obtain the curd from them, in return for which the men receive luxury items such as insulated leather boots.

Once the *zümbera* has been removed from the milk, only the yellowish, watery whey remains. In the valley this liquid is fed to the pigs and dogs of the households. If there are no pigs to be fattened in the mountains, the whey is thrown out; it is described as the residue of cheese (*arresta gazna*).

IV

According to the shepherds, their cheeses receive life from rennet; but in order to survive, a cheese must develop a rind and 'bone' (*ezürra*). Until these have been fully formed, a cheese is said to be as fragile as a new-born infant. After the initial salting, the cheese is rubbed with salt three times during the first forty-eight hours of its life. The salt serves two purposes: it is essential to the formation of a firm rind, and it conserves the interior, i.e. the bone and heart, of the cheese. Salt is also given to an infant at baptism to conserve (*konserbatzeko*) its body.

Like infants, newly made cheeses must be cared for and assisted (*soiñatu*) during the early stages of life. The shepherd assists a cheese by turning (*ützül-üngürü*) it once every day for at least one month if it is a house cheese, and for three months if it is a mountain cheese.

According to Lhande (1926: 554, 1026) *ützül* is the Souletine variation of *itzul*, which he glosses as the general notion of *tourner*, to turn, revolve, rotate; but, as I have argued, this notion is expressed as *üngürü* (verb *üngüratü*) in Sainte-Engrâce. By itself *ützüli* describes the action of turning something upside-down or inside-out in Sainte-Engrâce. Freshly cut hay and fern are *ützülikatü* with rakes so that their surfaces will be evenly and thoroughly dried by exposure to the sun and air.

When the terms *ützül* and *üngürü* are combined by the Sainte-

Engrâce people, they express the action of turning something over, revolving, inverting. In the Souletine dialect, the movement of the stars and other heavenly bodies is also expressed as *ützül-üngürü* (Lhande 1926: 1026).

A shepherd 'turns over' his cheese so that its upper and lower surfaces will dry evenly and that the interior of the cheese will harden and the rind become stronger.

During the first three months, a mountain cheese should be kept in the 'same space', i.e. in the cheese house of the hut. A young cheese will be physically injured if moved before the rind and bone have formed. A sudden, drastic change of atmosphere (*ideia*) before maturation is complete will also damage a young cheese. For these two reasons, most shepherds do not move their mountain cheeses from the hut to their houses until August.[4]

Several questions concerning new-born infants arose during the course of investigations about the making and maturing of mountain cheeses. The former are cared for and assisted exclusively by women in the female domain of the house; whereas the latter are cared for and assisted (*soiñatu*) exclusively by men in the male domain of the *olha* hut. First, were infants, like mountain cheeses, formerly kept in 'the same space' during the first three months of life? Second, given the fact that the bone of both cheeses and infants was formerly strengthened by means of the practice *hegitatzia*, were the bones of an infant also thought to be damaged by a sudden, drastic change of atmosphere (*ideia*)? Women answered the first question affirmatively but were uncertain how to answer the second.

During the period of maturation in the hut, the cheeses are in fact moved a few centimetres every day; and it was of particular interest to me to discover that they are moved in a clockwise direction around the cheese house and progressively higher on the shelves. (As I have explained, up is associated with clockwise movement in the rotation of both blessed bread and shepherds.) When a mountain cheese is made, it is placed on the lowest shelf to the right of the door (as viewed from within the cheese house) separating the *gaztantegi* from the main room of the hut. All the other cheeses on that shelf, which runs along the perimeter of the *gaztantegi*, are moved to the right. (The centre of the cheese house is taken as the point of reference.) The last cheese on the lowest shelf and on the left-hand side of

---

[4] In 1979 the Ligoleta shepherds did in fact remove their cheeses from the hut in early July. The cheeses had not yet matured, and some failed to do so properly once they were in the valley. The shepherds moved their cheeses because they were 'afraid that the tourists would steal them'.

the door is moved up to the second shelf. All the cheeses on this shelf are likewise moved one space to the right, as are those on the third shelf. Whenever a new cheese is made, the other cheeses move one space to the right and progressively higher on the shelves.

Mountain cheeses, like shepherds who take turns in the hut, are said to *aldikatü*, i.e. they replace one another by turns in time and space. (House cheeses are turned over daily, but they are moved neither upward nor in a clockwise direction.) But the shepherds themselves seemed not to recognize any connection between the daily clockwise and upward movement of their mountain cheeses and the clockwise rotation of either blessed bread or *olha* partners who travel between the valley and hut. Some men saw their practice of moving cheeses clockwise and upward merely as an 'old custom' which, for them, has no meaning. Others reasoned that the cheeses are moved in this manner 'to make space' for the newly made cheese, 'the little baby' of the Sainte-Engrâce shepherd.

PART FIVE

XII. THE CONCEPT OF CONCEPTION

THE primary aims of this chapter are to describe and to analyse the notion of conception collectively held by the men and women of Sainte-Engrâce; and, second, to show that there are not only linguistic but also ideological, sociological, and symbolic connections between human conception and the process of cheese-making in Sainte-Engrâce society.[1]

I

My interest in possible conceptual links between the notion of conception and cheese-making was initially guided by two factors: first, that the cheese-making shepherd in the *olha* is referred to as *etxekandere*; and second, that the verb *gatzatü* means both 'to curdle' and 'to conceive in the womb of a woman'.

Since I began this part of my research at the beginning of the transhumant season in 1977, I first raised questions about conception with the shepherds as they travelled to and from their huts and herded their flocks. The mountain trails and expanses of alpine pasture afforded us a privacy that is rarely attainable in the valley. From the very start, the shepherds were neither uneasy nor reluctant to share with me their own ideas about the conception and formation of a human foetus.

My first attempts to discuss the matter with women were largely unsuccessful. During the spring and summer, it is extremely difficult to find a woman alone for more than a few minutes in the day. When I did so and made a few tentative queries about idioms the shepherds had employed, the women became visibly uneasy and were anxious to change the topic of our conversation. My initial failure to gain their trust was, I think, partly due to the fact that they felt I was more interested in the world of the *olha* than in their own, and partly due to my own awkwardness with them, which I was later to overcome.

The pig-killing season in December of 1977 provided me with my

---

[1] Since the existing literature about modern peasant societies in Europe contains no information about notions of conception, I am unable to place the Sainte-Engrâce material in any comparative framework as far as Europe is concerned.

first opportunity to spend entire days with individual women. Their attitude towards me and my questions about conception changed considerably. Those who had previously feigned ignorance about 'making babies' demonstrated that they did after all have very clear ideas about conception. The *etxekandere* of one household was also willing—at all times—to discuss her ideas about conception and other physiological phenomena with me and her husband.

II

The notion of conception that I shall describe applies only to humans and not to animals. Whenever I employed an idiom commonly used to describe human conception within the context of animal pro-creativity, I was laughed at good-naturedly and quickly corrected. There is a highly specialized vocabulary by means of which human and animal are differentiated as categories. As I have mentioned previously, human semen (*brallakia*) is distinguished from animal semen (*azia*). Linguistic distinctions are also made between human sexual intercourse (*txikoka* or *aphainka*) and animal intercourse (*estali*), between a sterile woman (*dehota*) and a sterile ewe or cow (*antxü*), between a pregnant woman (*izorra*) and a pregnant animal (*ernai*). There is one term that is applied to both human and animal males: *xixkla* denotes a male that has not made a fertile female pregnant after repeated sexual intercourse.

In the local dialect, the only two terms which differentiate male from female—*kotxo* and *ürrüxa* respectively—are applied solely to animals. The category *jentiak* (people) is not divided into male and female, but into men (*gizonek*) and women (*emazteak*).

According to the women, one fundamental difference between themselves and female animals is that *ürrüxak* can conceive only when in heat. The fertility of female animals is periodic, whereas that of women is continuous from the onset of menstruation until menopause.

Differences in the duration and frequency with which female animals come into heat are recognized; and there is a special term for the heat of female animals which the Sainte-Engrâce people keep. The heat of a sow is *herüsi*; that of a mare is *giri*; that of a hen is *loka*; that of a bitch is *ogara*; that of a cow is *süsa*; that of a goat is *azkalda*. The women were horrified when I asked what the heat of a woman is called and denied its existence; but the men jokingly contended that a woman in heat is *amoros*, 'amorous'.

Linguistic distinctions are also made between the reproductive organs of humans and animals. The human penis is *pitua* or *pistoleta*; sometimes it is jokingly referred to as a 'tail' (*büztan*) or as a 'copulating stick' (*estal-txotx*). The penis of animals is generically referred to as *berga*. Human testicles are *barrabilak*, whereas those of animals are *koskoilak*.

There was some confusion, shared by both sexes, about terms for female reproductive organs. Three terms were given for the womb of a woman: *hümoia*, *humuntzia* (literally 'the baby container'), and *matrica*. Lhande (1926: 1002) records that the second of these terms denotes 'the placenta or membrane which contains the foetus'. In Sainte-Engrâce, I found that the placenta of a woman was referred to either as *khadana* or as *kaillatia*. *Khadana* also means animal placenta. *Kaillatia*, as I have explained, denotes the mass of curdled milk which forms after the first heating in the cheese-making process. Two words were used to denote the uterus of a woman: *ondokua* and *ondokutia*. The first of these also means 'descendant' and 'birthplace'.[2] *Alü* (or *alia*) and *mutxa* denote the vulva of a woman, whereas the vulva of all female animals was identified as *natura*.

The women were most uncertain how to translate *foetus* and *ovaire* in their own language; and it cannot be assumed that these words mean for them what they mean for us. After much debate, women finally concluded that the foetus is the *kaillatia*, which they had identified earlier as the placenta. The contradiction in terms exists for us, but seemingly not for them. The *kaillatia* is a curdled mass of blood, a portion of which is expelled at birth; the rest remains in the womb to form the body of the child.

Although Lhande (1926: 1025) glosses *ürrüthoi* as ovary, there is reason to suspect that this is conceptually a mistranslation as far as the Sainte-Engrâce Basques are concerned. The few men and women who recognized this term applied it exclusively to the ovaries of a sow. The only three households in the commune which breed pigs have all but one or two females in the litter spayed by the lowland veterinarian. The women of these households explained to me that the veterinarian removed the *ürrüthoik* so that the sows would be unable to conceive. But it was not at all clear to me that they, or many of the other women, had more than a vague notion of the role

---

[2] Azkue (1969: 113) and Lhande (1926: 809) gloss *ondoko* (a variation of *ondokua*) as posterior, heir, successor, descendant, and the afterbirth of a woman. M. Dominique Peillen has kindly advised me that, in standard usage, *ondoko*—not *khadana* or *kaillatia* —denotes the human placenta and that *dehota* may describe both a sterile woman and a sterile female animal. While I appreciate the advice of M. Peillen and recognize these standard denotations, I have translated *ondokua*, *khadana*, *kaillatia*, and *dehota* as these are understood by the Sainte-Engrâce people.

played by the ovaries in reproduction. My attempts to elicit information about an 'egg' in the womb were met with puzzled laughter. For lack of a better word, I used the term *arraultze*, which is applied solely to poultry eggs, and was teasingly reminded that women are not hens. If they have a notion of ovulation—or some similar process—it is apparently not seen as a necessary part of the reproductive cycle of women.

III

In Sainte-Engrâce, news of a pregnancy generates considerable excitement up and down the valley and travels rapidly. If the woman is unmarried, the news also gives rise to much speculation about the identity of the genitor, whether he will recognize his offspring legally in the presence of the town hall secretary, and whether or not he will marry the mother.[3]

Those who know the pregnant woman well as her close kin or 'first neighbours' greet her with the standard exclamation 'You have been curdled!' If the speaker is female, this is expressed as *gatzatü zion* (or *ziok*). If the speaker is male, he uses the verbal auxiliary *ziozü* which conveys the respect appropriate to her sex.[4]

As I have explained in Chapter XI, the verb *gatzatü* is also employed to describe the action of rennet upon milk. I have translated *gatzatü* as 'curdle' instead of 'coagulate' for two main reasons: first, the people themselves consistently glossed the word as *cailler* and not as *coaguler*; second, they stated explicitly that the action of rennet upon milk is identical to that of human semen upon the fecund red blood (*odol gorri*) in the womb.[5]

It was adamantly denied that animal semen has the same effect as human semen upon blood or as rennet upon milk; for, according to the people, animal semen lacks a property, found in both human semen and rennet, that causes a hot liquid to curdle. When I once

---

[3] In the past, as at present, it was not uncommon for a woman to bear her first child before her marriage. The pregnancy of an unmarried mother generates gossip, but it is not regarded as a disgrace to the woman or her household. According to the parish records, all but a few bastards were legally recognized by the genitor since the 1860s. In most cases, the genitor married the mother of his child or children in due course.

[4] I have not found a single Souletine Basque outside Sainte-Engrâce who has understood this expression as having anything to do with conception or a pregnant woman. Whenever people were told the meaning of the idiom, they laughed uproariously. For them, the notion that conception is in any way like the process of cheese-making seemed bizarre. The Tardets doctor, who has served the Sainte-Engrâce people for more than forty years, thinks that *gatzatü ziok* is an idiom unique to Sainte-Engrâce. He has never heard it employed by Basques from any other community.

[5] For a fascinating discussion of the word *gatzatü*, see Michelena 1966: 121–45.

asked a man if his cow had been curdled by the local bull, I was understood but corrected. A female animal is said to take (*hartzen*) the semen but is not curdled by it. The shepherd acknowledged that milk may be said 'to take' rennet when the liquid curdles but stead-fastly denied that animal semen is in any way like rennet.

The verb *gatzatü*, in the sense of human conception, is not an idiomatic usage unique to the Basques of Sainte-Engrâce. Michelena (1966: 144) reports that this meaning of the word is documented in two seventeenth-century prayer books (Etcheberri 1627; *Noelac* 1697).[6] Both Michelena and Azkue (1969: 334) cite the passage *gatzatü gineko gaua*, 'the night we were conceived', from Etcheberri's devotional.

Gatzatü provides us with the first key to understanding the con-ceptual links between human conception and cheese-making in Sainte-Engrâce ideology. From the point of view of both sexes, human semen (*brallakia*) curdles the hot red blood (*odol gorri*) in the womb in the same way that rennet curdles hot ewes' milk.

Lhande (1926: 785) gives the following range of meanings for *odol*: blood, life, race, related, humour, character, temperament. The Sainte-Engrâce people employ the word only in the sense of blood and figuratively in the sense of being related consanguineally, which they gloss as *sang* and *parenté* respectively. Womb blood, menstrual blood, and the blood which flows through the *zaiñak* (veins, nerves, and arteries) are three kinds of *odol*.

According to traditional notions of human physiology, there are two kinds of fecund blood: *odol gorri*, the 'red blood' in the womb contributed by the woman at conception, and *odol xuri*, the 'white blood' contributed by the man and contained in his semen. Human semen is thought to be white and viscid on account of *odol xuri*. In Sainte-Engrâce at least, *odol gorri* is conceptually distinct and physically separate from menstrual blood in the womb. With the onset of sexual maturity, the body blood in both sexes is thought to become hot and thereby to induce the flow of male white blood and female red blood that are essential to conception.

Conversations with women who are now in their twenties and thirties provided evidence to suggest that the conceptual distinction traditionally made between male white blood and female red blood is taking on a new form. These women stoutly maintained that a woman may have white blood in her womb; and that if this is so, her

---

[6] I have not yet had an opportunity to study these two texts, both of which are available in the Newberry Library, Chicago and in the library of the Basque Studies Program at the University of Nevada, Reno.

husband must have only red blood in his semen in order for the woman to conceive. White blood will not curdle white blood, nor will red blood curdle red blood.

In the traditional notion of conception, it is semen, not *odol xuri* alone, which curdles the red blood. The shepherds were especially adamant that I should understand this point, since, for them, only human semen has the same properties as rennet. I was often told that human semen is 'like rennet' (*presüra bezala*) by virtue of its *indarra* or power to curdle a hot liquid and its life-giving properties. From the point of view of the shepherds, however, human semen is not simply 'like rennet'; they draw a direct equivalence between these two substances. This conceptual equivalence was clearly expressed by one man who asked rhetorically 'what shepherd would put his rennet into the milk if he did not wish to make a cheese?' We were not discussing cheese-making but his reasons for practising coitus interruptus.

In order for semen to curdle the red blood in the womb, the latter must be both pure and hot; it should not contain any residue of menstrual blood. When the red blood has been curdled the substance (*materia*) of the foetus is amassed (*bildü*) in the womb. Both sexes explain this stage of conception in terms of the shepherd who amasses the substance of curdled milk to form a cheese.

Human semen not only curdles and gives form to the female material; it also contributes to the substance of the foetus. Once the red blood has been curdled, the male white blood separates from the semen and forms a solid mass with the red blood, i.e. the substance of the foetus consists of both male white blood and female red blood. As I have explained, the curdled mass is referred to as the *kaillatia*, employed in the sense of what we understand to be the foetus and placenta. The notion that part of the semen mixes with the red blood is wholly consistent with the particular form that the rennet/semen analogy takes in Sainte-Engrâce. According to the shepherds, rennet not only curdles milk, it also contributes to the substance of the cheese by itself becoming a part of it. That part of rennet which is said to give a cheese 'bone', i.e. its hard and dense interior, mixes with the substance of the cheese when curdling takes place.

All the major terms employed in descriptions of human conception (*gatzatü, materia, bildü, kaillatia*) are also used within the context of cheese-making. Stated in its simplest form, the Sainte-Engrâce concept of conception can be expressed by the following proposition:

rennet : milk : cheese : : semen : red blood : infant

Rennet curdles milk to form a cheese in the same way as human semen curdles red blood to form an infant.

IV

In Sainte-Engrâce, it is thought that conception can take place during menstruation. This contention is consistent with the apparent lack of any notion of ovulation. So far as I was able to determine, menstruation is not generally regarded as a deterrent to sexual intercourse; but conception during menstruation should be avoided by practising coitus interruptus. Before menstrual blood is expelled from the womb, it consists of small clots which will mix with, but will not become a part of, the red blood. These clots not only prevent human semen from curdling the red blood properly; they will not separate from the red blood once curdling has taken place and will become a part of the foetus. For reasons which people were unable to explain, menstrual blood gathers in the head of an infant during gestation and appears as a birthmark on its face. I was told that the two men in the commune who have fairly large birthmarks on their faces were conceived when their mothers were menstruating.

The majority of the people reasoned that white and red blood contribute equally to the formation of bones, skin, organs, etc. But some of the shepherds contended that bones are formed by semen, since this substance, like rennet, has certain properties which cause the solid curdled mass to harden. This view was also taken by one elderly woman, who broke convention by making cheese in her youth when there were no men in her household to perform the task.

Not many people were willing to speculate which part of the infant is formed first as the 'tiny, curdled mass' begins to grow in the womb. Some suggested that the head is made first, which may account for the notion that menstrual blood gathers there; others reasoned that organs (in an unspecified order) precede bones in foetal development. As I have explained previously, the soul of the infant comes from God through the priest at the sacrament of baptism.

In traditional notions of human physiology, the white and red blood contributed by the parents are fluids which also carry certain traits that are transmitted to the infant at conception. White powder (*pholbor xuri*), physical deformities (such as lameness and blindness), and the 'seed' of mental illness are some of these traits; in principle, they are manifested in the first and third generations but remain dormant in the second.

White powder, to which reference was made in Chapter VI, is

transmitted through either the white blood of the father or the red blood of the mother; it may be inherited by either sex. Like the 'seed' of mental illness, *pholbor xuri* is contained within the body blood and manifests itself during the procreative period, when the blood in the body is hot. The powder is activated by the heat generated by the body blood and is thought to give the person abundant energy and a *borthitz* (nervous, argumentative, and potentially violent) temperament. When the person experiences menopause, the body blood cools and the powder becomes inactive. The temperament of the individual changes accordingly from being *borthitz* to being tranquil, pacific, and patient.

The seed (*azia*) of mental illness may also be transmitted by means of male white blood or female red blood. The trait manifests itself in several ways: periods of severe depression which recur regularly once every six years, loss of a desire to live (which may result in suicide), alternating states of depression, silence, lethargy and extreme gaiety, garrulity, and frenzied activity, and lastly a desire to visit other households. [7]

The 'seed' of this illness is greatly feared by those whose parent or grandparent exhibited these symptoms; for the trait does not always miss a generation. I know of several cases in which the 'seed' was passed from parent to child at conception.

V

In Sainte-Engrâce, a woman is said to be 'curdled like milk' at conception and 'to rise like bread' during her pregnancy. The verb *altxatu* is applied to both the 'rising' of leavened bread and the 'rising' of the belly of a pregnant woman.

For the women, there is more than a visual similarity between the rising of bread and of the female abdomen. From their point of view, the process of fermentation activated by yeast is similar to the action of rennet upon milk and of human semen upon red blood. The Souletine word for yeast (*altxatürazia*) consists of the verb to rise (*altxatu*) and the noun *azia*, 'seed', 'animal semen', and formerly the gift of blessed bread that was given to the female first 'first neighbour'.

---

[7] The ways in which the 'seed' of mental illness manifests itself is a topic that lies outside the concerns of this book; but some mention should be made here of 'the desire to visit'. When the 'seed' becomes activated in the six-year cycle, the blood is thought to flow backwards, *arra-üngüratü*, i.e. counter-clockwise, through the veins and arteries. When a relapse occurs, the blood circulates backwards first too rapidly and then stops entirely for a few moments. This in turn is said to compel the person to gad about from house to house.

In Sainte-Engrâce, yeast is also commonly referred to as the rennet of bread (*ogi presüra*) and as the seed or animal semen of bread (*ogi azia*).

It was, however, pointed out to me by the women that yeast does not curdle dough 'as rennet curdles milk and human semen curdles red blood'. Yeast, rennet, and human semen are all life-giving substances by means of which solid matter is formed from a semi-fluid mass. Although there is clearly some conceptual link between these three substances, I was unable to uncover any general theory about the precise nature of that connection.

Leavened bread was formerly made by the elder *etxekandere* of the house. Although I was unable to watch the process (the women stopped baking during the 1940s), I was told that the addition of yeast was the most crucial step. Like the cheese-making shepherd with his rennet, the bread-making *etxekandere* was required to know exactly how much yeast was needed to make the dough ferment and rise slowly.

In some parts of the Basque country, the *etxekandere* recited an Our Father and the following prayer when she added the yeast to the dough: 'Rise, rise yeast, like the pure Virgin Mary who gave birth' (Castillo de Lucas 1966: 207). The Sainte-Engrâce women who made bread in the past say that they never recited this or any other prayer when the yeast was added.

The notion that the action of yeast upon dough is in some way analogous to that of semen upon the female material is by no means unique to Sainte-Engrâce. Albertus Magnus and Aristotle both make contrastive reference to yeast in their discussions of conception and embryonic development (Needham 1955: 55, 91).[8]

Until the late 1950s, the Sainte-Engrâce women gave birth in their houses. In most cases a woman was assisted only by one of her female 'first neighbours'. If a neighbour could not be reached in time, the husband of the pregnant woman frequently acted as her midwife. Men who served their wives in this capacity hold mixed views about their experiences. Some confided that they were greatly upset by the sight of the blood and of the suffering experienced by their wives. These same men claimed that they have no qualms about assisting their livestock during birth.

Other men were clearly proud of their skills as midwife and assured me that the birth of a child is no different from that of a lamb or calf. These men contended that being present at birth and assisting one's wife are emotionally rewarding experiences.

[8] See Aristotle's *De Generatione Animalium*, Book II, 755b.

Traditionally childbirth took place in the kitchen in front of the hearth. The woman squatted with her back to the fire. Her female *aizoa* or husband grasped her waist from behind and then pressed her belly to encourage the birth. When one couple demonstrated this for me, the husband squatted behind his wife and hugged her belly as they both leaned forward. The technique requires an extremely good sense of balance. When the infant was expelled, the midwife or husband cut the umbilical cord, squeezed the child's nose, and made the sign of the cross on its forehead. The infant was immediately turned (*hegitatü*) in front of the fire so that its bones would harden. The afterbirth was then buried in the garden, as were aborted foetuses and unbaptized stillborn babies.

Having rotated the infant in front of the fire, the midwife swaddled it in white cloth and bound the baby with strong cotton bands, which were known as *troxa-khordak*. (The verb *troxakhordatu* means to swaddle or to bind up.) The cloth was changed twice daily but was not removed until the infant was two years old. In the traditional way of thinking, the *troxa-khordak* were one other means of strengthening the bones of the child and protecting its body in much the same way as a rind protects cheese.

Until roughly twenty years ago, the women were ritually purified by the priest after childbirth. After having given birth, a woman was expected to remain in her house until she was strong enough to walk to the church to receive her purification. In most cases purification took place the day after birth—rather than after the forty days formerly prescribed by the Church. I know of no other Souletine community in which the latter prescription was not observed.

In Sainte-Engrâce, the woman was required to travel alone to the Senta church, where she was met on the steps by the priest. In her left hand she carried a blessed candle. With her right hand she touched the surplice of the priest, who then blessed her and offered prayers for her and her new-born child. Having been blessed, the woman took the candle in her right hand and waited for the priest to light it. She did not enter the church but returned unaccompanied to her house.

From birth until the age of four or five a child is cared for exclusively by the two *etxekanderak* of the household, who assume full responsibility for its feeding, toilette, and supervision. The father of an infant characteristically expresses a keen interest in his offspring, upon whom he bestows considerable affection; but because his proper social and economic domain lies outside the house in the fields, barns, and mountains, he is excluded from the routine of caring for and raising his infant child. Most fathers do, however, share responsibility with their wives for the spiritual welfare of the child. When an infant is put into its cradle at night, the father and mother generally recite a prayer asking God to bestow His blessings upon the child and its parents.

At present, as in the past, considerable emphasis is placed upon breast-feeding. Breast milk is considered to be vastly superior to cow's milk, which traditionally supplemented the former. The older men and women are extremely sceptical about the powdered milk now available in the chemist's shop in Tardets and used by many young mothers. Among the older generation, it is widely thought that powdered milk induces anaemia.

Until roughly forty-five years ago, a woman who was unable to suckle her infant contracted the services of a wet-nurse (*ünhüdea*). The selection of a wet-nurse was generally guided by practical considerations, such as the proximity of her house to that of the infant; but a preference was expressed for employing a wet-nurse who was 'without marriage' and who had an ample supply of milk. The women with whom I discussed this custom reasoned that an unwed mother was favoured because, without a husband to support her, she had greater need of the small payments in cash and food than a married mother.

No named relationship existed between a wet-nurse and the infants whom she suckled. From the point of view of the infant's household, the wet-nurse was no more than a 'female servant' (*neskato*) in their temporary employment.

Named relationships did exist between those who were suckled by the same wet-nurse in infancy. Men who had a wet-nurse in common were *egüzanaiak*, literally 'breast brothers'. (The root *egüz-* is a variation of *ugatz*, meaning 'breast'.) From the point of view of a man, a woman suckled by his wet-nurse was his *egüzarreba*, 'breast sister'. Women who were 'breast sisters' were called *egüzahizpak*. These same terms are still applied to those having a godparent in common, i.e. the spiritual relationship between 'breast siblings' has survived. I have not uncovered any evidence which might explain the connection (if indeed there was one) between secular and spiritual 'brothers and sisters of the breast'.[9]

According to the elderly women, an individual sometimes had an affectionate regard for his 'breast siblings' and wet-nurse which he retained for the duration of his life; but the women stressed that his

[9] It may be that milk was once associated with the Holy Spirit. See Warner (1976: 192–205) for an interesting discussion of the symbolism of the Virgin's milk.

relationships with these people were not an important basis of association in their society. (For example, 'breast siblings', unlike age-mates, were not invited to each other's weddings.)

In order to increase her supply of breast milk, a woman should eat soup with bread in it and drink cow's milk. She should avoid foods that are *borthitz*, such as tomatoes, garlic, pepper, or house cheese that has not matured properly. According to the older women, she should also take care to wet her wrists before breast-feeding so as to cool the milk which would otherwise be too hot for the infant to drink. Infants are generally weaned after ten months.

VI

The husband–wife (*senharr–emazte*) relationship is the procreative union upon which the preservation of the household depends. In the first quarter of this century, at least six and sometimes as many as fourteen children were commonly born into a house.[10] Those who are now past sixty years of age reason that two major incentives encouraged them to have as many offspring as possible. First, before the advent of modern farm machinery, children were an invaluable source of labour. Second, the old people contend that having at least six children improved their chances of securing an heir or heiress who was 'of the house' (*etxenko*), i.e. a son or daughter who takes a keen interest in performing the tasks appropriate to his or her sex, expresses a willingness to work hard and to co-operate with the other *etxenkuak*, to marry and to remain in the house.

Since the Second World War there has been an increasing tendency for women to bear only two or three children. Considerable emphasis is still placed on the procreative union of husband and wife; but young couples, and especially the wives, now in their twenties and thirties argue that having more than three children is no longer economically necessary. Unlike their elders, they do not seem to be concerned about the demographic consequences of a declining birth rate and population.

Of the thirty-two households in the upper community, only six or seven are judged to have a child 'of the house' through whom the household may survive. From the point of view of many young couples, it is now futile to argue that having a large family increases the likelihood of producing an *etxenko*. As one young woman queried, 'What difference will it make if I have three or thirteen children? As

[10] My sources were the town hall records and an 1881 register, which M. and Mme. Joseph Lascoumes of Sainte-Engrâce kindly lent me.

soon as they grow up, they all want to go down to the towns, to have motor cars and expensive clothes. So they will need money. What can they earn here? You can't expect them to stay.'

Of households into which children were born but none has remained it is said that 'no children are being curdled in the house' (*haurrak ez dizie gatzarazi etxen*). Couples whose offspring have all left the community receive much sympathy from their more fortunate neighbours and are not critized for having failed to produce an heir or heiress. Childless couples, on the other hand, are often both criticized and condemned. When a couple is judged by others not to want to 'make babies', their failure to do so is most often attributed to their shared greed and selfishness. But when a couple is thought to want children, their failure to have any offspring is generally attributed to a physiological defect in the husband which makes him *xixkla*, i.e. unable to curdle his wife because his semen lacks *indarra* (procreative force). Although a *xixkla* husband is the traditional and most commonly cited reason, I have also heard people say that a particular couple is childless 'because the wife has been permanently sterilized by the pill'.

A childless couple has recourse to one morally, socially acceptable alternative—adoption, preferably of a nephew or niece. In one contemporary case, a couple has refused to take this course of action. They are judged to have one of the wealthiest and largest properties in the commune and are sometimes accused of having wilfully prevented conception in order to retain exclusive ownership of it. Their imputed avarice is regarded as a serious moral offence.

Until recently, the only method of preventing conception was coitus interruptus; and, for the majority of the men, this is still the only morally acceptable method. I know of a few young women who have obtained diaphragms. In their understanding, the device prevents their being curdled by sealing off the womb and thereby keeping the red blood and semen separate.

Contraceptive devices such as the pill and coil are generally feared by the majority of men and women because they are thought to interfere with the normal blood flow within the woman's body. The actual manner in which these contraceptive methods prevent conception is widely misunderstood. Many men and women reasoned that the pill curdles menstrual blood into a permanently solid mass and that this in turn may result in permanent sterility.

One other means of birth control has been employed by a few women, often in spite of protests from their husbands. These women have had either their ovaries removed or their Fallopian tubes tied. From the point of view of many men, permanent female sterilization is an anathema; but for some women at least, an 'operation' not only ensures that conception cannot occur. It is also regarded as an effective means of avoiding the 'crisis' of menopause.

VII

For women, the procreative period begins with the onset of menstruation. According to traditional notions of female physiological processes, red blood is formed in the womb when a woman experiences her first menstrual period; she becomes hot-blooded and fertile. Her red blood continues to 'flow' as long as she menstruates. The age at which menstruation begins ranges from eleven to eighteen, but the average age seems to be about fourteen.

In Sainte-Engrâce, neither menstruation nor menstrual blood is thought to be polluting, although there are certain restrictions on a woman's activities during her periods. A menstruating woman does, however, perform most tasks normally allotted to her in the house. She may prepare food, do household chores, and have contact with the livestock.

Neither the men nor the women seemed to have any strong objection to having intercourse during a menstrual period; but, as I have already mentioned, conception during menstruation should be avoided by practising coitus interruptus so that the menstrual blood and fecund 'red blood' will not mix in the womb.

Women of all ages take a fairly casual view of menstrual blood and its disposition. Formerly, a woman merely pinned her skirts between her legs during her period, or 'bad week', and it seems that she made little attempt to conceal her condition from others. Among the women, menstruation is regarded as an uncomfortable nuisance that is talked about without embarrassment; it is also an experience which occasionally gives rise to ribald joking among women. During the pig-killing season when I was seen wearing an apron spattered with blood, one of my most unabashed informants drew me into her house, cackled, and tugged my apron. 'What's all this? Have you got the bad week, eh?' She repeated her joke to all of her female neighbours, who warned me that my 'bad week' was due to last one whole month. (Among the women, the pig-killing season is referred to as the 'bad month'.)

In the traditional way of thinking, a menstruating woman should not do any 'wet work', i.e. she should not wash anything in cold water. Women now in their fifties and sixties who observed this precaution explained that cold water makes both menstrual blood and body blood stop flowing.

The body part most sensitive to hot/cold contrasts are the wrists. When the wrists are exposed to hot and cold liquids, the blood in the *zaiñak* (which collectively denotes veins, arteries, and nerves) is heated or cooled accordingly. The hot or cold blood is then circulated through the body by means of the *zaiñak*.

During menstruation both the menstrual blood and body blood are thought to be extremely hot. For this reason it is said that a menstruating woman is unable to make mayonnaise. The heat generated by the menses is so intense that it causes the eggs and oil to curdle.

During her period, a woman may do 'dry work', i.e. any task inside or outside the house that does not bring the woman into contact with liquids. Hot/cold contrasts, such as cooking near a hot fire and then going outside into cold air, do not affect either menstrual or body blood when a woman does 'dry work'.

According to traditional views of male physiological processes, men have neither menstrual blood nor fecund red blood; but they do have semen and white blood, neither of which a woman possesses. Since men do not menstruate, the precise time at which they can be accurately assessed as having reached sexual maturity is difficult to determine. Most people reasoned that the virility of a man is not publicly evidenced until he 'curdles' a woman.

For men, as for women, the onset of sexual maturity is thought to make the body blood hot. This in turn is said to induce the flow of white blood that is essential to conception. So long as the blood of a man is hot and his white blood is flowing, his semen has *indarra*, in this context a procreative power or force. Men between the ages of twenty and thirty are thought to have the most powerful semen and hottest blood; and, on account of their hot blood, men in this age group tend to be more nervous, impatient, and quick-tempered than more sexually mature men and women. When the blood of a man cools and his white blood stops flowing, his semen loses its *indarra*, and the man becomes *xixkla*.

VIII

In Sainte-Engrâce, menopause is experienced by both men and women. With the onset of menopause, the procreative abilities of both sexes are terminated. Fifty is the average age at which this occurs. No linguistic distinction is made between male and female menopause, both of which are referred to as 'the stopping of the blood' (*odol ükhüratzia*). The verb *ükhüratü* is a variation of *ekhüratü*, which means to become tranquil, peaceable, resigned, patient.

When menopause occurs, the blood in the body begins to cool and is thought to flow first too rapidly through the veins and arteries and then to stop entirely for a few moments. The time it takes for the blood to become cold varies from one individual to another. For some, the process lasts only a few days; for others, it may last as long as six months.

The cooling of the body blood generally has three effects on both sexes. First, it causes the fecund fluids of male white blood and female red blood to stop flowing; second, it induces hot/cold flushes and fainting spells; and third, it is thought to make the person more tranquil and patient. This last effect is most pronounced in those to whom 'white powder' was transmitted at conception.

The 'stopping' of the fecund blood generally has two effects on both sexes. First, it renders a person sterile. When a man experiences menopause, he may continue to have sexual intercourse; but he is no longer able to curdle a woman, for his semen lacks both white blood and the procreative *indarra* that are essential to conception. In a similar manner, a woman who experiences menopause is unable to conceive since she is no longer able to contribute the material, i.e. red blood, upon which human semen acts during conception. The stopping of the fecund blood also often results in a physical or mental crisis. Male menopause is most commonly manifested by a heart attack. Both sexes may suffer from severe depression, and this is the most common form which the female crisis takes. I have recorded one case in which the suicide of a woman was attributed to her menopausal depression.

If depression, hot and cold flushes, or fainting spells persist for several weeks, the individual may be sent to a clinic to receive treatment for a 'mixed head', an expression applied to both depression and mental illness. One elderly man, who suffered a severe and prolonged period of depression, spent several weeks in hospital before his white blood stopped flowing and his body blood circulated normally again.

In Sainte-Engrâce, the Basque term *odol ükhüratzia* (the stopping of the blood) is often used interchangeably with *retour d'agea* (from the French *retour d'âge*); and there are at least two senses in which menopause is a 'return'. For the Sainte-Engrâce people, menopause is not merely a change of life; physiologically it marks a return to the human condition into which an individual is born and in which he remains until puberty. Those who experience menopause, like infants and pre-pubescent children, have 'cold blood' (*odol hotz*) and are infertile.

For men who experience a crisis at menopause, 'the stopping of the blood' also necessitates their 'return' to the female domain of the house, where they spend the majority of their time among the women and children. Men who had a crisis are considered, and consider themselves, to be too weak to participate in the activities in which hot-blooded, virile men engage. They generally cease to work with the younger male head of household on the farm. The menopausal crisis also marks the end of their active participation in the male world of the *olha*; they no longer ascend to the mountains to herd or to make cheese during the months of summer transhumance.

One old man who experienced a particularly severe depression during his menopause spends his days sitting on a stool in front of his house or in the kitchen beside the hearth. Another man in the community, who is also resigned to the consequences of his crisis, whittles wooden cups, shoes, and flutes while he chats with his boisterous wife in their kitchen.

There is one man in his sixties who has not yet experienced menopause and to whom I have already referred. He has fathered two children since the age of fifty. He has not suffered any crisis and continues to herd and to make cheese in the mountains with his younger comrades. Among the men, he is greatly admired and respected for his physical strength and shepherding skills. The younger men are also impressed by his sexual prowess, for which the women pity his wife. She has conceived thirteen children.

The women also express pity for those of their sex who have not experienced menopause by the age of fifty. During the past forty years three women in their late fifties have given birth. In two cases the child was born 'weak' and suffered from ill health. These physical infirmities were attributed to the abnormal blood flow in the mother's body. Like the blood of a woman who carries the 'seed' of mental illness, that of a woman who fails to experience menopause is thought to alternate (*aldikatü*) between flowing too quickly and stopping entirely. In both instances, menopause is thought to be the only means by which the blood circulation can be restored to normality.

For women, as for men, menopause cools the blood within the body; and this in turn alters the temperament of the individual. Women who have experienced menopause are generally regarded as more tranquil and patient than those who are still fertile, menstruating, and hot-blooded.

Menopause has a much less drastic effect upon the daily lives of women than it has upon men. Having experienced her crisis, a woman generally continues to assist the younger *etxekandere* with domestic chores and child-rearing; but she is rarely expected or permitted to continue working outside the house—the ideologically and socially female domain in Sainte-Engrâce society.

IX

In my analysis of the Sainte-Engrâce notion of human conception, the following proposition was offered:

rennet : milk : cheese : : semen : red blood : infant

I would like now to re-consider this set of analogies within the context of the separate social and ideological domains of men and women—namely, the *olha* in the mountains and the house in the valley—and to expand the proposition as follows:

rennet : milk : cheese : *olha* : male procreativity : :
semen : red blood : infant : house : female procreativity

During their procreative period, men and women are sexually, socially, and economically active; conceptually they belong to two separate domains within which the same fundamental ideals of co-operation, 'mutual assistance', and amicability are realized: the male domain of the *olha* and the female domain of the house. Even as male procreativity is symbolically associated with the *olha*, where 'cheeses are curdled' (*gaznak gatzarazi olhan*), female procreativity is symbolically associated with the house, where 'children are curdled' (*haurrak gatzarazi etxen*).

As 'the woman of the house', a shepherd fulfils the domestic and social role traditionally assigned to the elder female head of household in the valley. As the maker of cheese, he symbolically fulfils the procreative role of the younger female *etxekandere*, upon whose fertility the survival of the household depends. The significant point of difference between making a cheese and 'making a baby' (*haurr egitea*) is that in the former instance the man provides not only the 'seed' (in the form of rennet) essential to the formation of the cheese; he himself amasses his 'baby', symbolically gives birth to it and cares for it, none of which he is either socially or physiologically able to do as the father of his children. In this respect, the cheese-making shepherd in the mountains is like the bread-giving female *etxekandere* in the valley who ritually gave a gift of blessed bread symbolizing a substance that women are physiologically incapable of contributing to the foetus at conception: the life-giving substance of semen. As one symbolic expression of female fecundity, the ritual giving of 'female semen' by women in the valley was complementary and opposed to cheese-making by men in the mountains.

X

The concept of conception described and analysed in this chapter is not unique to the Basques of Sainte-Engrâce. The notion that the action of rennet upon milk is the same as that of semen upon the red blood of the womb and that the formation of a foetus is analogous to the formation of a cheese closely parallels theories of conception proposed by a variety of scholars with a range of philosophical, theological, and scientific interests in the subject of human embryogeny.

The notion that the formation of a foetus is analogous to the curdling of milk into cheese takes a variety of forms in time and space. Among historians of science, the best known of these forms is the Aristotelian 'cheese analogy' of conception.[11]

When the material secreted by the female in the uterus has been fixed by the semen of the male (this acts in the same way as rennet acts upon milk, for rennet is a kind of milk containing vital heat, which brings into one mass and fixes the similar material, and the relation of the semen to the catamenia is the same, milk and the catamenia being of the same nature)—when, I say, the more solid part comes together, the liquid is separated off from it, and as the earthy parts solidify membranes form all round it; this is both a necessary result and for a final cause, the former because the surface of a mass must solidify on heating as well as on cooling, the latter because the foetus must not be in a liquid but be separated from it (*De Generatione Animalium*, Bk. II, 739b, 22–31).

The proposition that rennet : milk : : semen : catamenia also appears in Book I (729a, 7–14):

Whereby, too, it is plain that the semen does not come from the whole of the body; for neither would the different parts of the semen already be separated as soon as discharged from the same part, nor could they be separated in the uterus if they had once entered it all together; but what does happen is just what one would expect, since what the male contributes to generation is the

---

[11] For a detailed examination of the ways in which the Aristotelian 'cheese analogy' of conception closely parallels the Sainte-Engrâce notion of human conception, see Ott (1979).

form and efficient cause, while the female contributes the material. In fact, as in the coagulation of milk, the milk being the material, the fig-juice or rennet is that which contains the curdling principle, so acts the secretion of the male, being divided into parts in the female.[12]

The Aristotelian cheese analogy and variations of it were incorporated into the works of a variety of classical and medieval scholars (cf. Needham 1959). Clement of Alexandria, for example, 'adopts the Peripatetic view that generation results from the combination of semen with menstrual blood, and uses the Aristotelian illustration of rennet coagulating milk' (Needham 1959: 76). The Aristotelian cheese analogy is also mentioned in the treatises of the Brethren of Sincerity which were written during the late tenth century at Basra in Iraq (Needham 1959: 82).[13]

One form of the cheese analogy appears in the *Liber Scivias* of St Hildegard (1098–1180), who had a vision in which she:

saw upon earth men carrying milk in earthen vessels and making cheeses therefrom. Some was of the thick kind from which firm cheese is made, some of the thinner sort from which porous cheese is made, and some was mixed with corruption and of the sort from which bitter cheese is made ... As for those whom thou hast seen carrying milk in earthen vessels, they are in the world, men and women alike, having in their bodies the seed of mankind from which are procreated the various kinds of human beings. Part is thickened because the seed in its strength is well and truly concocted and this produces forceful men to whom are allotted gifts, both spiritual and carnal ... And some had cheeses less firmly curdled, for in their feebleness they have seed imperfectly tempered and they raise offspring mostly stupid, feeble, and useless ... And some was mixed with corruption ... for the seed in that brew cannot be rightly raised ... and makes misshapen men (Needham 1959: 84–5, translation by Singer).

A better known example of the cheese analogy appears in the Wisdom Literature.[14] 'Remember, I beseech thee, that thou hast

---

[12] The argument that the different parts of the semen could not be separated in the uterus is difficult to follow. In Chapter 18, Book I, of *De Generatione Animalium*, Aristotle suggests that the separation of the parts would be like splitting up a single animal into several. As Platt observes, this argument is terribly inconclusive.

[13] Although Needham (1959: 66) reports that Aulus Gellius also refers to the cheese analogy, Peter Dronke of Clare Hall, Cambridge has kindly informed me that no specific or clear association between cheese-making and the formation of a foetus is made by Aulus Gellius.

[14] In Basque the passage 'Hast thou not poured me out as milk, and curdled me like cheese?' is expressed as *Ez othe nauze esnea bezala hegitu eta manthoina bezala gatzarazi?* (*Bible Saindua* 1972: 536). In the Labourd dialect, *manthoin* denoted 'curdled milk' (Lhande 1926: 712); but the Sainte-Engrâce shepherds told me that *mathua* (the Souletine equivalent of *manthoin*) means 'a young, newly made cheese'.

fashioned me as clay; and wilt thou bring me into the dust again? Hast thou not poured me out as milk, and curdled me like cheese?' (Job 10:10). The comparison of the formation of the embryo with the clotting of milk into cheese also appears in certain Indian embryological texts (cf. Needham 1959: 27).

The wanderings of the cheese analogy during the Middle Ages may be attributed in part to the impact that Aristotle and his Arabic commentators had on those scholars who knew *De Generatione Animalium*, which was first translated from Arabic and Greek in the thirteenth century, or texts in which the Aristotelian analogy was employed; but this view fails to consider two possibilities. First, the cheese analogy of conception may have been, in some cases, an independently invented idea; and, second, it may have been part of local folk traditions with which certain scholars were familiar.

In the case of St Hildegard, who could not have had access to translations of the embryological works of Aristotle or Clement of Alexandria, it seems likely that she knew the cheese analogy as a piece of popular lore (personal communication, Peter Dronke).[15] The cheese analogy may also have been part of a folk tradition with which Aristotle was acquainted and which existed before he incorporated it into *De Generatione Animalium*.

The extent to which the cheese analogy, or variations of it, formed a part of folk theories of conception during the Middle Ages has not yet been determined; but we have, at least, one fourteenth-century example of the rennet/semen analogy from the Occitan village of Montaillou.

Worried by the prospects of an illegitimate pregnancy, the concubine of the village priest asks her lover what she will do if she becomes pregnant. 'I have a particular herb,' Pierre says to Beatrice, 'If a man carries it when he mixes his body with that of a woman, he cannot beget nor can she conceive.' True daughter of the country and the cheese-making sheds, in spite of her noble extraction, Beatrice immediately suggests a folk analogy to her lover. 'What kind of herb is this?' she asks Pierre. 'Is it the one that the cowherds place in the pan of milk in which they have put rennet to prevent the milk from curdling, so long as this herb stays in the pan?' Mocking her folk analogy, Pierre Clergue says that she shouldn't mind which herb it is but that it is a particular herb which will be effective (Le Roy Ladurie 1975: 247–8, my translation).

---

[15] Needham (1959: 85) suggests that St Hildegard obtained the cheese analogy from Constantine the African, whose translation of Haly-Abbas's *Liber Totius* (between 1070 and 1085) was called *Liber de Humana Natura*. Peter Dronke (personal communication) reports that Constantine does not in fact mention the cheese analogy.

As Le Roy Ladurie points out, the rennet of a hare, taken three days before the menstrual period, was used as a contraceptive in the Middle Ages. But in the folk tradition of the Ariège, rennet was not seen as a contraceptive but as the equivalent of 'that which causes both cow's milk and the semen of a man to curdle, and which makes, accordingly, a cheese or a foetus. The magical herb of Pierre Clergue, the Montaillou priest, prevents the solidification of milk and semen; it is anti-rennet; hence contraceptive' (Le Roy Ladurie 1975: 248).

The analogy between rennet and semen also appears in a Montaillou custom called *cherchez le berger* or *cherchez la femme*, in which a malevolent shepherd put a certain herb into the rennet of another shepherd in order to prevent his milk from curdling. 'A similar herb was placed on the stomach of a woman to prevent the semen of a man from curdling to form a foetus. The semen was magically sterilized' (Le Roy Ladurie 1975: 580).

These examples show the historical depth and spatial distribution of an analogy that is central to the Sainte-Engrâce notion of human conception—namely, that rennet : cheese : : semen : infant. The modern existence of the cheese analogy of conception in one French Basque community is itself an interesting phenomenon; but my main aim in this chapter has been to understand the ideological, sociological, and symbolic connections between human conception and the process of cheese-making in Sainte-Engrâce society. So far as I know, Sainte-Engrâce provides us with the first European example of a phenomenon that has been reported in a variety of forms for many different societies outside Europe—namely, an attempt by men, in an institutionalized framework, to fulfil symbolically the female procreative role and to re-enact symbolically the physical creation of children in a male domain from which women are excluded. In Sainte-Engrâce, this also involves a reversal of male and female sociological roles, i.e. the cheese-making shepherd performs the socio-domestic role of the female head of household and recreates the ideologically female domain of the house in the male domain of the mountain herding hut.

PART SIX

XIII. CONCLUSION

I

SEVERAL different aspects of Sainte-Engrâce society have been examined in this book, and, wherever possible, the traditional form of an institution or custom has been contrasted with its modern one with a view to showing the transformations that have taken place. In my analyses of both traditional and modern aspects of the society, certain themes have recurred and certain patterns have emerged.

First, repeated reference has been made to the fundamental ideals of co-operation and 'mutual assistance' (*alkharr lagüntza*) to which the Sainte-Engrâce people adhere more or less uniformly inside and outside the household. Within the household these ideals are articulated in the carefully balanced division of labour between male and female, as well as between elder and younger heads of household. Outside the household, the twofold obligation to co-operate and 'to assist mutually' is the essential basis of two sets of institutionalized relationships: the 'first neighbour' relationship in the valley, by means of which individual households are permanently linked as interdependent and mutually supportive socio-economic units; and *txotx* partner, *etxekandere/neskato* relationships among shepherds in the *olha*.

In Sainte-Engrâce, systematic co-operation and reciprocity between households and between individuals belonging to different households are made possible by two factors. First, there are institutionalized frameworks in which these ideals can be realized. Second, there is a moral basis, expressed in the obligation 'to assist mutually', which stresses the need for co-operation and reciprocity between individuals who share common interests and aims.

The permanence and structure of 'first neighbour' relationships provide one framework in which these ideals are realized in a variety of ritual, social, and economic activities. 'First neighbour' relationships—as distinct from generalized neighbour relationships commonly found outside the Basque country—are systematically ordered and characterized by institutionalized forms of reciprocity.

213

In Sainte-Engrâce society, the asymmetric ordering of 'first neighbour' relationships also reduces the likelihood of competition for assistance within the neighbourhood; for no two households have the same three 'first neighbours'. Competition is also denied by the shared assumption that 'first neighbours' will take turns helping one another and that no household will be without a *lagün*, a companion and assistant, when one is needed.

The ideals of co-operation and reciprocity are also realized in the *olha*. Like the members of a household and 'first neighbours', the members of an *olha* are obliged to give 'mutual assistance'. Systematic co-operation between shepherds belonging to different households (and in many cases to different settlements or *quartiers*) is made possible for two reasons: the *olha* is a permanent corporation, and it has a formal organization in which relationships between shepherds are fixed and their pastoral roles systematically ordered.

One other theme which has recurred in this book is the importance —which the people themselves recognize—of two ordering principles in Sainte-Engrâce society: *aldikatzia*, which I have translated as serial replacement, taking turns, or alternation, according to context; and *üngürü*, rotation. But so far no attempt has been made either to summarize the variety of contexts in which these principles appear or to consider their general importance as organizing notions in the society.

Aldikatzia, in the sense of alternation, was shown to be an ordering principle in the following contexts. In the traditional method of selecting godparents, the respective natal households of the child's parents alternated (*aldikatü*) in providing a godfather and godmother. The same rule of alternation between the natal households of parents applies to the selection of Christian names. Alternation also operates in the *olha* ligoleta.

In the traditional notion of female physiological processes, the blood of women who carry the 'seed' of mental illness or who fail to experience menopause by the time they reach their early fifties is thought to alternate (*aldikatü*) between flowing too quickly through the body and stopping entirely.

The notion of alternation has also appeared in my accounts of the local religion and ritual practices. The High Mass alternates between the upper church and the lower chapel; and formerly the priest and vicar took turns celebrating it. In the 'old religion', male and female heads of household took turns attending the early Mass on Sunday. If the *etxekandere* represented the house at the early Mass, the *nausi* attended the late Mass. Male and female heads of household also alternate in providing companionship for the soul of a deceased 'first neighbour' and for his survivors during the obligatory two-night vigil. At a community-wide level, the 'first neighbours' of all Sainte-Engrâce households are said to alternate in providing mortuary services for one another. In all but one of these examples, reciprocity is a necessary feature of *aldikatzia*.

In the sense of serial replacement, *aldikatzia* was employed in the following contexts. Formerly, households took turns in serial succession using the mill in which they own a share. Until the 1950s, fixed groups of 'first neighbour' and neighbour households replaced one another serially (*aldikatü*) as hosts of the threshing party in August. In the traditional *olha* system, the shepherds progressed serially through the six hierarchical roles until they became the cheese-making *etxekandere* and returned to the valley. *Aldikatzia* orders the movement of sheep in winter, as well as the use of winter pastures in the valley. *Aldikatü* also describes the movement of mountain cheeses as they replace one another serially on the shelves of the 'cheese house' in the *olha* hut.

The same principle formerly structured two ritual activities in the valley. In the annual processions on Corpus Christi and Ascension, the male heads of household whose land the pilgrims crossed took turns carrying the church crucifix and replaced one another serially in line. In the blessed bread ritual, the *etxekanderak* of the commune took turns giving their gift to the church and to their female first 'first neighbour', i.e. they replaced one another serially as bread-givers.

The principle of rotation (*üngürü*) is also an important organizing notion in Sainte-Engrâce society. The noun (*üngürü*) is also employed in the sense of a circle, a circumference, a circuit. The verb form (*üngüratü*) means to surround, to encompass, to recite the rosary, as well as to rotate.

The people of Sainte-Engrâce conceive of the space in which they live as 'the circle of mountains' (*bortüko üngürü*). Formerly, the special funeral cloths of the house were hung *üngürian* around the deathbed. In the traditional method for curing skin rashes, a blessed candle was rotated above the affected area. Formerly, both newly made cheeses and new-born infants were rotated in front of the fire 'to strengthen their bones'. When the blessed bread of Easter finds the body of the drowned, it 'makes one rotation' (*üngür bat egiten*).

In these contexts, *üngürü* is applied to the positioning or movement of physical objects; but in this summary, I am chiefly interested in examining the more abstract uses of *üngürü* as an ordering principle.

First of all, we have seen that *üngürü* was a fundamental ordering principle in the blessed bread ritual. The gift of blessed bread transmitted from female 'first neighbour' to female 'first neighbour' is said to have formed an *üngür bat*, a circle, when the two-year cycle of exchange was completed. At a community-wide level, rotation was also shown to order the exchange of first 'first neighbour' mortuary services, though few of the people themselves visualize this cycle of exchange as an *üngür bat*. At a community-wide level, *üngürü* also ordered turns, in alternate years, to thresh and to recruit *aizoak* during the wheat harvest. We have seen, too, that rotation orders the movement of shepherds between the valley and the mountains during the period of summer transhumance, when the shepherds are said to be 'in the *olha* rotation', and turns to use a mill.

When we consider and compare the contexts in which the principles of *aldikatzia* and *üngürü* are employed, we find the following general pattern: that *aldikatzia*, in the dual sense of serial replacement and alternation, orders relationships and roles within systems; whereas *üngürü* is a principle by means of which systems are ordered. The former operates at the visible level of reality, the latter at an abstract level.

As serial replacement, *aldikatzia* necessarily entails an asymmetric ordering of relationships and roles within systems. As we have seen, the transmission of blessed bread and that of first 'first neighbour' mortuary obligations constituted two overlapping cycles of asymmetric exchange moving in opposite directions. Asymmetry also defined the ordering of hierarchical roles in the traditional *olha* system.

There are certainly not any remarkable correspondences between Sainte-Engrâce social and symbolic orders, such as have been found in asymmetric systems among the Purum of Indo-Burma (Needham 1962) or in eastern Indonesia (Barnes 1974). There are, however, other societies outside Europe where systems of exchange closely parallel those of Sainte-Engrâce, i.e. where asymmetry orders the transmission of certain 'valuables' and ritual services which move in opposite directions. But only one example of asymmetric exchange can be drawn from the existing literature about European societies outside the Basque country. In southern and eastern Serbia, *kumstvo* or godparenthood relationships constitute a 'unilateral flow of prestations' between patrilines (Hammel 1968: 75, 77). The fact that Sainte-Engrâce provides us with the first reported European example of two unilateral systems of exchange defined by asymmetry and moving in opposite directions is of theoretical interest and importance.

One other recurring theme in this book has been the conceptual importance of right/left distinctions and—in particular—the clockwise aspect of rotation in Sainte-Engrâce society. Right/left distinctions are central to the ordering of 'first neighbour' relationships and, consequently, to the ordering of bread-giver/bread-taker relationships and 'first neighbour' mortuary obligations. The clockwise aspect of rotation is recognized and expressed by the people in terms of movement from left to right. Formerly, turns to thresh wheat in *ogi joitea* were transmitted in a clockwise direction every other year; new-born infants and newly made cheeses were rotated in a clockwise direction in the practice of *hegitatzia*. The blessed bread of Easter rotates in a clockwise direction when it finds the body of the drowned. The members of an *olha* make a clockwise rotation as they move between the valley and the mountains. In the *olha* hut, mountain cheeses are rotated around the storage room in a clockwise direction.

The counter-clockwise aspect of rotation is expressed not in terms of movement from right to left—for 'only evil things go to the left'—but as a 'backwards rotation' (*arra-üngürü*). When the fixed order of turns to thresh wheat in *ogi joitea* was reversed in alternate years and, conceptually, followed a counter-clockwise direction, turns were said 'to rotate backwards' (*arra-üngüratü*). The expression *arra-üngürü* is also employed by those few people who recognize and acknowledge the counter-clockwise transmission of first 'first neighbour' mortuary obligations.

II

Although there are many European societies in which ethnographers have been unable to isolate any formal ordering principles, there is evidence to suggest that principles similar to those of *aldikatzia* and *üngürü* do in fact order systems and relationships within systems in some European communities outside the Basque country. In the existing literature a few ethnographers provide accounts of activities and duties ordered by 'rotation'; but it is not always clear in their reports that 'rotation' is an accurate translation of the concept held by the people whom they have studied, nor is it clear whether their informants made any conceptual and linguistic distinctions between principles of rotation, alternation, and serial replacement.

In his study of Kippel, an Alpine village in south-western Switzerland, Friedl (1974) reports three different contexts in which 'rotation' orders relationships between individuals or households: in the traditional alp associations, irrigation associations, and in keeping the 'fire watch' at night.

Every member of an alp association has a house-sign carved in wood (*Tesseln*). These house-signs are 'strung together and are . . . used to determine the rotation of herding duties on the alp, the obligation passing from one man to another according to position on the string of *Tesseln*' (Friedl 1974: 34). Turns to tend the combined herd of cattle owned by the members of an alp association are reckoned 'according to a system of rotation based on the number of cows each [member] has on the alp' (Friedl 1974: 55).

A string of house-signs is also used to determine the order in which members of irrigation associations take turns using the irrigation canals in Kippel. 'Each member . . . has one piece of wood, and when all are strung together an order is established' (Friedl 1974: 36). Friedl does not tell us whether these pieces are strung together in a random order or whether the order of turns is in fact systematically determined by factors such as the spatial orientation of the members' houses or fields.

House-signs carved into the 'fire watch stake' also determine the order in which households take turns keeping the fire watch at night. 'Theoretically the fire watch stake, and thereby also the duty, makes one complete round of the village every eighty days or so, depending upon the exact number of house-signs carved in it' (Friedl 1974: 36). A photograph of the house-signs on the fire watch stake is provided; but we are not told whether the order of these house-signs is fixed from year to year, what factor or factors determine the ordering of house-signs and turns, or whether the rotation of turns follows any particular direction around the village. Friedl does not provide us with any native gloss for the English term 'rotation'.

For the Castilian hamlet of Valdemora, Freeman (1970: xv) reports that 'taking turns—or "alternating", as it is called—is the order of the day'. In Valdemora, a number of responsibilities are rotated on the basis of the *vecinos*' house order in the village.

Beginning at an arbitrary starting point and following a fixed succession through the irregular streets, some duties are handled in turn by the various families. This rotation is known as the *adra*, a word meaning 'turn' deriving from the Arabic . . . The *adra* in Valdemora is always a rotation based on house order rather than any other kind of order (Freeman 1970: 33).

Freeman cites ten different contexts in which the *adra* traditionally operated. The *adra* determines irrigation turns in the village; 'Valdemorans used to feed and house itinerant beggars by *adra* when such people passed through the town'; *vecinos* are called by *adra* to work on communal properties when few participants are needed; the *adra* is automatically activated for grave-digging when a member of the burial society dies; 'regulations call for activation of the *adra* in attending the sick, and in cases of prolonged illness representatives of only two households are present each day. Keeping the wake with the family of the deceased . . . is mentioned in older documents as falling by *adra* to two members of the [burial] society at a time.' Formerly, a house-order *adra* was sometimes established which required families to send individuals to tend the draft animals for a stated number of days. Formerly, the duties of the *hornero*, custodian of the oven, were filled by *adra*. On San Roque the feast 'once activated four *mayordomos* annually, rotating by house order [*adra*], who supplied bread and cheese for all present'. The semi-weekly cleaning of the public laundry-place is performed in rotation (by *adra*) by the women who use it. After the wheat has been harvested 'the dried grain is brought to the individual threshing floors . . . and the machine is taken from one to the other by *adra*' (Freeman 1970: 36, 37, 38, 39, 42, 56, 62, 112, 166, 184).

Freeman (1970: 33) also reports that irrigation turns in Valdemora were once rotated on the basis of plot order and that 'this distinct ordering principle was called the *sortia*'. Another example of rotation by plot order is provided by Dias (1953), who reports that turns to thresh wheat are rotated according to plot order in Rio de Onor (Tras-os-Montes) in northern Portugal.[1]

Other forms of rotation are reported by Homans (1941) in his study of English champion villages in the thirteenth century. 'There is . . . reason to guess that there was once in England a system of laying out strips of different holdings in a regular order of rotation, and that the order was related to a conventional conception of the direction of the course of the sun' (Homans 1941: 96). A similar system existed until recently in Denmark and Sweden, where it was called *solskift*, 'sun-division'. One feature of the *solskift* was that the order of arable strips corresponded to that of the houses in the village which owned the strips. Homans (1941: 96–7) also reports

[1] João de Pina-Cabral (personal communication) of Linacre College, Oxford, has kindly informed me that two ritual goods—the church cross and images of the Holy Family—are rotated annually around the two halves of a parish (Lavradas) in northern Portugal. The cross, which is carried by the priest, and the images pass from neighbour to neighbour in a fixed order. The Lavradas people describe the movement of these ritual goods as 'going in the direction of the sowing' or 'towards the right'. Although the movement of these goods is in fact circular at a community-wide level, the people conceive of their rotation in terms of a spiral.

that both house sites and the regular rotation of strips corresponding to the house sites were thought to be ordered in a clockwise direction around the village.

Of the ethnographers whose works I have cited, Freeman is the only one who identifies 'a principle of rotation'. She does not, however, tell us where 'the proper starting point' of the *adra* lies or what 'the traditional order of rotation' by houses is in Valdemora. But the facts which she does provide suggest that the *adra* is a concept of the same order as *aldikatzia* in as much as it, too, is a principle by means of which a range of obligations and rights are systematically ordered.

It is hoped that the cases of 'rotation' cited and my own more detailed examination of two Basque ordering principles will encourage other ethnographers working in Europe not only to pay close attention to indigenous concepts of the same order as the *adra*, *aldikatzia* and *üngürü*, but also to consider carefully the ways in which such principles systematically order phenomena. Furthermore, these principles seem to have so much in common with those reported for non-European societies to suggest that Europe is not as unique, in its lack of formal modes of organization, as so much of the ethnography seems to imply.

APPENDIX

DEMOGRAPHIC TRENDS IN SAINTE-ENGRÂCE SINCE 1831

year	population
1831	1,349
1836	1,457
1841	1,402
1846	1,340
1851	1,451
1856	1,337
1861	1,229
1866	1,231
1872	1,174
1876	1,045
1881	1,013
1886	999
1891	994
1896	941
1901	941
1906	902
1911	883
1921	851
1926	727
1931	815
1936	772
1954	589
1962	566
1968	529
1975	510

Sources
Annuaire administratif, judiciare et industriel du département des Basses-Pyrénées (1831–1911)
Dénombrement de la population (1921–36)
Recensement, population du département des Basses-Pyrénées (1954–75)

BIBLIOGRAPHY

Aristotle
1972 *De Generatione Animalium*, trans. Arthur Platt in *The Works of Aristotle*, Oxford: The Clarendon Press.

Azkue, Resurrección María de
1935 *Euskalerriaren Yakintza*, vol. i, Madrid: Espasa-Calpe.
1969 *Diccionario Vasco–Español–Frances*, 2 vols., Bilbao: La Gran Enciclopedia Vasca, 1st edn., 1905–6.

Barandiarán, José Miguel de
1922 'Fiestas populares', *Anuario de Eusko-Folklore*, vol. ii, 131–8.
1947a 'Matériaux pour une étude du peuple Basque: À Uhart-Mixe', *IKUSKA*, nos. 4–5 (May–Aug.), 107–25.
1947b 'Uhart-Mixe', *IKUSKA*, nos. 6–7 (Sept.–Dec.), 165–75, 177–84.
1948 'Materiales para un estudio del pueblo vasca en Liginaga', *IKUSKA*, nos. 10–13 (May–Dec.), 78–84.
1949 'Materiales para un estudio del pueblo vasca en Liginaga', *IKUSKA*, iii, nos. 2–6 (Mar.–Dec.), 33–49.
1955 'Notas sobre la vida pastoril de Ibarre', *Anuario de Eusko-Folklore*, vol. xv, 39–46.

Barnes, R. H.
1974 *Kédang, a study of the collective thought of an eastern Indonesian people*, Oxford: The Clarendon Press.

Bible Saindua
1972 vol. ii, Bilbao: Editorial la Gran Enciclopedia Vasca.

Bonaparte, Prince Louis-Lucien
1883 'Carta linguistica del Principe L.-L. Bonaparte', *Euskal-erria*, vol. ix, no. 116, San Sebastián: J. R. Baroja.

Bourdieu, Pierre
1962 'Celibat et condition paysanne', *Études Rurales*, nos. 5–6 (Apr.–Sept.), Paris: Mouton, 32–135.

Campbell, J. K.
1964 *Honour, Family and Patronage*, Oxford: The Clarendon Press.

Caro Baroja, Julio
1971 *Los Vascos*, 3rd edn., Madrid: Ediciones ISTMO.
1974 *De la vida rural vasca*, 2nd edn., San Sebastián: Editorial Txertoa.

Castillo de Lucas, Antonio
1966 'La pintadera del pan', *Homenaje a Don José Miguel de Barandiarán*, vol. ii, Bilbao: Publicaciones de la Excma. Diputación de Vizcaya, 199–218.

Cavaillès, Henri
1910 'L'association pastorale dans les Pyrénées', *Le Musée Social, mémoires et documents*, no. 3 (Mar.), Paris: A. Rousseau, 45–80.
1931 *La Vie pastorale et agricole dans les Pyrénées des Gaves, de l'Adour et des Nestes*, Paris: Librairie Armand Colin.
Colas, Louis
1923 *La Tombe basque*, Paris: Champion.
Cuzacq, René
1972 *Sainte-Engrâce en Soule*, 2nd edn., Bayonne: Rapid' Offset.
de Goñi, Karmele
1975 'Estudio etnográfico del pueblo de Zerain, Guipúzcoa', *Anuario de Eusko-Folklore*, vol. 26, San Sebastián: Sociedad de Ciencias Aranzadi, 255–442.
Dias, A. J.
1953 *Rio de Onor, comunitarismo agro-pastoril*, Porto: Instituto de Alta Cultura.
Donostia, P.
1961 'Quelques notes au sujet des médecins et médecines populaires au pays basque', *Gure Herria*, vol. 33, no. 1 (Jan.–Feb.), 14–32.
Douglass, William and Bilbao, Jon
1975 *Amerikanuak, Basques in the New World*, Reno: University of Nevada Press.
Douglass, William
1969 *Death in Murélaga*, Seattle: University of Washington Press.
1975 *Echalar and Murélaga, Opportunity and Rural Exodus in Two Spanish Basque Villages*, London: C. Hurst.
Echegaray, Bonifacio de
1932 'La vecindad. Relaciones que engendran en el País Vasco', *Revista Internacional de los Estudios Vascos*, vol. xxiii, no. 1 (Feb.–Mar.), 5–26, 376–405, 546–564.
Etcheberri of Ciboure
1627 *Manual devotionezcoa*, vol. i, Bordeaux: G. Millanges.
Etchegoren, Jean
1935 'Artzañak bortian', *Gure Herria*, vol. 15, no. 5 (Sept.–Oct.), 402–9.
Fay, Dr H. M.
1910 *Lepreux et cagots du Sud-Ouest*, Paris: Librairie ancienne honoré champion.
Foix, Abbé Pierre
1921 'Sainte-Engrâce', *Gure Herria*, vol. i, no. 12 (Dec.), 705–12.
1922 'Sainte-Engrâce', *Gure Herria*, vol. ii, no. 4 (Apr.), 207–15; no. 6 (June), 339–47; no. 9 (Sept.), 493–504.
1923 'Sainte-Engrâce', *Gure Herria*, vol. iii, no. 2 (Feb.), 77–85; no. 3 (Mar.), 124–36; no. 4 (Apr.), 222–32; no. 5. (Sept.), 565–75.
1924 'Sainte-Engrâce', *Gure Herria*, vol. iv, no. 7 (July), 429–38.

Freeman, S. Tax
  1970   *Neighbors, The Social Contract in a Castilian Hamlet*, Chicago:
         University of Chicago Press.
  1979   *The Pasiegos, Spaniards in No Man's Land*, Chicago: University of
         Chicago Press.
Friedl, John
  1974   *Kippel: A changing village in the Alps*, New York: Holt, Rinehart
         and Winston.
Gèze, Louis
  1873   *Éléments de grammaire Basque (dialecte Souletin)*, Bayonne: Veuve
         Lamaignère.
Gómez-Ibáñez, Daniel A.
  1975   *The Western Pyrenees. Differential evolution of the French and
         Spanish borderland*, Oxford: The Clarendon Press.
Goyheneche, Eugène
  1961   *Notre terre Basque*, Bayonne: IKAS.
Greenwood, Davydd
  1976   *Unrewarding Wealth: The commercialization and collapse of agri-
         culture in a Spanish Basque town*, CUP.
Hammel, Eugene A.
  1968   *Alternative Social Structures and Ritual Relations in the Balkans*,
         Englewood Cliffs: Prentice-Hall.
Hardon, John A., S.J.
  1975   *The Catholic Catechism*, London: Geoffrey Chapman.
Haristoy, Abbé P.
  1893   'Monographie de l'antique abbaye de Sainte-Engrâce', *Extrait du
         Bulletin Diocésain de Bayonne*, Bayonne.
Hélias, Pierre-Jakez
  1978   *The Horse of Pride: Life in a Breton village*, New Haven: Yale
         University Press.
Hertz, Robert
  1928   'Saint Besse, Étude d'un culte alpestre', *Mélanges de sociologie
         religieuse et folklore*, Paris: Librairie Felix Alcan, 131–91.
Homans, G. C.
  1941   *English Villagers of the Thirteenth Century*, Cambridge, Mass.:
         Harvard University Press.
Idoate, Florencio
  1973   *Documentos sobre agotes y grupos afines en Navarra*, Pamplona:
         Excma. Diputación foral de Navarra.
Igantetan Elizan
  1970   Published by E. Laxague, vicaire général.
Irigaray, L.
  1963   'Chikitoak', *Igela*, no. 2 (Mar.–May), Paris: D. Peillen, 5–8.
Ispitzua, Tiburcio de
  1922   'Fiestas populares', *Anuario de Eusko-Folklore*, vol. ii, 73–9.

Jaury, Pierre
1938 'Phettirien lehen astia zouhourteko olhan', *Gure Herria*, vol. 18, no. 4 (Oct.–Dec.), 296–301.

Lefebvre, Theodore
1933 *Les Modes de vie dans les Pyrénées atlantiques orientales*, Paris: Colin.

Le Roy Ladurie, Emmanuel
1975 *Montaillou, village occitan de 1294 à 1324*, Paris: Éditions Gallimard.

Lhande, Pierre, S. J.
1926 *Dictionnaire Basque-Français*, Paris: Gabriel Beauchesne.

Littré, Émile
1963 *Dictionnaire de la langue française*, Éditions Universitaires.

Löpelmann, Martin
1968 *Etymologisches Wörterbüch de baskischen Sprache*, 2 vols. Berlin: Walter de Gruyter.

Michelena, Luis
1966 'Tradición viva y letra muerta', *Homenaje a Don José Miguel de Barandiarán*, vol. ii, Bilbao: Publicaciones de la Excma. Diputación de Vizcaya, 121–45.

Needham, Joseph
1959 *A History of Embryology*, CUP.

Needham, Rodney
1962 *Structure and Sentiment*, Chicago: University of Chicago Press.

Noelac Eta Berca Canta Spiritual Berriac
1697 Bayonne: Maffre. First known ed. 1630.

Nussy Saint-Saëns, Marcel
1955 *Le Pais de Soule*, Bordeaux: Clèdes et fils.

Ochkach, B.
1935 'Eskualdunak artzain', *Gure Herria*, vol. 15, no. 1 (Jan.–Feb.), 7–16.

Ott, Sandra
1979 'Aristotle Among the Basques: The "Cheese Analogy" of Conception', *Man*, vol. 14, no. 4 (Dec.), 699–711.
1980 'Blessed Bread, "First Neighbours" and Asymmetric Exchange in the Basque Country', *Archives Européennes de Sociologie*, vol. xxi, 40–58.
forthcoming. 'Egalitarianism in the Basque Household', in *Seven Studies of the Family in Southern Europe*, ed. J. K. Campbell, Oxford: The Clarendon Press.

Peillen, Dominique
1962 'Xikitoak (Zuberoko artzainen pertsoak)', *Igela*, no. 2 (May), Paris: D. Peillen, 27.

Peillen, Jean and Peillen, Dominique
1965 'L'élevage ovin dans le pays de Soule', *Bulletin du Musée Basque*, no. 28, 49–60.

Pitt-Rivers, Julian
1974 'Mana' (inaugural lecture), Welwyn Garden City: The Broadwater Press.

Sallaberry, Jean-Dominique-Julien
  1870 *Chants populaires du pays basque, paroles et musique originales,* Bayonne: Veuve Lamaignère.
van Gennep, Arnold
  1946 *Manuel de folklore français contemporain,* vol. i (2), Paris: J. Picard.
  1947 *Manuel de folklore français contemporain,* vol. i (3), Paris: J. Picard.
Veyrin, Philippe
  1975 *Les Basques,* 1st edn., 1943, Paris: Arthaud.
Vinson, Julien
  1882 *Les Basques et le pays basque,* Paris: Librairie Leopold Cerf.
Warner, Marina
  1976 *All Alone of Her Sex: The myth and the cult of the Virgin Mary,* London: Weidenfeld & Nicolson.
Webster, Wentworth
  1901 *Les Loisirs d'un étranger au pays basque,* Châlon-sur-Saône: E. Bertrand.
Whiteway, M. A. R.
  1901 'The Pyrenean Neighbour; or the Vicinal System of the Western Pyrenees', *The Archaeological Journal,* vol. lviii, no. 230, London: The Royal Archaeological Institute of Great Britain and Ireland, 182–98.

GLOSSARY

aizoa : the 'first neighbour'; pl. *aizoak,* 'neighbours' and, more specifically, the second and third 'first neighbours'

aldikatzia : alternation, serial replacement; verb form *aldikatü,* to alternate, to take turns, to replace serially

alkharr lagüntza ; 'mutual assistance'

antxü : sterile; a ewe that is neither carrying a lamb nor lactating

antxüzain : the shepherd in charge of the non-lactating ewes

arra-üngürü : a 'backwards rotation'; verb form *arra-üngüratü*

artzain-mithil : the servant shepherd

artzain-nausi : the master shepherd

artzanide : the annual meeting of a shepherding syndicate

askazi : one's consanguineal kin (collaterally as far as third cousins) and close affinal kin

axurzain : the guardian of the lambs

azia : animal semen, vegetable seed, the gift of blessed bread given to the female first 'first neighbour'

bigerren aizoa : the second 'first neighbour'

borthitz : the taste of acidic foods such as tomatoes, of garlic, salt-cured ham, and green peppers; nervous, argumentative, and potentially violent (said of a person's temperament)

bortü gazna : mountain cheese

brallakia : human semen

bulta : the mountain pasturage of a shepherding syndicate

cayolar : a shepherding syndicate and its mountain hut (Gascon)

elizako etxekandere : literally, 'the woman of the house of the church' who gave blessed bread

erortu : to die as a result of falling off a precipice in the valley

eskerritik eskuñilat : from left to right

etxalte : the sum total of all movable and immovable property that is transmitted intact from elder to younger heads of household

etxe : house

etxe gazna : house cheese

etxekandere : the female head of household in the valley and the cheese-making shepherd in the mountains; pl. *etxekanderak*

etxenkuak : the members of a household

ezko benedikatia : a thin, coiled candle of beeswax blessed by the priest

ezküandere : 'the candle woman'; in Soule, the female first 'first neighbour' who takes the blessed candles given by the 'first neighbours' and domestic group of the deceased to the church for his funeral

gatzatü : to curdle, to conceive in the womb of a woman

gaztantegia : the room in which cheeses are matured and stored in the mountain herding hut

haurr ordarizka : literally 'child exchange'; when two siblings from one house marry siblings from another house and each couple establishes post-marital residence in one of these two houses

hegitatzia : the practice whereby both newly made cheeses and new-born infants were rotated in front of the fire 'to strengthen their bones'

hirugerren aizoa : the third 'first neighbour'

indarra : physical strength; jural power and authority; the power to compel by moral suasion; life-force; procreative power; supernatural power; the power and force of the natural elements and of certain substances (such as semen and rennet)

kaillatia : the curd formed after rennet has been added to hot milk; the placenta of a woman; a human foetus

kaillatü : to coagulate

konskritak : age-mates; persons born in the same year and who received their First Communion together

lagün : assistant, comrade, companion

larrütü : to die as a result of falling off a precipice in the mountains

lehen lehen aizoa : the first 'first neighbour'

manex : a person, word, or ewe that is not Souletine Basque

nausi : literally 'master'; the male head of household

neskato : literally 'female servant'; a woman employed as a domestic servant in a household; a shepherd who acts as a 'female servant' in the herding hut

odol gorri : the fecund 'red blood' in the womb of a woman

odol ükhüratzia : 'the stopping of the blood'; male and female menopause

odol xuri : the fecund 'white blood' contained in the semen of a man

ogi benedikatia : blessed bread

olha : a Souletine shepherding and cheese-making syndicate; their mountain herding hut; pl. *olhak*

olha-barreia : the ritual dispersal of mountain cheeses on Sainte-Madeleine

olhakuak : the members of a shepherding and cheese-making syndicate

ondokua : descendant; birthplace; 'womb place'; the uterus of a woman

ordari : dyadic reciprocity; verb form *ordarizkatu*, to exchange reciprocally, to compensate, to recompense

pholbor xuri : 'white powder'

presüra : rennet

Santaztarrak : the people of Sainte-Engrâce

senharr-emazte : husband and wife

soiñatu : to care for, to assist

tortxa benedikatia : a long, straight, blessed candle used in mortuary rituals

txotx : a unit of fifty or sixty milking ewes

txotx lagünak : shepherds who were partners in the shepherding and cheese-making syndicate and who were obliged to contribute the same number of milking ewes and rams to make a *txotx*

üngürü : circle, circuit, circumference, rotation; verb form *üngüratü,* to rotate, to encircle, to encompass, to recite the rosary

xerrika : 'the pursuit of the pig'; the pig-killing season

xixkla : a man or male animal who fails to make a fertile female pregnant after repeated sexual intercourse

zorra : debt, duty, obligation; pl. *zorrak,* 'first neighbour' mortuary obligations

zümbera : a soft curd removed from the milk after a cheese has been made

INDEX

adoption, 43, 203

adra (see also under rotation), 218–20

age-mates, 78, 78n, 125, 202, 228

aldikatzia (see also alternation, 'serial replacement', taking turns), vii–viii, 6n, 27, 35, 35n, 69, 214–17, 220, 227; in attending Mass, 82, 214; in blessed bread ritual, 104–105, 111, 113, 215; of blood, 207, 214; Christian names, in selection of, 58, 214; godparents, in selection of, 58, 214; of Mass, 85–6, 214; mill, in use of, 32, 215; in mortuary services of 'first neighbours', 128, 214–215; of mountain cheeses, 189, 215; in municipal council, 27; in *olha*, 136, 145, 151, 154, 156–8, 161–7, 165n, 189, 215; ordering principle of, 214–17, 220; in Rogation Procession, 90, 215; in wheat threshing, 71, 215; of winter pastures and sheep, 34, 215

'alp reckoning', 146n

alternation (see also *aldikatzia*), 154, 164–5, 165n, 166n; in attending Mass, 82, 214; of blood, 207, 214; of Christian names, 58, 214; godparents, in selection of, 58, 214; of Mass, 85–6, 214; of mortuary services by 'first neighbours', 128, 214–15; in *olha*, 154, 160, 164, 166–7, 214

Aristotle, 199, 199n, 209, 209n, 210, 210n, 211, 222

Ascension, 90, 215

asymmetric exchange, vii–viii, xii; of blessed bread, 92, 103–106, 113–14, 116–17, 216; of first 'first neighbour' mortuary services, 117, 128–30, 216; outside the Basque country, 216

asymmetry, 67–8, 113, 117, 129, 166, 216

azia, 227; as animal semen, 109; as 'female semen', 109; as gift of blessed bread, 198; in mental illness, 198

Azkue, R. M. de, 63, 71n, 100, 114–15, 193n, 195, 222

'backwards rotation' (see also under rotation, counter-clockwise), 71, 98, 113, 129–30, 198n, 217

baptism, x, 30, 40, 75–7, 119, 187, 197

Barandiarán, J. M. de, 64, 114n, 126n, 140n, 222

Barnes, R. H., 216, 222

Basque country, *agotes* in, 114; charters in, 66; land area of, 16; provinces of, 1, 1n, 2

Basque language, ix–xi, 1, 1n, 12, 15, 26–7, 29, 57

Basque nationalism, 28–9

Basque Studies Program (of the University of Nevada, Reno), ix, xi, 195n

Basse-Navarre, xi, 1, 2, 45, 63, 65, 140n; village in, Saint-Michel, ix, 45, 65

bastards, 194n

Béarn, 5, 9, 11, 16, 26, 33, 43n, 51, 67n, 114; 'first neighbours' in, 66–7; houses in, 21

Bible Saindua, 210n, 222

Bilbao, J., xi, 114n, 223

birth, 64, 75–6, 173, 199–200

blessed ash, 96–7

blessed bread, xii, 41–2, 45, 56, 69, 96, 101, 104, 115, 117, 228; asymmetric exchange of, 103–106, 113–14, 116–17, 129; cheese, as opposed to, 208–209; of Easter, 100, 215; as 'female semen', 208–209; givers of, 103–104, 107–109, 113–14, 120, 160; *indarra* of, 87, 96, 100; ritual giving of, 71, 81, 85–6, 92–3, 93n, 97–8, 100, 103–16, 126, 130; rotation of, 105–106, 123, 156, 188, 215–16; 'serial replacement' in ritual of, 104–105, 111, 113; takers of, 103–104, 108–109, 113, 119–20; Üngürütürü, role in ritual of, 105

blessed candles, 46, 76, 96–8, 103, 113, 120–22, 124, 126, 129, 139, 148, 183, 200, 215; *indarra* of, 87, 97, 122; rotation of, 97–8, 215

blessed fire, 93, 96–7; change in ritual of, 99–100

blessed laurel, 41, 44, 90, 96–9, 121, 123, 139, 148, 183; *indarra* of, 87, 99

blessed things, class of, 45, 87–8, 96–8, 139

231